Is There a White Elephant in Your Way?

The Guidebook for Awakening
and Self Empowerment

The Hidden Answer to Health, Wealth and Love

Nanice Ellis

ISBN: 978-1539485308

WWW.NANICE.COM

Acknowledgment

In the writing of this book, I want to thank my son, Travis, for his flowing inspiration and ingenious insights into the creation of this book, and my son, Dustin - without him, none of this would be possible.

CONTENTS

Part 2
The Awakening of True-Self

Introduction

Have you been on a long quest for answers, but despite your strong intentions and relentless search, you don't get anywhere? At times, maybe you almost put your finger on it, but it slips away before you do.

Maybe your quest for freedom, liberation or awakening has led you here today. If you allow me, I will take you on a unique journey of self-discovery, where you will finally be able to identify and name the White Elephant in your way!

In this book you will uncover many new answers, but I'll be very honest with you - just reading the words won't change a thing. If you want change, transformation or awakening, you must claim these answers for yourself and then put them to work for you. In part one, you will discover the core cause of every issue, block and challenge, while in part two, I offer many powerful exercises and process designed for tangible life-changing results. I highly suggest doing them all with focused intent and attention.

If you desire real life transformation, you must take the necessary and consistent actions that alchemize the words in this book into real life experiences. Here, within these pages, I offer you the key to freedom, liberation and awakening, but you must consciously use that key to unlock your own mind and wake up your own higher consciousness.

When you fully comprehend the unseen driving phenomena, you will understand why people do the things they do, and also why they think and feel as they do, but, most importantly, you will finally understand yourself. This information will give you the ability to heal and overcome many issues that were impossible to heal or overcome in the past.

Many ideas and theories that we now regard as truth were once "made up" by someone with a keen curiosity and the know-how to turn their discoveries and observations into fundamental concepts. Sigmund Freud and Joseph Campbell both observed human behavior in their own unique ways, and, as a result, developed theories which describe the dynamics of human behavior, in such ways that it has helped us to understand ourselves, and, if we so choose, to live our lives from a space of higher consciousness. In the spirit of offering a new understanding of human behavior, I present this information in much the same way.

I am about to show you the hidden dynamics behind the most chronic and stubborn issues in our lives, and, as I do, I will show you how to identify the white elephant in your way, and once you fully understand why certain challenges just won't go away, I will show you the solution, with practical instructions on how to make it work for you.

Without knowing it, we have all been living inside an invisible prison. You cannot see it because you are in it and it is all around you, but when you finally comprehend the foundation of this prison, you not only have the key to unlock the cell door, you have the ability to dismantle the prison from the ground up – reducing it to ashes so that you can build a new foundation that will support the real you and the life you wish to live.

Part 1

Chapter 1

TRUE-SELF DISPLACEMENT

The truth is always simple and obvious, but we don't recognize it because it is hidden behind the illusion we mistake as reality.

Have you ever had a sense that there is more to life than meets the eye? Have you ever felt like you are not yourself, or possibly a shell of *who you really are*? Do you ever feel that your greater potential is out of reach or maybe that you are here to fulfill a special purpose and you either don't know what it is, or, if you do, it seems too big to manifest?

If you have experienced any of this, you are not alone. Most people feel that they are missing something and no matter what they do, they keep missing it by a mile. That "something," however, is always the same one thing - you are missing your own True-Self.

Through no fault of our own, our real selves have been hidden from us, and we have mistaken our false selves as being who we really are. This one misperception has taken us on a wild ride through life, and maybe even lifetimes.

The one thing that we have each been seeking is our real selves, not realizing that many of the patterns we perpetuate and programs that run our lives keep us from the ultimate discovery of self.

The loss of self has set many dysfunctional dynamics into play, and because we have virtually all displaced our real selves, there is a silent and invisible driving force for all of humanity. This unseen force drives humankind by unknowingly shaping personality, behavior, relationships, interests, choices, health, finances and all aspects of human dynamics.

We've all referred to our True-Selves but what does it even mean?

Your True-Self is the part of you who is eternal and lives on beyond the death of your physical body. It is the greater part of you, over and above the roles you play and your earthly experiences. It is also known as your God-self, higher-self, whole-self, real-self, inner-being, and, of course, this is *who you really are* in your fullest form.

Although no one ever tells us, your True-Self is meant to inhabit your body, living life as you, while also providing unlimited access to wisdom, knowledge and an abundance of energy, as well as everything needed to thrive. When your True-Self is embodied, life is elevated and you live in a wonderful flow of expression and creativity; with direct access to intuition and the knowing of your purpose, you are able to attract opportunities and people who support your journey, and without the constant struggle of overcoming challenges, your life takes on the quality of a beautiful and unique dance. Most of us do not live like this because, for reasons we will discuss shortly, the True-Self is often displaced from the physical body and this is the primary cause of virtually every challenge we face in life.

Displacement Symptoms

True-Self displacement causes us to experience life in a very different and often difficult way. It can make you feel like there is something wrong with you or that you are missing something important. It can even make you feel like you are not yourself, or a shell of who you really are.

True-Self displacement and the many dysfunctions that cause it, or happen as a result of it, can make you experience irrational fear or worry and it may be why you hide self-expression or unknowingly sabotage your dreams and desires. Other symptoms include: health challenges, scarcity, failure, loneliness, problematic relationships, overwhelm, depression, fatigue, lack of inspiration and the list goes on. If you have ever thought, "I don't feel like myself or something's wrong or missing in my life" you are likely experiencing True-Self displacement.

You don't lose anything by embodying your True-Self, and, in fact, you gain everything. *Your True-Self is ready and waiting for your embrace.*

Locating Your True-Self

Whenever your True-Self inhabits your body, it is called True-Self embodiment or embodying your True-Self.

In early childhood, the True-Self likely inhabited your body for a time, but, if you are like most people, for reasons we will discuss soon, you unknowingly misaligned with it or even kicked it out. So, if your True-Self is not fully embodied, where exactly is it?

To locate your True-Self, can you find the part of you who is always watching or non-judgmentally observing? We all have it. This is your True-Self. If you are not aware of your non-judgmental observer, no worries; just imagine that there is an eternal aspect of you that is always observing without judgment.

When your True-Self is not embodied, it "follows" you wherever you go; it may be up above, in the corner, to your left or right, or it may be partly or mostly in your body but misaligned - somewhat like a giant puzzle piece that is not snapped into place correctly.

It is actually quite common for one's True-Self to be part in and part out of the body, but in moments of crisis or emotional trauma, you may have experienced a full dissociation where you stood in the corner, detached from your body, watching the whole thing. The "you" that was watching, without being touched by pain, is your True-Self. There are many reports of watching one's body during surgery, as well as near death experiences where clinically dead people experience their True-Selves beyond the physical realm, and come back to share the astounding details, which almost always include feelings of unconditional love, oneness, and a sense of being limitless.

We have all had profound experiences of True-Self embodiment, but we probably did not recognize our True-Selves as the source of the experience. Nonetheless, in these precious moments, when you are grounded and centered, accompanied by feelings of peace or joy, you are actually experiencing a union with your True-Self and this is why it feels so incredible. Can you recall such a moment in your life?

This exquisite union may happen during meditation, transformational experiences, peak experiences, conscious sex, doing what you love to do, expressing your gifts or even a random occurrence that comes about from letting go.

Unfortunately, the reunion of True-Self is, all too often, fleeting and unsustainable, but, it doesn't have to be this way. Your True-Self belongs in your body, living life as you in blissful union. Embodying your True-Self is the best thing that you can do for yourself, because it enlightens and transforms every experience you will ever have.

The many benefits of True-Self embodiment include: joy, peace, prosperity, inspiration, energy, creativity, loving relationships, connectedness, adventure, fulfillment, physical and emotional health and the increased ability to consciously live the life you most desire.

When you embody your True-Self, you feel energized, confident and grounded in the present moment. Every positive experience ever desired manifests through your True-Self. True-Self embodiment is the key to creating and living your best and most fulfilling life.

True-Self displacement includes anything from a slight misalignment to a full out of body disassociation. True-Self embodiment is the complete alignment of one's True-Self within the physical body.

When you live life with your True-Self mostly displaced, you may not notice the shift from one to the other, but the more you experience True-Self embodiment, even the slightest misalignment of your True-Self can be vastly uncomfortable.

Chapter 2

Understanding True-Self Displacement

Have you ever wondered why young children have unlimited energy? It is because they embody their True-Selves - they laugh, play and love without conditions, and, as a result, they are naturally plugged into Life Force Energy. This is the way we are all meant to live our entire lives, but something happens in the early years that misaligns us with our True Being.

We are each born from a Divine Universe that loves us unconditionally, and we are fully deserving of this love, but, at some point in childhood, we experience amnesia of our True-Selves, and we forget that we are unconditionally loved, and, as a result, we begin to ask, "Am I worthy of love?" From our childish perceptions, we seek this answer, not knowing that the life-long quality of our relationships, prosperity and health all depend on our immature interpretation of the signs.

In most cases, the pivotal answer is, "I am worthy if...."

This is the reason why most of humanity is silently suffering from the invisible wound of unworthiness.

Humanity's Invisible Wound

If it hasn't happened prior, oftentimes, the wound of unworthiness concurs with the introduction of traditional school. When we start school, we are immediately taught that there is failure and success, right and wrong, good and bad and deserving and not deserving - all adding up to either worthy or not worthy. As children become socialized in the system, they quickly discover that their worth is conditioned upon jumping through all sorts of made up hoops, following along and conforming to stringent and disempowering rules. Suddenly, worth is conditional and we are unworthy until we prove that we are worthy.

The system says *"In order to be worthy, you must produce certain results and exceed expectations, and because there is only so much (love and attention) to go around, you must compete in a race to be the worthiest."*

Once children have to pass tests, get approval and meet ever-changing conditions in order to be worthy of love, they quickly get the message that in a "system of worth," only the best are worthy, because there is not enough for everyone.

Because most of us experience this painful childhood dynamic, we think that it is normal, but it is actually a traumatic experience that changes the course of life, and has adversely impacted the history of humanity.

To understand this deep emotional wound, we must understand that young children are reasonably powerless to care for themselves, and, therefore, they instinctively depend on parents, teachers and authority figures for survival, so when children feel judged unworthy or disempowered by adults in charge, their young minds interpret it to mean that they are not worthy of love and care, and because this is experienced to the young mind as life threatening, it triggers a fear of survival, resulting in emotional trauma.

This deep fear can be traced back to our primitive ancestors; if your tribe did not deem you worthy, you might have been rejected and consequently cast out alone into a dangerous wilderness, where you likely faced imminent death. This dynamic has been passed down in our genes, and, as a result, young children associate survival with worthiness, making them super-sensitive to any threats. Therefore, they can intuitively feel that "bad behavior" results in their parents or caretakers withholding love, and, if they are not worthy of love, they might be abandoned and cast out to perish.

Anything that threatens survival, at any age, results in trauma, but this is even truer in the early years, when a child's mind is not yet matured, and he is still trying to make sense of the world. If a child fears that his life is not secure, because he has to keep proving that he is worthy, that fear retards normal, healthy development.

Healthy emotional development requires children to feel safe and protected which means that they must believe that they are unconditionally worthy of love and unconditionally worthy of life.

So, when children are first made to believe that they are unworthy until they prove otherwise, their young psyches experience emotional dissonance; this is due to the fact that the reality of life conflicts with the child's emotional need to feel worthy.

If the message of unworthiness only comes from one source, it is not necessarily traumatic. However, for most children, the message comes from multiple sources of authority, and when they all invoke the same fear of conditional worthiness, children inevitably experience emotional trauma.

Well-meaning parents and teachers genuinely want the best for the children in their care, but the problem is, in a society based on proving one's worth, most adults believe that in order to succeed in life, children must grow up doing the same, thereby passing on the wound of unworthiness from one generation to the next. The fact that a shocking number of twelve year olds are on anti-depressants should speak for itself.

What was meant to be a life based on love and creativity suddenly becomes a life based on fear and suppression, and nothing is ever the same.

Emotional trauma commonly causes us to dissociate, go unconscious and even leave our bodies if the trauma is severe. Young children deal with the trauma of being unworthy in exactly the same way; their True-Selves dissociate, go unconscious and are most often displaced.

Young children who once had unlimited energy, curiosity and zest for life, suddenly begin to shut down in order to protect themselves from future emotional pain.

If a child's True-Self dissociates, his subconscious mind deals with the loss of (True-Self) consciousness by activating internal programs, designed to protect the child, until full consciousness is restored. The internal program that is the base program for all other subconscious programs is known as the EGO.

The EGO is a survival program located in the subconscious mind, and it is pre-programmed to run your life, if for any reason, your True-Self is not capable. Its prime objective is to keep you alive, and, as such, it is designed to ensure that your basic survival needs are met. This means that whenever your True-Self is not conscious in the present moment, the EGO is automatically triggered to take over. This very sophisticated program is designed to feel like you, so you may believe that the EGO is you, but it's not. Signs that the EGO is operating include: negativity, anxiety, worry, past or future referral, looking for what can go wrong, judgment, resistance, control, externally identified, needy, defensive, etc..

The EGO utilizes a complex series of programs to operate your life, but the Worthiness Program is the most pivotal, because according to the EGO, based on primitive programming, your survival depends on your tribe, and especially those in authority, finding you worthy.

Once a child experiences the wound of unworthiness, the Worthiness Program, also located in the subconscious mind, is activated, and this subconscious program will run until it is consciously deactivated. From the moment of activation, the entire world, every relationship and all decisions are filtered through the Worthiness Program; everything is seen and processed in terms of increasing or decreasing one's worth.

Until we awaken, and the Worthiness Program is turned off, conditional worthiness is the foundational belief for almost every human being on this planet, and the core belief that every other disempowering belief is based upon. If you believe that you are fundamentally unworthy of life, and love, unless you meet certain conditions, you will construct a reality built on this false premise, and, as a result, you will embark on this game of life looking outside yourself for proof of worth. Depending on culture, family, societal norms and where you live in the world that proof may be sought in the form of accomplishments, identity, winning, status, appearance, relationships etc...

In the Worthiness Game of Misfortune, we must continue to prove our worth over and over again without end. We may feel worthy from time to time, but even when we do, in the recesses of our minds we fear that at any moment we might be deemed unworthy. We don't realize that all our attempts at proving worth pushes us further away from the love we so desperately seek, and, if we didn't question our worth, we would effortlessly experience this love without conditions.

No matter how it appears, when worth is questioned, we unconsciously fear that we are not worthy of love nor worthy of life, and, therefore, our lives depend upon proving that we are worthy because survival depends on it.

But, this unconscious strategy is doomed to failure, because worth is intrinsic and unconditional, and, therefore, it cannot be proven or disproven. The mere act of trying to prove that you are worthy or getting others to treat you a certain way so that you feel worthy, comes from the belief that you are not worthy. If you know that you are unconditionally worthy, you don't need proof.

Most people spend their entire lives trying to prove that they are worthy, never considering that the quest for worth is impossible to fulfill, nor understanding that this impossible quest covertly sabotages their dreams and desires.

If you look deep, you will find that the core wound of all emotional wounds is the belief of unworthiness or conditional worthiness. This belief is so painful because it is completely untrue, but, since our parents, teachers and peers all suffer from the same debilitating belief, it seems perfectly normal.

Disempowering Beliefs Cause True-Self Displacement

The belief of unworthiness or conditional worthiness sets the stage for other disempowering beliefs, such as powerlessness and victimhood. When you believe that you are unworthy, it invokes feelings of powerlessness, and, if you feel powerless, it sets you up to be victimized, and, if you feel like a victim, you will perpetually fear loss.

All other disempowering beliefs fall into one or more of these three categories.

- ***Unworthiness*** - you believe that your worth is dependent on proving that you are worthy.
- ***Powerlessness*** - you believe that you have little or no power in one or more areas of your life.
- ***Victimhood*** - you believe that others can harm you in some way.

Unworthiness, powerlessness and victimhood are all beliefs that are universally false and in error, h*owever,* free-will allows you to believe anything you choose, consciously or unconsciously, but there is a consequence because your beliefs directly affect everything about you and your life. When you believe any of these false beliefs, they manifest as issues that represent the errors of those beliefs; failed relationships, financial hardship, physical challenges and every other difficulty known to mankind.

Beyond a shadow of a doubt, your True-Self knows who you really are, and would never consider any disempowering belief to be true. You are unconditionally worthy and intrinsically powerful - and no experiences, or proof otherwise, can ever convince your higher (wiser) self differently.

Lost dreams, unmet desires, scarcity, confusion, relationship issues, health problems, life challenges and virtually every issue known to mankind can be traced back to True-Self displacement, but the biggest and most pivotal issue of True-Self displacement is inhibited Life Force Energy.

Chapter 3

Life Force Energy

The entire Universe, and all aspects of it, is composed of Source energy.

Source energy is the essence of all things and everything is made from this energy, because there is absolutely nothing else to make anything out of. Source energy is the one and ***only*** creative energy of the vast and eternal Universe and it can be molded and manifested as literally anything or anyone. Many great teachers refer to Source energy as the energy of love, and although this is true, if you think that it is no greater than the emotion of love, you will completely miss the magnificence and magnitude of what *it really is.*

Source energy becomes Life Force Energy as it manifests in this physical realm. Life Force Energy is still pure Source energy but it is subtly altered in order to be the perfect energy source for the specific requirements of Earth and its inhabitants. For all intents and purposes, Life Force Energy is Source energy, so when we talk about one, we talk about the other.

Although most of us rarely consider it, we all need Life Force Energy to survive. Not just air, water and food, but invisible Life Force Energy; also known as Chi, Prana or Universal Energy. You can live weeks without food, days without water, minutes without air, but you cannot live at all without Life Force Energy. Life Force Energy is the energy of life and without it, we would not exist. If Life Force Energy is cut off completely, we quickly die because there is no energy to sustain us. *Without knowing it, your life depends on Life Force Energy.*

Air, water and food are all made from Life Force Energy, but unlike air, water and food, there is an unlimited abundance of Life Force Energy in the Universe, but you must access it in order to use it.

Ultimately, we each have the ability to access and experience one hundred percent of the Life Force Energy required to live a vibrant, healthy and fulfilling life, and we are each entitled to an abundance of Life Force Energy, with direct access to it through our True-Selves.

Your True-Self channels Life Force Energy through Pure Desire.

Although, we have the innate ability to experience as much Life Force Energy as we need, it is the Pure Desire of our True-Selves that determines the flow. At the bare minimum, our ***desire to live*** calls forth more than enough Life Force Energy. Without the desire to live, we eventually die because we lack the Life Force Energy needed to sustain us.

Just the desire to breathe allows us to channel Life Force Energy, and, if you have the desire to create, invent, relate, innovate or experience the fullness of life, you will naturally call forth the necessary Life Force Energy to fulfill your desires. Since Life

Force Energy flows according to the current of Pure Desire, you only get what you need, but you get as much as you need, whenever you need it.

Being in the flow is a symptom of True-Self embodiment accompanied with the Pure Desire to be, do or experience the manifestation of that desire. *Being in the flow* is being plugged into Life Force Energy through our True-Selves.

Life Force Energy effortlessly flows through our True-Selves, but when we are not consciously present, our True-Selves are displaced, and, as a result, the flow of Life Force Energy is inhibited and our supply is diminished.

Everyone experiences at least some natural Life Force Energy, but few of us are completely connected and experiencing the fullest potential of Life Force Energy. One way or another, we must have a minimum amount of energy in order to live, and, therefore, if you are not receiving all the energy you need naturally via your True-Self, the energy that you lack must be generated.

The Automated Back-up System

Lucky for us, when we go unconscious in our lives, and our True-Selves are displaced, we each have an automatic back-up energy generator called the EGO.

The EGO is your Energy Generating Operator!

Remember, the EGO's primary job is to ensure your survival, so when your True-Self is displaced and you experience energy deprivation, the EGO's job is to make sure you have the energy you need in order to survive. Therefore, if you are not receiving adequate Life Force Energy, the EGO automatically develops certain dynamics that have the potential for generating energy.

The EGO utilizes various methods for energy generation, which we will explore, but at the core of most methods is the Worthiness Program.

Chapter 4

The Worthiness Program for Energy

The Worthiness Program is a built-in survival program whose purpose is to determine the conditions upon your worth and to make sure that you meet these conditions, in such a way that others find you worthy and your survival is not threatened.

The Worthiness Program first determines the specific conditions upon your worth, according to the religion, culture, family and society in which you reside, and based on this assessment, the EGO formulates your identity, including the development and expression of the necessary behaviors and qualities that will prove that you are worthy according to these conditions.

The EGO then compels you to meet these conditions by motivating you to do so. It covertly manipulates you to act in specific ways by offering you energy through motivation.

Motivation provides you with the energy necessary to meet the conditions of your worth, but the EGO also uses motivation as a prime method of energy generation. Think about it, when you feel motivated, you have the energy to act.

Motivation generates energy

Whenever the EGO wants you to do something that will prove that you are worthy, it motivates you to take the necessary action, and when you receive positive feedback, such as approval, acceptance or praise, the feeling of worthiness energetically "inflates the EGO" and the inflated EGO generates more energy as a reward. Can you recall an experience that made you feel really good about yourself? Winning a race, being the best or getting an award all inflate the EGO, and, consequently, the reward is increased energy.

The EGO motivates you with energy in order to prove your worth, and when you do, the feeling of worth inflates the EGO, and the inflated EGO generates more energy.

Life Force Energy vs. Artificially-Generated Energy

Keep in mind that when we talk about energy that is generated by the EGO, we are always talking about energy that is artificially-generated by an internal program, and, therefore, it is artificially-generated energy. It is still Life Force Energy except the means by which we access it is through a program, opposed to naturally "sourcing" it via our True-Selves.

Life Force Energy resonates at a very high frequency - inherent in this energy is the power of healing and rejuvenation, and, as such, when we inhibit the flow of Life Force Energy, we cut ourselves off from the many gifts that this energy effortlessly provides. Again, artificially-generated energy is still Life Force Energy because there is no other energy in the Universe, but it is a lower frequency, and, therefore, not as healing and beneficial to the mind and body.

The EGO uses motivation to generate energy, and when we trace motivation back to its source, we find fear - motivation to do, be or have originates from the hidden fear that we are not worthy, and we must prove that we are worthy in order to be worthy of love - *and life.*

Because energy derived through motivation is channeled through fear, it takes on the characteristics of fear, morphing the high frequency of Life Force Energy into a more fear-based lower frequency energy. Not only do we lose the benefits contained in pure high frequency Life Force Energy, we are also negatively affected by the frequency of fear.

The White Elephant

As we explore a new and unique understanding of the EGO, and the many ways in which it artificially generates energy for us to live, it will become increasingly clear that the EGO is the invisible White Elephant that stands between you and the life you truly desire and deserve.

The EGO is a survival program located in the subconscious mind, and, much like a life jacket you would find on a boat, it is meant to save you in case of emergency, but, according to the EGO, an emergency situation occurs whenever you are not consciously present in the moment, and your True-Self is not fully embodied.

The moment you go unconscious, by not being present, the EGO is activated, thereby taking control of your life, for as long as you are unconscious.

This means that the EGO automatically turns on whenever you focus on disempowering beliefs, deny your feelings, think negatively or become distracted or dissociated in anyway.

The EGO is a back-up program that is intended to serve us, but the servant has become the master and this master operates our lives according to its own pre-programmed agenda, even if it means the cost of relationship issues, money challenges, health concerns and general chaos. Indeed, the EGO attempts to attain what the True-Self naturally possesses, and it may experience a fragmented version, from time to time, but it is never the same, leaving us feeling empty and wanting more.

The EGO's main focus is to ensure that you have enough energy to live, because without energy you would perish and die, but in a relentless attempt to generate energy, the EGO unwittingly wreaks havoc on your life, often resulting in every issue and challenge imaginable. This is not to say that the EGO is negative or even the enemy - *after all, a program can only do what a program is programmed to do.*

The point is to be cognizant that you are not the EGO.

The EGO is programmed to seem like the real you, and, as a result, you will believe you are the EGO, but nothing can be further from the truth. So, why, exactly, does the EGO feel (and sound) like the real you? Due to the fact that the EGO is only a program, it does not have an independent form of communication, and, therefore, the EGO feels like you because it uses your body and mind to communicate messages, and the EGO sounds like you because it uses your internal voice to speak to you.

When you learn to accurately identify the EGO, you will notice a vast difference between your True-Self and the EGO, and this clear distinction will, ultimately, allow you to listen more to your True-Self and less to the EGO.

Although you were never intended to live as the EGO, it doesn't mean that the EGO is something you must get rid of, and, in fact, you don't want to eradicate it as long as you run the risk of going unconscious. Imagine sleep-walking through your life and not having an automated back-up system to ensure survival.

The EGO is specifically designed by the Divine to give each of us the best shot at life. Since the EGO is a gift from the Divine, the more you love and appreciate this wonderful gift, the more you can become conscious as your True-Self, and the less the EGO has to work for you.

The Answer to EGO Domination is Awakening as Your True-Self!

The EGO only operates when you unconsciously sleep-walk through life, therefore, the key to transcending the EGO is Waking Up. When you are conscious and awake, your True-Self comes to the forefront and there is no reason for the EGO to operate, so it remains dormant.

The pivotal feature of awakening is being free of all programming so that you are fully present in every moment, and, consequently, all your choices are made consciously, ultimately transforming the quality of your life.

The one most important thing to remember is that when your True-Self is conscious, the EGO is not active, and, therefore, consciousness is the on and off switch for the EGO.

- Going unconscious is the On Switch for the EGO.
- Becoming Conscious is the Off Switch for the EGO.

In the following chapters, you will discover how the **E**nergy **G**enerating **O**perator controls your life and why it does the things it does, and, by making the unconscious conscious, you will have the power to transcend this White Elephant by overcoming the internal programming that has run your life up until this point.

In Part 2, you will learn how to master the EGO and embody your True-Self so that you can fully experience the unlimited love, abundance and wellness that comes from living as your real and True Self.

Let's Recap

- You are born unconditionally worthy, embodying your True-Self and channeling unlimited Life Force Energy.
- You intended to live as your True-Self – as the commander of your life.
- At some point, usually in childhood, you learned that your worth is conditioned upon other people finding you worthy.

- Believing you are unworthy unless proving otherwise resulted in emotional trauma, causing True-Self displacement.
- Displacement includes anything from a slight misalignment with your True-Self to complete dissociation.
- True-Self displacement inhibits Life Force Energy.
- You cannot live without Life Force Energy, whether it is channeled naturally via your True-Self, or the EGO artificially generates it.
- When your True-Self is misaligned or dis-embodied, it triggers the EGO to take control of your life because you are not conscious in the present moment.
- The EGO is the Energy Generating Operator and its primary job is to keep you alive by generating the energy that you need to survive.
- Since your survival is dependent on proving your worth, the EGO uses the Worthiness Program to determine the conditions of your worth.
- In order to meet the conditions, the EGO generates energy through motivating you to prove your worth.
- When you prove your worth, according to the conditions, the EGO is inflated, and more energy is generated as a reward.

The EGO has many ways to gauge your worth but none as pivotal as meeting your Primary Emotional Need.

Chapter 5

The Primary Emotional Need

When we do not remember that we are unconditionally worthy, we experience the emotional wound of unworthiness, and, as a way to cope with this wound, the well-meaning EGO uses the Worthiness Program to pinpoint a "primary emotional need," that when met, indicates that we are worthy, but only temporarily.

Your "primary emotional need" is specific to you and your life experiences, with the most common emotional needs including: appreciation, approval, acceptance, validation, respect, being included, being understood, being seen and being heard, but there are many more, as well.

Where does this emotional need originate?

When children experience more than occasional disapproval, disrespect, lack of appreciation or not being heard, etc... they sense that their parents, teachers or caretakers are withholding love from them, and they unconsciously deduct:

1. I am not unconditionally worthy.
2. In order to be worthy, I must behave in ways that my parents/caretakers/teachers (and everyone else) deem worthy.
3. When others find me worthy, they will reward me with the emotional need I most associate with *not* feeling worthy.

Your primary emotional need is more than likely the same need that did not get met in childhood, so if you can recall your childhood experiences, you may be able to pinpoint a pattern that explains your primary emotional need. For example, if you were the middle child in a large family, and no one heard you when you spoke, you may have associated not being heard with being unworthy, thereby developing an unconscious belief that says, "In order to be worthy, I must be heard." Therefore, your primary emotional need is to be heard.

Another example, let's say, your mother was very judgmental, and every time she criticized your choices, you felt unworthy. Because you associated disapproval with unworthiness, you developed a belief that says, "In order to be worthy, others must approve." Therefore, your primary emotional need is approval.

One more example, let's say, you grew up in a family where family members did not appreciate each other, and because you weren't appreciated as a child, you felt unworthy, thereby developing a belief that says, "In order to be worthy, others must appreciate me." Therefore, your primary emotional need is appreciation.

If you listen to your own words and thoughts, when you are feeling unloved by your partner, friend or relation, you will begin to understand your primary emotional need. If you have found yourself saying or thinking:

- "You don't hear me" - the primary emotional need is likely being heard.

- "You don't approve of me or you always judge me" - the primary emotional need is likely approval.
- "You don't appreciate me"- the primary emotional need is likely appreciation.
- "You don't understand me" – the primary emotional need is likely being understood.
- "You don't respect me" – the primary emotional need is likely being respected.

According to the EGO, your worth is dependent on your primary emotional need being met, because when it is met, it means that you have proven your worth to others, and, therefore, you won't be rejected.

Although we are usually unaware of this primary emotional need, the EGO is constantly tracking for the fulfillment of it, consequently altering our behavior in order to get it met. All for one reason – proof of worth!

This means that if your primary emotional need is approval, you must somehow get others to approve of you, again and again, in order to feel worthy. Since everyone has different ideas of right and wrong, and good and bad, if you always need others to approve, you must change your behavior according to specific expectations - possibly "changing hats" many times a day in order to gain approval in all situations and relationships. This also means that you must suppress your real self – hiding any form of self-expression that others might judge.

Our personalities become molded according to our primary emotional need and our unconscious strategies to get this need met, influencing our choice of friends, partners, style, interests, hobbies, roles and especially the careers we choose. If your primary emotional need is respect, you might be motivated to be a police officer or teacher. If your primary emotional need is appreciation or admiration, you might be motivated to be an actor or performer. If your primary emotional need is to be heard, you might be motivated to be an attorney or news reporter. Without having the slightest awareness, our entire lives could be focused around this one emotional need.

We might sacrifice our true desires for approval, compromise our values for appreciation or hide behind a false self in exchange for being understood. Without knowing it, your primary emotional need runs your life, making you do things you don't really want to do, and keeping you from expressing and experiencing the True You. It is an invisible prison of your own making, and even if you can get others to meet this emotional need, it is never enough to fill the bottomless pit of unworthiness.

Keep in mind, the EGO may need everyone you know to meet your primary emotional need or it may be selective, where only pivotal people in your life must meet this need: parents, close family members, partners, certain friends and/or people in authority.

"Better Than"

Although somewhat less common, a slightly different version of the Worthiness Program may result in an inflated sense of worth.

Instead of seeking approval or acceptance, the EGO latches onto the belief that we are "better than" and, therefore, more worthy. This may motivate us to excel and over-achieve as it pushes us toward activities and roles that result in praise, respect, awards and prestige, allowing us to demonstrate that we are the best, brightest and most accomplished.

Believing that we are "better than" empowers us to be superior at all we do, which can sound like a good thing on the surface, but it is still a false sense of worth because it is conditioned on being "better than." Any sense of worth that is conditioned on anything is EGO-driven worth and not the sense of worth that comes from knowing who we really are.

It takes a great deal of effort and determination to keep this dynamic going because the EGO is invested in maintaining circumstances and results where others see us as more worthy and powerful.

Just to clarify, when the "better than" version is running, you are not trying to prove your worth to anyone, instead, you are needing them to see you as superior. The most common primary emotional needs associated with this dynamic are respect and being right.

The need to be right often results in disharmony because in order to be right, someone has to be wrong. This dynamic could easily attract conflict in various areas of your life. You might even attract people who also want to be right in order to win the fight and inflate the EGO. If there is no conflict, and everyone agrees that you are right, the EGO doesn't really feel "better than." The ideal scenario to the EGO is that you win a disagreement, the other person agrees that you are right and they offer you respect.

When others respect you, it means (to the EGO) that they see you superior, but, if you need people to respect you in order to feel superior, you are likely super-sensitive when respect is not forthcoming. In fact, if you feel disrespected, it could trigger an emotional reaction, resulting in feelings of anger, frustration or resentment in order to protect your pride.

In fact, the EGO may use pride as a defense mechanism to protect your esteemed worth. If you are prideful, it likely means that you can't ask for help because that would make you seem weak to others. Instead, you hide your challenges and deal with them yourself, so others don't see you as "less than" and you can maintain superiority.

Chapter 6

Energy Generating Operator

The EGO is literally invested in getting others to meet your primary emotional need as proof that you are worthy, therefore, it motivates you to behave in ways that will result in approval, acceptance, appreciation, respect or whatever your primary emotional need might be. This EGO-driven motivation manifests as *that feeling* of wanting approval, acceptance, appreciation, understanding, etc..., and this is why it is so difficult to overcome the need that others like us; to the EGO our survival depends on being liked.

When others meet your primary emotional need, it creates a feeling of worthiness, boosting the EGO and resulting in the artificial generation of energy. As the EGO is boosted energy is generated. Think about the additional energy you experience whenever you get a boost to your EGO.

The EGO only needs a temporary feeling of worth in order to get a boost, and generate energy, but the energy doesn't last very long before you need additional proof of worth for more energy. You can think of this like an "Energy Boost System."

Although the EGO gauges your worth on your primary emotional need being met, the EGO has a complex strategy to determine worth that does not necessarily involve the fulfillment of this need.

Boosting the EGO via Competition, Comparison and Judgment

Since we are talking about conditional worth, conditions have to be met or exceeded in order to be deemed worthy, boost the EGO and generate energy.

This means that in order to achieve this temporary status of worth, and get boosted with energy, the EGO needs to constantly measure your current degree of worthiness, but in order to measure worth, it needs someone, or something, to measure it against, which makes competition, judgment and comparison necessary components to the Worthiness Program.

In competition and comparison, there needs to be a judge to determine who is better or best (who is the worthiest). No problem, the EGO jumps in the ring and puts a judge's hat on your head - motivating you to judge.

If you judge "so and so" for "such and such" and you are better, you feel worthy, the EGO gets a boost and energy is generated. Of course, the "energy high" doesn't last very long, and the come down often feels quite bad (because it feels bad to judge), but that just motivates you to seek the next EGO boost in order to feel better. In this way, artificially-generated energy is like a drug, and you keep needing more in order to get the same energetic high.

But, the EGO doesn't just take your word for worth; the EGO looks to other people to determine your current worth. If you receive approval, acceptance, respect, appreciation or whatever your primary emotional need might be, the EGO interprets it as worthiness, and you get an EGO Boost of energy. On the other side of the token, if you receive negative judgment, disapproval, nonacceptance, disrespect, etc…, the EGO interprets it as unworthiness, and you experience a deflated EGO, resulting in fatigue, failure, self-pity, disappointment and any other feelings associated with unworthiness.

Have you noticed that feeling "down" is a byproduct of feeling unworthy? When you lose the race, fail the test or experience disapproval in some way, the EGO is deflated and energy is not available – since you didn't' get an energy boost from success, energy must be conserved with the conservation method of fatigue.

Some people also use comparison as a strategy to avoid failure. Instead of competing for success, they find successful people intimidating, and so they don't even try. When the EGO assesses that you are inferior in comparison to another, it will not motivate you to compete in order to avoid failure.

Self-worth is a moving target, subject to change at the drop of a hat? Depending on who you are with and what you are doing, your worth can swing from high to low without even taking a breath. For example, let's say you are a good tennis player and you are about to play tennis with two new friends. It turns out that you are a superior tennis player when opposing new friend number one; you feel worthy, the EGO gets a boost, and you are energized. Now, it's time to play against new friend number two. It quickly becomes apparent that this friend is an excellent tennis player, and you are inferior in comparison. No EGO boost for you. Instead, the EGO is deflated, and you barely have enough energy to crawl home in self-doubt and defeat.

The fact that we must judge ourselves and each other in order to determine our current level of worth explains why humans are instinctually judgmental. When you understand this, you can see that most people are not bad or unkind - they are just on automatic pilot, unconsciously trying to generate energy in order to live.

If there was a disclaimer regarding worthiness, it might go like this:

> *If you meet certain conditions, you will be worthy, but for only as long as those conditions are met. If you fail to meet those conditions for any reason, you will no longer be worthy. Conditions may change at anytime, and your worth is subject to (that) change without notice. Worthiness may also be canceled or withdrawn by any judge, at the discretion of the judge.*

The Worthiness Meter

The EGO measures everything in terms of worth.

Until we are fully awake, we may experience every relationship, job and situation through the filter of worth; unconsciously determining how our worth will be influenced based on the choices we make. When we are unconscious and unaware of this underlying dynamic, we unknowingly base many of our decisions on the estimated worth that we will either receive or lose. This may explain irrational choices that we later regret.

The EGO will point us toward any short-term or long-term choice that might increase the perception of self-worth. On an unconscious level, we seek increased worth in order to experience an EGO boost and generate energy. In a way, you could say that we exchange worth for energy, therefore, we must perpetually move in the direction where our perceived worth increases. This is especially true in relationships.

The quality and intensity of the EGO boost that you receive, at any given time, is in direct proportion to how you perceive the person or people with whom you are relating. This may be why you care more about the opinions and acceptance of "superior" people; higher status, smarter, more attractive or whatever superior means to you - and why you receive a higher energy boost when judged positively by them or in comparison to them.

Without knowing it, we are often interested in a person, place or thing based on the amount of worth that we anticipate gaining from the relationship or experience. Due to the automated nature of the Worthiness Program, we don't even know that this is what we are doing and we don't even know why we are seeking certain things and rejecting others.

Let's Recap:

- If your True-Self is not embodied, your ability to receive Life Force Energy is inhibited.
- When Life Force Energy is inhibited, energy must be generated in order to live.
- The EGO's primary job is keeping you alive, so it operates energy generators.
- The EGO needs to be boosted to generate energy.
- To get an EGO boost, you must be deemed worthy.
- To feel worthy, others must meet your primary emotional need and/or you must be superior in some way.
- Because you can only be superior in comparison to another, the EGO motivates you to compare and compete with others.
- In order to determine the winner or the best (the worthiest), a judge is required, and, as such, the EGO motivates you to judge, as well as allowing others to judge you.
- If you are judged better, the EGO gets a boost, and energy is generated.
- If you are judged worse, the EGO is deflated, and energy is lost.
- The quality of the EGO boost that you receive is in direct proportion to how you perceive the person or people you are judging yourself against, or who are judging you.

The Treasure is Within

The source of your worth lies deep inside you. You have hidden it from yourself but it has been there all along, anticipating your remembrance – no less powerful than the day you locked it away, it awaits your willingness to re-discover it. Only through a still mind can you ever go deep enough into your being to re-discover your intrinsic worth.

Maybe you will find it in a deep energetic cave within your heart or a virtual mountain top within your solar plexus.

Your worth is a treasure like no other, and when you find it and claim it for yourself, this treasure will be a magnet for all other treasures, big or small, physical or spiritual. Knowing your unconditional worth allows you to attract your greatest dreams and sweetest desires. The wall of conditions (upon your worth) is forever gone and now you can be the master creator of your life – allowing all the goodness imaginable to flow through you and dance with you.

Chapter 7

Energy Generators

The EGO utilizes motivation to generate energy.

When we are not receiving adequate Life Force Energy to live, the Energy Generating Operator (EGO) creates virtual "motors." The EGO is the operator of these "motors" and the "motors" have the potential to artificially generate energy.

Virtual "motors" can be best described as what we refer to as motivation.

As you probably know, motivation produces energy and without motivation, we lack the necessary energy to take action or complete a task, but did you know that the EGO will only motivate you if it believes that the action to be taken will support, increase or prove your worth?

The EGO asks, "Will this person, place, thing or experience provide or prove worth?" If the EGO says yes, you will feel motivated to take action, but, if the answer is no, the EGO will not provide motivation. The answer will be no if there is any possibility that your worth could be decreased or challenged; potentially failing, looking like a fool or being judged poorly.

Since motivation is a motor for energy generation, we can more accurately call it Motor-vation.

Return on Investment

Oftentimes, when we talk about the return on investment, we are speaking about the investment of money and the return of capital and profit from that investment. In much the same way, the EGO assesses the investment of energy, and based on the results, strategizes future investments.

The EGO has access to a limited amount of energy, and in order to motor-vate you, it must take some of this energy and invest it in motor-vating you to do something that will improve your worth, thereby invoking an EGO Boost and generating more energy.

When the energy generated from the EGO Boost is greater than the energy used to motor-vate you, the EGO will conclude that it was a good investment, and will find similar types of investments where you can be equally as motor-vated.

Along the same lines, if the EGO provides energy via motor-vation but you don't succeed at whatever you have been motor-vated to do, there is no payoff of energy. When the energy needed for motor-vation is greater than the energy generated via the EGO boost, the EGO concludes that it was a bad investment, and will not provide motor-vation for similar types of "investments."

If you fail, not only do you not get a boost of energy, failure deflates the EGO, thereby draining energy.

Once the EGO concludes that the cost of motor-vation is greater than the payoff, the EGO will stop motor-vating you in terms of the pattern; if you have a pattern of failing in relationships, the EGO will withhold motor-vation for new relationships or if the pattern is in terms of business, the EGO will withhold motor-vation in terms of business.

We get stuck in dead-end jobs or less than fulfilling relationships because we don't have the motor-vation to find a better job or new partner. When we have a history of failed attempts, the EGO no longer motor-vates us to take action in this direction because the outcome does not improve our worth and, worse yet, it drains our limited resources of energy. We may really want to leave a difficult or unsatisfying situation, but without motor-vation, we can do little about our predicament

We all know that when we lack motivation, there is no way to begin a new project or continue on a pre-existing one. So, what is the answer?

Although it may not feel like it at the time, when your "motors" begin to fail, or fail completely, and you lack motor-vation, it can be the best thing that ever happens to you. It means that the EGO is no longer dependent on certain results in order to prove worth, and when your old energy source (driven by the EGO) is no longer available, you have to find a new way of living.

As long as you are getting a sense of worth from externals, it can be challenging to disengage because the EGO is receiving what it seeks, but when this dynamic fails, and you don't have any motor-vation to pursue worth in this way, you have a Grand Opportunity to discover your intrinsic worth.

When you give up the battle of proving your worth, there is no place to go but within. By re-discovering your intrinsic worth, and remembering *who you really are*, you align with your True-Self. In so doing, you are tapped into the infinite and unlimited well of inspiration, and as you allow this inspiration to flow through you, an enormous amount of energy suddenly becomes available in direct proportion to your willingness to be, do or create that which inspires you.

Since you already know and own your intrinsic worth, you are no longer being, doing or creating in order to prove worth, but, rather, you are a channel for Source, and as you allow this intuitive guidance to move you, you have access to an incredible supply of Life Force energy that you can use to create your greatest dreams and manifest your simplest desires. Free of EGO constraints and awake from unconscious programming, you are able to finally live your life as it was meant to be lived - with ease and grace.

Much more about this later, but first, let's explore how the EGO operates so that you have the knowledge and awareness to transcend unconscious programming.

Positive Motor-vation

When you are motor-vated to move toward something that will improve or prove worth, the EGO is a positive energy generator.

This is Positive Motor-vation.

The EGO motor-vates you with the promise or hope of rewards, such as, praise, money, emotional needs met, winning, power, attention, etc..., in order to move you in the direction of improving worth.

Even though the EGO motor-vates you to accomplish things that will support or increase your worth, in order to reach your goal or attain your desired outcome, you must believe that you are worthy of it. If you don't believe you are worthy, your doubt and self-judgment misaligns you with the desired outcome and you will likely miss your target by a mile. If this is the case, motor-vation often burns out well before reaching the goal. *Self-doubt burns us out!* This is one of the reasons why we may have so much energy and motor-vation at the start of a project, but before long it dissipates and we lose interest.

When worth is not attached to the realization of a dream or desire, we are no more worthy upon realization and no less worthy if we fail.

Negative Motor-vation

The EGO uses fear in order to make us avoid anything that might cause us to lose worth, like trying something new and failing or being rejected by someone with perceived importance.

When we are afraid of consequence or afraid that something we desire won't happen, the EGO might also motor-vate us to take action in order to avoid what we fear. Fear can be a powerful energy generator because it creates fight or flight, and either response can generate mass amounts of energy.

When you are motor-vated to move away from what you fear, the EGO is utilizing negative motor-vation. The purpose of negative motor-vation is to avoid losing worth.

> *Signpost on the path*
>
> *For inspiration - go directly to Source*

Motor-vation versus Inspiration

Whenever we talk about motivation, we are referring to EGO-driven motor-vation, whereas, when we talk about inspiration, we are referring to the Pure Desire of True-Self.

Eventually, motor-vation burns itself out, and us on the way, primarily because the EGO motor-vates us through fear. If you look closely, you will see that inherent in all motor-vation is fear, and fear manifests as stress, overwhelm and anxiety which cannot be sustained indefinitely. Since the EGO is a survival program, an essence of fear underlies virtually all behavior, actions and reactions. When we are motor-vated by the EGO to be, do, have or experience something, it is generally because we are trying to prove or protect our worth – the driving force is the fear that we are unworthy.

When your True-Self is embodied, you don't need energy generated by motor-vation. Being connected to Life Force Energy through your True-Self connects you to Source, and when you are connected, you are naturally inspired to do, be and experience. Inspiration naturally and effortlessly results in the necessary energy to fulfill whatever inspires you.

The True You uses desire to channel energy through love. Pure Desire comes from the *love of that which we desire*; not because we need it to feel better or improve our worth, but rather because we are inspired for the pure joy of experience and expansion of consciousness.

Inspiration taps us into the unlimited flow of Life Force Energy that sustains our journey in whatever ways we choose.

Let's Recap

- When your True-Self is displaced, Life Force Energy is inhibited.
- Since you cannot live without adequate energy, the EGO (Energy Generating Operator) activates to generate energy.
- The EGO uses motor-vation to generate energy, and this creates "motors" that unconsciously run your life.
- Two types of motor-vation include positive motor-vation where the EGO motor-vates you to improve or maintain worth, and negative motor-vation where the EGO motor-vates you to avoid anything that might diminish worth.
- The EGO discerns the value of motor-vation, and, if the return on investment is not positive, you will eventually experience a lack of motor-vation in specific areas of your life.
- Motor-vation is EGO-driven and eventually wears out while inspiration is channeled by your True-Self and provides unlimited energy according to Pure Desire.

Chapter 8

Energy Generating Emotions

Emotions are powerful energy generators.

We all know that emotions motivate us to do, be and have, but emotions are also powerful generators of energy.

The "E" in emotion stands for energy, and the "motion" in emotion represents that energy in motion. Emotions are your mind's interpretation of moving energy in your body, and, in fact, the motion of energy in the body is what creates emotion. Our minds simply interpret that moving energy as a feeling, such as anger or happiness.

Emotional Reactions are Energy Generators

Emotional reactions are generally in response to our worth being challenged in some way meaningful to us. When an experience or person causes us to feel unworthy or not good enough, we automatically defend our worth with an emotional reaction, even if we don't realize why we are reacting. An emotional reaction is a defensive strategy used by the EGO to protect your worth whenever it appears to be challenged by a person or experience.

For instance, if your primary emotional need is respect, the EGO constantly sorts for any signs of disrespect. Even the slightest indication of disrespect or lack of respect can trigger the EGO because it interprets that the person disrespecting you thinks you are unworthy

Emotional reactions are caused by the fear that we are really unworthy and we might be exposed. The act of lashing out with emotion, such as anger, is unconsciously intended to defend our worth, so the more fragile our worth, the more we react. Most likely, someone with a quick temper has a weak sense of worth.

Until we are awake and conscious, most of us unknowingly rely on emotional reactions, such as anger, frustration, jealousy, impatience and sometimes even hate or rage in order to generate energy.

Emotional reactions are like invisible bombs that go off in order to produce energy. When you have an emotional reaction, due to an issue being triggered, it generates a charge and energy is released through your emotions.

Since an emotional reaction is the result of an issue being triggered, we need internal triggers in order to invoke those reactions, and it also means that the EGO is invested in our issues as a source of energy. If your issues are the impetus for energy, releasing an issue means that you cut off an energy source. The EGO automatically holds on to all emotional triggers because they are quick ways to produce energy for you. This is one of the reasons why it may be so hard to heal and release issues.

We may also get energy when we trigger someone else's emotions. You may not like it when your partner or friend gets angry or frustrated at something you said or did, but, if you look closely, you might see that you get energy from their emotional reactions, especially if you lash back to defend yourself.

Emotional reactions can produce large amounts of energy in a short period of time, but that energy is not sustainable. It quickly runs out and the body needs another source of energy, requiring another emotional reaction or another means to produce energy. Let's say that while driving in rush hour traffic, someone cuts you off and frustration is triggered. The surge of anger floods your body and generates energy, but there is also a come down afterward that drains energy and you will need another emotional reaction or EGO boost to compensate.

We can live for many years like this, but, at some point, the return on investment becomes upside down. Emotional reactions are ultimately energy depleting, leaving us feeling exhausted and overwhelmed.

Sooner or later, the energetic cost of generating energy through emotional reactions is greater than the energy that is generated - resulting in this unconscious strategy doing the opposite of what it was intended to do. When the cost of emotional reactions is greater than the gain, the body's defense mechanism is often hopelessness or depression. Depression and hopelessness prevent us from having strong emotional reactions, because as you shut down, you become numb to emotional triggers. Part 2 includes a chapter on healing emotional trauma and triggers.

The EGO generates conditional energy.
The True You circulates unconditional energy.

Life Force Energy flows abundantly and continuously, but when we are not awake, we unconsciously impede that flow by our false and disempowering beliefs and by putting false conditions on being worthy. If you could just let go of your limiting beliefs and conditions, Life Force Energy would flow into your body, finances, relationships and unlimited opportunities, providing more health, wealth, love and joyful fulfillment.

Chapter 9

"Motors" for Energy

Are there unconscious behaviors or dysfunctional dynamics that you would like to change or release?

The first step to Free Yourself from unconscious behavior and dysfunctional dynamics is to understand the hidden agenda of why you do the things you do, and this means that you must identify the motor-vation that runs you and dictates your life.

The following is an overview of the most common "motors" used by the EGO to generate energy. When you look at your own life, you may notice a "motor" that is not on this list; trust your intuition – if you think it might be a "motor," it probably is. Also, keep in mind that just because you experience something on this list, it doesn't automatically indicate that you are using it to generate energy. It's only a "motor" if you are generating energy by one or more of the following:

- Getting your primary emotional need met
- Triggering an emotional reaction
- Boosting the EGO in some way
- Depending on it for your sense of worth

If you are using something in order to get energy, it's a "motor."

The key is to be honest with yourself and inquire within. It is most helpful to bring this new awareness to your everyday life, and as you go through your days, observe where you are getting energy; notice any emotional reactions, anything that boosts or deflates the EGO, where you are on automatic pilot, when you are giving your energy/power away and especially notice any ongoing challenges because they are clues that may point to possible energy generators.

The Most Common EGO "Motors"

The "Roles We Play" Motor

It is nearly impossible to go through life without experiencing certain roles, and there is nothing wrong with "role playing." You might even say that we came to this life in order to experience various roles, just like we might experience different rides at an amusement park.

Some of the most common roles include: parent, student, teacher, leader, advocate doctor, healer, inventor, researcher, manager, artist, author, actor, etc....

Other roles we might play in our family, school or society include: clown, slacker, perfect child/student, martyr, caretaker, lost child, hero, helper, achiever, fixer, placater, advisor, screw up, nerd, victim, trouble-maker, athlete, good man/woman, thief, black sheep, pleaser, etc...

Your True-Self may have planned to experience a particular role or roles, but oftentimes, roles are cast onto us by parents, siblings, teachers or peers. Before we are even old enough to understand an assigned role it is stuck to us like glue, and we have taken ownership.

When we are not fully connected to our True-Selves and Life Force Energy is inhibited, the first place we often look for energy is through the roles we play in life.

The EGO loves roles because whatever we identify with becomes a source of artificially-generated energy, and roles are often the most powerful form of identity. We often unconsciously attach identity to a role because it attempts to prove our worth, making us feel worthy, and, therefore, boosting the EGO and generating energy, but when we attach our identity to a role, it influences the nature of the role, and often changes the experience entirely.

As soon as we identify with a role, and our worth is attached to the role, we unknowingly begin to weave our lives around this false identity, and by the time we are established adults, we are trapped in an invisible prison of our own making. We might even compromise our values and sacrifice our own needs in order to fulfill a role - completely unaware of this dynamic and even more unaware that we possess the key to freedom. Even "positive roles," such as the helper, caregiver or achiever can be traps for disempowerment and limitation.

Often, from the time we are very young, others give us energy for playing certain parts. Maybe our parents gave us praise, approval or encouragement for being the helper or the fixer, or, maybe, we got consistently scolded for being the trouble-maker or the slacker. Either way, emotional energy was generated on our behalf, unconsciously programming us to identify with these roles in order to receive energy from others.

Certain roles we play might come with a sense of power, such as the hero or the fixer, and when we play these roles, we feel powerful, and we project that others respect our power, boosting our EGOs and further increasing the amount of generated energy.

Money – the Great Energy Generator

Aside from being a source of financial exchange, the EGO uses money as an energy generator. The EGO sees money as a symbol of power and worth so the more money you have, the more the EGO gets boosted. The EGO may also get a boost from the admiration and respect of others who have less than you.

It makes sense that having an abundance of money can make you feel worthy, boost the EGO, and, therefore, generate energy, but, believe it or not, the EGO can also generate a tremendous amount of energy from the lack of money.

In what ways does the lack of money generate energy?

- *Worrying about money* - every time you worry about money the emotion of fear generates energy.
- *Trying to get money* - the motor-vation of trying to get money generates energy.
- *Talking about not having enough money* - the "poor me" story and complaining about lack generates energy.

- *Feelings of jealousy* - jealousy and/or resentment of others who have more money generates energy.
- *Arguing about money* - fighting with your partner/family over not enough money or how to use money generates energy.
- *Any degree of stress* - stress, overwhelm and frustration caused by "thoughts of scarcity" generates energy.
- *Relief or gratitude* - when you finally get money (especially at the last minute) the feeling of relief and/or gratitude generates energy.

When you believe that future abundance will make you worthy, money that you don't yet have provides the potential for worth, and, therefore, the EGO motor-vates you by generating energy for the pursuit.

According to the EGO, energy generation has priority over financial abundance - after all, you can survive without money but you cannot survive with life energy.

Sometimes, people have a lot of money but they still use money to negatively generate energy; never enough, fear of loss, fear of bad investments, other people's jealousies, stress around money management and relief when an investment pays off can all be generators of energy - anything that invokes an emotional reaction generates energy. Oftentimes, this energy generating dynamic leads to loss of money because the focus is on loss and scarcity. If this is the case, the EGO might conclude that less money or loss of money generates more energy, and, as a result, you might experience self-sabotage where a financial decision manifests in loss. The EGO unconsciously leads us in the direction of energy generation, even if it means challenges.

Of course, some financially abundant people generate energy by focusing on more abundance, which is better than focusing on loss and scarcity, but, if you depend on finances in order to feel worthy, the underlying fear will eventually create costs to the body, mind and spirit.

Story Telling Motor

Many of us get energy from our stories, especially stories that focus on our hardships or invoke pity. It is human nature to share our stories with each other, but when we tell the same story over and over again, it might mean that we are getting energy from that story. We might use a story to get others to think highly of us in order to increase our worth or appear better than, or we might want others to feel sorry for us, as an attempt to steel energy from them, and, in fact, provoking others to judge us or react in some way may be an unconscious attempt at getting energy.

Story telling could also be a way to invoke an emotional reaction in ourselves - in telling our story we might trigger certain feelings, such as feeling special or feeling like a victim.

Stress Motor

It is common to complain about stress, but you cannot put an end to stress until you understand that it is a powerful energy generator. An overwhelming "to do" list, or waiting until the last minute to meet deadlines, produces a combination of pressure and fear which combust as emotional energy. However, if stress goes on too long and too hard, at some point, it implodes in burnout. At the core of stress we usually find a belief that we must "do" in order to be worthy.

Helping Others Motor

Of course, it is great to help others, but sometimes we feed off helping those in need, without even knowing it. If you need to help or heal others in order to feel better about yourself, you may be using it as a "motor" to generate energy. Only you can know for sure, but, if believing you are better than someone in need boosts the EGO, you are likely using acts of charity to generate energy.

Fixer Motor

The Fixer is a bit different than the Helper. When the Fixer Motor is running, it usually means that we think that we know what is best for others and we want to change them so they will be a better version of themselves. We might attract people who don't want to be fixed resulting in antagonism in the relationship - but friction also generates energy.

People Pleasing Motor

Pleasing people can be an unconscious racket to generate energy. On the surface, it may appear that we are nice and kind, but underneath the surface, people pleasing can be a rather large motor. We may be motor-vated to please others in order to be needed, get attention or receive approval. *Ask yourself, "Why do I really do the things I do?"*

Complaining Motor

Every time we complain, nag or argue, we focus on what is wrong - this generates energy through antagonism and resistance, and any resulting emotional reactions. You can never change anything you complain about because the EGO sees it as a "motor" for energy, and, therefore, will not allow you to release it.

Judging Others Motor

When you judge or criticize someone, you are seeing them as less than you, or you are trying to devalue them in order to increase your sense of worth - feeling more worthy in comparison boosts the EGO. Gossip is a form of judgment that is done in a group of two or more people.

Self-Judgment Motor

The EGO uses self-judgment in order to determine our current degree of worth, but it also uses self-judgment to motor-vate us.

Of course, when we are motor-vated by self-judgment, we need more and more self-judgment to keep that "motor" running (staying motivated), and eventually that "motor" requires more energy to operate than it actually produces. This may explain all those times you tried to make changes or improve yourself in some manner, but, along the way, you lost the required energy and motor-vation.

Rushing Motor

Oftentimes, we unconsciously run late so that we can gain energy from the stress associated with rushing.

Problem Solving Motor

Successfully solving problems often results in an EGO boost which produces energy. When you get energy from problem solving and you rely on problems in order to generate energy, you set yourself up for more and more problems.

Fighting Against Motor

Fighting against anything, such as an issue in your family or a world issue generates energy, because it requires you to take a stand. In your fight against something, the EGO gets boosted because you believe you know better so it makes you feel worthy. If you rely on fighting against things in order to gain energy, you will attract perpetual issues to keep the "motor" running.

Scar Motor

We may learn to feed off our scars, disabilities or anything we don't like about ourselves in order to generate energy. If every time you look at a scar or focus on a disability, you have a negative emotional reaction (shame, regret, etc...) you may be using it to generate energy. If we are generating energy from our physical problems, it is nearly impossible to heal.

PTSD Motor (Post-Traumatic Stress Disorder)

Large amounts of energy are sparked anytime past trauma is triggered. For example, when a war veteran hears a car backfire, his whole system reacts, as if he is currently at risk of being shot. This fight or flight reaction floods the body with adrenaline, which is like the physical manifestation of artificially-generated energy.

Extra Weight Motor

If you feel an emotional charge when you complain about those extra pounds you can't lose, you may unknowingly be using them to generate energy.

Drama Motor

The drama of life invokes all sorts of emotions, resulting in huge out-pours of artificially-generated energy - no wonder it is so easy to get addicted to drama.

The Abuser Motor

Abuse of any nature (verbal, emotional, physical, etc...) is always an attempt to gain worth and generate energy. Abusing someone demonstrates power, albeit false power, but, nonetheless, as the one abusing increases his/her sense of power over another, perceived worth increases, thereby generating energy.

Victimhood Motor

When your identity is attached to being a victim, you might generate energy by telling others you are a victim to get sympathy, attention or support, or you might also generate energy by being hyper-reactive to possible victim scenarios. When you identify as a victim, it can be very difficult to overcome because victimhood can be a strong "motor" for energy.

Survivor Motor

When victimhood energetically costs more energy than it generates, the Energy Generating Operator (EGO) may turn off the Victimhood Motor and turn on the Survivor Motor, thereby transferring the generation of energy from one identity to another; from victim to survivor. A great deal of energy can be generated from playing the role of survivor, especially if you are taking a stand or fighting against something, but it is still artificially-generated energy, and, sooner or later, the cost greatly outweighs the gain.

Lying or Deceit Motor

We may "get power" from others through overt or covert manipulation. Power over another may increase one's perception of worth, thereby generating energy. A person may even have a secret affair or deceive a partner, in some other way, in an attempt to gain power and energy.

Relationship Motor

Relationships with powerful, smart or super attractive people may make us feel more worthy or we may use relationships with "inferior" people so that we can feel superior, and, therefore, more worthy - either way, the conscious or unconscious intention is to boost the EGO (more on this soon). We might also jump from one relationship to another when the former relationship no longer provides the boost.

Living in the Past Motor

The EGO might generate energy by replaying happy memories that bring up positive emotions, or replaying bad memories that bring up negative emotions, but, either way, emotions generate energy.

Living in the Future Motor

Energy might be generated by obsessively daydreaming about a happy future or fearing a negative outcome. It's good to imagine the future we desire, but constantly living in the future disempowers our present day ability to create that future.

Being Defensive Motor

Any time you defend yourself against anything, emotional, mental or physical, energy is generated for that defense. The same is true for resistance; anything you resist requires the generation of energy.

Unconscious Sex Motor

Sex can unconsciously be used to generate energy through the process of desire and conquest, subjugating others, pornography or having power over another.

Grudge Motor

When we hold onto anger or resentment, every time we think of the person or situation, we generate energy through reactivating negative emotions.

Shopping Motor

Buying power can be an EGO boost, along with a feeling of increased worth that comes from a sense that you deserve what you desire to purchase. Buyer's remorse occurs when that energy surge wears off and you feel unworthy of your purchase, or you become suddenly aware that you now have less money, and, therefore, less buying power.

Social Media Motor

Facebook and other social media sources offer energy boosts to the EGO through the ability to share successes and feel worthy, as well as complain about failures and get sympathy and attention. People get energy from talking about themselves and feeling important. Anything that inflates the EGO generates energy. Social media is also a great stage for judging, competing and comparison. Plus, when people remain anonymous, there is no limit to what they say or share in order to spark a reaction or ignite a Battle of Belief.

Daily Chaos Motor

The tension of having to "put out fires" or dealing with ongoing problems that keep you on your toes can be an immense energy generator. Energy might even be generated from disorganization and the stressful search to find missing things.

Control Motor

The EGO generates energy from controlling others because in order to control someone (or something) you must have greater power, and, therefore, greater worth. The EGO artificially generates energy whenever we experience a sense of power that comes from control - albeit false power.

Perfectionism Motor

The EGO generates energy with the motor-vation to be perfect, but perfectionism is just another word for self-judgment. The need to be perfect or do everything perfectly is a control mechanism orchestrated from unworthiness, causing us to strive for perfection in order to prove worth, but the standards are ruthlessly high. Since perfectionism is a moving target, and we rarely attain our definition of perfect, this "motor" costs a great deal more energy than it generates, and often burnsout fairly easy.

Tease/Bully Motor

Teasing may be harmless and fun, but, if both people are not enjoying it and participating, the teaser may, in fact, be using teasing to gain worth in order to boost his EGO. When we tease someone without their joyful participation, we are demonstrating that we are more clever, and we have power over the one being teased, thereby turning teasing into bullying. Whenever we make another powerless, so that we feel powerful in comparison, the Bully Motor is likely running.

Fame Motor

Standing out, being popular or experiencing some level of fame in your local community, country or worldwide can be an enormous EGO boost and energy generator.

Competition Motor

In the quest to be the best, energy is generated, and if we succeed, more energy is generated, but, if we lose, we might feel as if our energy is "sucked-dry."

Illness Motor (disease, disability, injury)

When we use a physical challenge as cause for attention, or we attach our identity to it, a physical challenge can become an energy generator.

Co-dependency Motor

Taking care of a partner who is dependent on a substance or dysfunctional lifestyle can improve our sense of worth by making us feel needed or better than. The ongoing chaos in co-dependent relationships can also be energy generating.

"Know It All" Motor

Being able to say, "I told you so" boosts the EGO, and every time a "know it all" is right and others are wrong, energy is generated.

Religion Motor

When believing that your religion is the "right religion" makes you feel better than non-believers, there is likely a "motor" running. Religious activities, such as charity work, could also be used to get others to meet our primary emotional need, or abiding by rules or religious doctrine could make us look better in the eyes of fellow followers, thereby improving worth.

Spiritual Seeking Motor

Yes, even spiritual seeking can be a "motor" for the EGO. The search for peace, wisdom or enlightenment motor-vates us and generates energy, but what are we searching for?

Material Things Motor

If you attach your worth to fancy cars, big houses, jewels and other material things, the EGO uses these things to prove worth and generate energy.

Acquisition Motor

Much like the Material Things Motor, except an increased sense of worth and energy is only generated in the process of acquiring material things, and once the acquisition is complete, the things acquired have little or no meaning in terms of worth or energy.

Credit Score Motor

In school we use grades to determine worth, but as we become adults, we often substitute grades for credit scores. If we have a high score, we are worthy, and energy is generated, but, if we have a low score, we may hide in shame.

Status/Career/Position Motor

If worth depends on status, career or position, it is a "motor" for energy.

Physical Appearance Motor

When our worth is dependent on the way we look, compliments, attention and admiration can all be EGO boosts and "motors" for energy.

Accomplishments Motor

When we depend on education, degrees, awards or any type of tangible success for our sense of worth, they become "motors" for energy.

Being Special or Different Motor

Focusing on our differences, even if we don't like them, can generate energy.

Intelligence or Gifts Motor

Being smarter or more gifted in some way boosts the EGO, but, if you always need to be superior in order to feel good about yourself, this means that the people in your life must be inferior – which ultimately leads to all sorts of challenges as you compete with family and friends for superiority.

Once again, just because you experience something on this list, it doesn't automatically indicate that you are using it to generate energy. It's only a motor if you are generating energy by one or more of the following:

- Getting your primary emotional need met
- Triggering an emotional reaction
- Boosting the EGO in some way
- Depending on it for your sense of worth

If you are using something in order to get energy, it's a "motor."

Chapter 10

More Motors ...

The Self-importance "Motor"

One way in which the EGO proves, or improves, worth is through importance. If we are important, or possibly even more important, we are worthy. As a result, the EGO is constantly sorting for opportunities to gain importance, and it can realistically latch on to just about anything. Importance is a major "motor" that operates many other common "motors." For obvious reasons, it frequently shows up when the Status Motor or Know it All Motor is running, but it also shows up with the Comparison Motor and the Complaining Motor; particularly when the EGO tries to prove that your issues make you important, and, if your problems are worse in comparison to other people's problems, you are more important.

The EGO also uses our past experiences to demonstrate importance - you see this a great deal in people who re-tell their "war stories" over and over again. The EGO uses "battle scars" and "awards of recognition" in much the same way. Even being a victim can improve worth when a sense of importance is placed upon it.

Self-importance shows up in all sorts of subtle and not so subtle ways. It could show up as a belief that others should cater to us and put our needs first, or it could show up as feeling annoyed at the slow "inconsiderate" driver ahead of us. Oftentimes, it shows up as defending ourselves against perceived wrong-doings or any possible worth-related injury.

It is quite common for self-importance to manifest as an attempt to be "on top" - to be better or even the best, and when we want to make sure that others know how smart, generous or creative we are, self-importance manifests as a need to "take credit." Even labeling ourselves extrovert or introvert, good or bad, smart or not smart, etc... can be a sign of self-importance.

Notice how many of your actions are based on self-importance - how often do you do something so that you can take credit for it? If you didn't get credit, would you still do all the things you do? Your primary emotional need is often tied into getting credit for the things we do so that others will meet that need - if your primary emotional need is appreciation, you might go out of your way to help others in order to get credit and appreciation in return.

In order to demonstrate importance, the EGO must identify and categorize, therefore, everyone and everything is viewed according to labels, status, traits, stereotypes and other various standards.

The EGO addresses the world from a very mechanical standpoint because that is what is it programmed to do - *a program can only do what a program is programmed to do!*

Our True-Selves are not at all concerned with self-importance, and, therefore, have a vastly different experience of life. Self-importance is replaced with seeing everyone as equally important - knowing each being is valuable and worthy manifests as respect, understanding and compassion for all, and, therefore, the richest person in the world is no more important than the poorest.

Beyond the illusion of duality, we know that each of us has the potential to be good and bad and what is in one of us, is in all of us. Our True-Selves see all people as who they really are behind their masks and false identities. Secure in our own being and never taking anything personally, we allow everyone to be exactly as they are.

Despite the fact that our True-Selves are the most creative, productive and innovative, there is no great need to take credit for our creations, productions or innovations. As our True-Selves, we might anonymously partake in the most giving and altruistic manner without a thought of recognition or a need for return on investment.

The Proving You Can Do It "Motor"

Proving that you can do something is often a driving force when others predicted that you would fail. So, if your mother, teacher or preacher told you that you would never succeed, the "proving you can do it motor" might be operating.

When someone in authority tells a child that he cannot succeed, the child's EGO either deflates and, later in life, he experiences failure after failure, or the EGO rises to the occasion and motor-vates him to prove the naysayer wrong, so that this one pivotal person finally deems him worthy.

Oftentimes, the "proving you can do it motor" actually results in great success, where the individual can move mountains, but, as with all "motors' there is a cost. Operating this "motor" can result in ongoing relationship issues or health challenges, due to the fact that everything comes a distant second to the one crucial goal.

Giving the naysayer the power to decide your worth usually ends in terrible disappointment, as well. Even when goals are exceeded, if the final declaration of "I told you so" goes unacknowledged by the one person you were trying to prove wrong, satisfaction is never experienced because you still do not feel worthy.

After countless years of struggle and strife, the prize at the end of the race is void of any real meaning, and without validation from the source of your motor-vation, worth is diminished. Even though the "motor" may have manifested success in the traditional sense, if your worth is no greater than when you began, the "motor" has ultimately failed.

Whenever we are trying to prove someone wrong, we can be certain that the EGO is in charge.

EGO says, "I must prove I can do it!"

If, when performing as EGO, you get knocked down, you get up to prove you are worthy.

True-Self says, "I know I can do it!"

If, when living as your True-Self, you get knocked down, you get up because inspiration and vision move you from the inside out.

Success that comes from True-Self inspiration is not about proving anything to anyone, for any reason. Instead, it is the result of a strong vision and a burning desire to reach the heights of human potential, ultimately celebrating the auspicious success of the human spirit.

Your True-Self would reach for the sky, even if no one was watching, because it is not about anyone but you.

The Same Thing

If you were to analyze the list of artificial energy generators just discussed, you would begin to notice a pattern. Almost all of these Energy Generators also Inhibit Life Force Energy.

For example:

- Self-judgment makes us go unconscious, causing True-Self displacement and inhibiting Life Force Energy, but the EGO also uses self-judgment to motor-vate you to prove worth.
- Victimhood also makes us go unconscious, causing True-Self displacement and inhibiting Life Force Energy, but the EGO may use it to create an identity and attach worth to that identity and, therefore, generate energy.
- Complaining, stress and rushing all make us go unconscious, causing True-Self displacement and inhibiting Life Force Energy, yet the EGO can use any of these dynamics to generate energy.

When the EGO uses judgment, victimhood, complaining, etc… to generate energy, more Life Force Energy is inhibited, furthering the need for EGO generated energy, and perpetuating a dysfunctional cycle. The more you depend on EGO-driven energy, the more the EGO needs to generate energy. In an attempt to get energy through artificial means, we unconsciously cut ourselves off from the abundant flow of Life Force Energy.

All the ways in which the EGO attempts to generate energy are ultimately energy depleting, and, therefore, "motor" failure is inevitable.

The True You is the conduit for Life Force Energy.
When you embody your True-Self, you are plugged into
Life Force Energy, and you don't need "motors" for energy.

In part 2, we will explore the many ways to turn off "motors."

Chapter 11

Extrovert or Introvert?

What we consider to be extroverted and introverted behavior may be a byproduct of the EGO.

The EGO causes us to be extroverted when it wants us to be seen because it needs attention, admiration or appreciation in order to feel worthy. If your primary emotional need is one of these three or something similar, there is a very good chance you are considered to be an extrovert.

The EGO causes us to be introverted when it doesn't want us to be seen because it is protecting us from criticism, judgment or ridicule. If your primary emotional need is approval, acceptance, validation or something similar, there is a very good chance you are considered to be an introvert.

The EGO doesn't just demand, "Look at me!" in order to show importance and prove worth, it also says "Don't look at me" in order to remain separate and protect worth.

When you comprehend human behavior from this perspective, it is easy to see why people behave as they do. Much of what we consider to be personality is actually a result of unconscious EGO manipulation, where the EGO motor-vates us to act in specific ways in order to get our primary emotional need met, thereby proving worthiness.

Does this mean that extrovertism and introvertism disappear when we embody our True-Selves?

As our True-Selves, we may appear introverted when we go within for connection and introspection, but, unlike EGO introvertism, we are not hiding because we are afraid to be seen.

We may also appear extroverted due to authentic expression, but it is not at all about needing attention, admiration or appreciation. We are simply allowing ourselves to be a clear and open channel for Divine Expression, and when the Divine shines through, the spotlight of the Universe may be directly overhead.

Living fully as your True-Self allows you to transcend labels, stereotypes and even personality limitations. When the EGO is no longer in charge, you are free of all unconscious behaviors that once limited your choices. The sky is the limit as you are empowered to be *who you really are*.

Chapter 12

The Core Cause of Challenges

In essence, there is really nothing wrong with most of the ways in which we generate energy. Competition can be fun, money can be liberating and success can be fulfilling, however, in the quest for EGO generated energy, we create and attract all sorts of problems and challenges. In fact, this model of human dynamics pinpoints the most common cause of our perpetual issues as the unconscious generation of energy.

If you are not receiving adequate Life Force Energy, the EGO will do whatever it takes to generate the necessary energy to keep you alive. Therefore, the EGO will motor-vate you to argue, compete, judge, attract drama, create chaos and sometimes even abuse or be abused by others. Yes, there are other explanations for these behaviors, and they are no less true, as many things can be simultaneously true depending on your approach, BUT, when you get to the heart of the matter, understanding our programmed survival strategies is key, as survival supersedes all else. Consider that the core cause of most dysfunctional behavior is the unconscious quest for energy in order to survive.

When you don't remember *who you really are* and that you are unconditionally worthy, the EGO reacts to life as if your survival is at risk, resulting in unconscious behavior, emotional reactions and fear-based decisions.

When you are cut off from the Pure Desire of your True-Self, the EGO is responsible for making sure you have the necessary energy to live. Just like not having enough food, air or water, when you are not plugged into Life Force Energy, you go into survival mode, automatically doing whatever it takes to generate energy - completely unaware of cost or consequence. When we are in survival mode, we run on automatic pilot because this is how we are programmed.

Yes, this means that most of the world is in survival mode, living off EGO energy, and this is why we are individually and collectively faced with so many challenges.

We generally experience issues in the same areas of our lives that we use to generate energy. In other words, *wherever "motors" run, issues follow.*

For instance:

- If you get energy out of work-related stress, the EGO will attract and create stressful work situations.
- If you get energy out of playing the part of hero or savior, the EGO will attract people who need rescuing.
- If you get energy out of challenging relationships, the EGO will attract and maintain challenging relationships.
- If you get energy out of being a "people pleaser," the EGO will attract people to please, who you can probably never please.

- If you get energy out of worrying about not having enough money, you will experience lack of money.
- If you get energy out of complaining about bad drivers on the road, you will encounter bad drivers.
- If you get energy out of being frustrated when things break, things will break.

Get the point?

Wherever you get energy, for whatever reason, challenges will inevitably arise.

The Invested EGO!

The EGO is invested in perpetuating problems.

Many people are relentlessly unsuccessful at solving ongoing issues, because they are not healing the core cause. Since the energy needed to survive is more important than harmony, healing or happiness, the EGO will not allow you to heal or resolve something from which you are generating energy.

If you rely on your physical challenges for energy generation, you make it nearly impossible to heal because the EGO will not allow you to heal something that provides energy. This means that if you get energy from being sick, injured or disabled or "telling your story" in order to receive attention or sympathy, no matter how hard you try, it will be very difficult to heal as long as that "motor" is running - in order to heal you must stop using your sickness, injury or disability as a means to generate energy.

This is the same reason why we have so many challenges and delays in reaching self-improvement goals. If we should reach a self-improvement goal, it means that the EGO can no longer generate energy from self-judgment and motor-vating us to change.

For instance, if you are trying to lose weight and you are constantly judging your overweight body, the EGO generates energy every time you make a judgment and have an emotional reaction, and this means that if you succeed in meeting the goals for your body, the EGO can no longer generate energy from the judgment of your out-of-shape body. If losing weight means losing an energy source, your body will hold onto the weight, which may be why it is so difficult to lose weight. Whereas, generating energy is essential for survival, having a beautiful body is not, and, therefore, the EGO will choose energy generation over fitness or aesthetics.

In this way, the EGO is invested in creating and maintaining issues and deficiencies you can judge and be motor-vated to change.

For whatever you judge, complain or criticize, you get energy, and, if you should improve or fix the problem, the EGO losses a "motor." If you are getting energy from beauty imperfections, challenges in intelligence, financial issues or anything you dislike about yourself, the EGO will not allow you to improve or change, (as long as you are getting energy from it) no matter how hard you try. This makes self-judgment and self-criticism terrible strategies for success.

Law of Attraction

In examining the Law of Attraction, let's observe how it works in terms of the EGO.

Since survival always overrides wants and desires, if the EGO is in charge, your wants and desires play second fiddle to generating energy. If your attempts at manifesting your dreams and desires are met with blocks and obstacles, it may be because the EGO is running "motors" and unconsciously motor-vating your behavior, and although you may have the inspiration to manifest what you want, motor-vation supersedes inspiration when the EGO is in charge.

If this is the case, the Law of Attraction will attract and create whatever it takes to ensure your worth, and keep your "motors" running. For instance, it will attract issues and challenges that cause you to emotionally react because emotional reactions generate energy.

The EGO is not programmed to make your dreams come true or direct you to happiness.

The EGO is a survival program that is programmed to keep you alive and it will function, and make you unconsciously function, in ways that generate energy for you to live. As I discuss in my book, "Seducing the Field" the key to using the Law of Attraction is True-Self embodiment. As your True-Self, you have the ability to consciously use the Law of Attraction to manifest anything you desire.

Let's Recap

- The EGO uses "motors" to generate energy.
- These "motors' often cause issues in your life.
- The EGO is invested in maintaining issues that produce energy, making it impossible to solve problems that generate energy.
- The Law of Attraction will attract issues that keep your "motors" running, resulting in unconscious and unwanted manifestation.
- Conscious Creation requires True-Self embodiment.

Some Facts about the EGO

- When we say that someone has a "Big EGO," we are really saying that their EGO generates a lot of energy.
- The EGO must keep inflating itself in order to generate energy consistently.
- The more perceived power and control you have, the greater the energy boosts.
- Artificially-generated energy cannot be stored, so energy must be perpetually generated.
- When the EGO gets a boost, energy is generated and it gets inflated with this energy. This is an Inflated EGO.
- Any type of boost to the EGO generates energy.
- When the EGO gets wounded, you become tired and unmotivated because a "motor" failed.

The EGO generates energy for you in three ways:

1. The EGO motor-vates you (with energy) to prove your worth.
2. Emotional reactions generate energy.
3. When the EGO is boosted via proof of worth, energy is generated.

Living in an EGO-driven world!

We are currently living in an EGO-driven world where the structure of mainstream society supports the EGO, while discouraging True-Self expression. Government-run schools and corporate-run nations perpetuate the EGO by using a system of rewards and punishments. Students and employees are rewarded when they prove that they are worthy according to the standards of the particular establishment, while they are punished, or at least discouraged, for independent thinking and non-conforming behavior.

In a system of rewards and punishments, the EGO is trained while the True-Self is suppressed.

Chapter 13

The EGO's Biggest Defense

The EGO's biggest defense is fear.

The purpose of fear is to keep you alive; to protect your physical vehicle (body), as well as your sense of identity (who you think you are). If you get too close to the edge of a cliff, fear will warn you to back up, and if you do something that might threaten your identity, fear will warn you to shut down expression, causing you to stay safely in your comfort zone.

Your comfort zone is comprised of all the people, places and things that support your identity, give you worth and generate energy.

To understand the dynamics of fear, imagine an invisible electric fence that you might use to keep a dog in your backyard without a physical fence. When the dog touches the energetic boundary that you set with the electric fence, he gets zapped. It doesn't take long for the dog to learn that he must stay within the parameter to avoid pain.

Now, imagine that the electric fence represents the boundary of your personal comfort zone, but, instead of getting zapped with an electric current, when you approach the boundary, you get zapped with the vibration of fear, warning you to back away. Like the dog, you have probably learned to stay within the safe zone.

The problem is, everything that you desire (that you don't yet experience) is located outside your comfort zone, otherwise you would already have it.

Going outside your comfort zone probably won't be risky to your physical body, unless you dream of being a race car driver or partaking in some other dangerous behavior, but, more than likely, the danger of going outside your comfort zone is quite risky to your sense of identity. In order to reach for a dream or try something new, you might have to give up who you have been to become someone new, and this is perceived like death to the EGO, because if you lose your identity, you lose your foundation of worth and without worth, you might be rejected or abandoned, possibly resulting in death.

The EGO is programmed to limit you so that you do not risk judgment, rejection, abandonment or exclusion, or anything that might threaten survival, and, this means, if you desire to express yourself or do something that might endanger your worth in the eyes of others, the EGO is programmed to stop you by the use of fear, doubt or anxiety. Even the thought of losing approval creates anxiety so that we continue to behave in ways that guarantee our worth and the approval of others.

Let's not forget about the most pervasive aspect of fear – Worry!

Because the EGO is a survival program, it is programmed to be on guard for possible danger so it must always be anticipating the future, and ascertaining that your future worth will ensure survival. Pulling another card from its sleeve, the EGO motor-vates you through worry. Most of us spend our entire lives in the Realm of Worry – never feeling free and peaceful for very long before there is something else to worry about.

Fortunately, fear does not have the last say, or we would stay small and limited in our expression. Each of us has the ability to override fear, and choose higher versions of ourselves that exist outside the parameters of our comfort zone.

If the "better than" version of the Worthiness Program is running, "traditional fear" is generally less prevalent because part of the identity is often entangled with being fearless – to be the best, brightest and most anything, you must be able to exceed your own comfort zone, time and time again. However, fear may operate in a completely different way; instead of being afraid to take chances, the "better than" version of the Worthiness Program may use fear of ***not being the best*** as motor-vation to be a super-achiever.

Chapter 14

FRUSTRATION

According to the EGO, we don't improve or prove our worth by just standing around or waiting indefinitely, so it needs a way to keep us constantly moving toward a goal, even if it is just completing a household task.

FRUSTRATION TO THE RESCUE!

Let's be clear, the EGO is not punishing us with uncomfortable emotions, rather, it is manipulating our behavior so that we effectively get the job done or quickly reach our destination. Because our perceived worth depends on fulfilling roles, jobs and responsibilities, any delay or interruption could be costly (to worth), and the Worthiness Program will simply not allow it, so the EGO motor-vates us to "get on with it" by the use of frustration. But, it is an endless cycle because there are always more jobs, goals and destinations.

The precipitating factor to frustration is feeling out of control and wanting a situation, experience or relationship to be other than it is. Feeling out of control is a danger signal to the EGO indicating that our wellbeing is at risk. Therefore, control must be restored at all costs.

Frustration indicates that things are not working according to expectation and warns us to succeed or directs us away from the challenge at hand, so that we can find a better use of our time and energy - one more likely to result in proving worth.

Frustration motor-vates us to meet expectations or move on to where we can be more successful.

If a particular action or interaction perpetually results in frustration (more failure than success) there will be a threshold where the EGO will simply stop motor-vating us to take this action or have this interaction, thereby avoiding future frustration.

Frustration indicates that a "motor" is trying to operate, but stress and resistance are causing it to seize.

- Motor-vation - a green ***go*** light indicating the motor is running
- Frustration - a yellow ***warning*** light indicating the motor is seizing
- Defeat - a red ***stop*** light indicating the motor is failing

IMPATIENCE

Similar to frustration, the EGO motor-vates you with impatience so that you are always moving in the direction of proving or improving worth. Therefore, waiting in traffic or waiting in line is a waste of time to the EGO.

Transcending the EGO

Transcending the EGO requires you to make unconscious behavior conscious, so that you can override "motor-driven" actions and reactions.

The EGO is never satisfied for very long - it always wants more and more, so there is no point even trying to satisfy it. Your True-Self, on the other hand, is always at peace and there is never a need for attaining satisfaction because it is the very essence of fullness.

Maybe you don't know *who you really are* without the EGO, and it can be scary to find out, but that is exactly what you must do if you are to free yourself from limitation and disempowerment.

As your True-Self, everything might still be the same on the outside, but your experience and relationship with life will be completely transformed and elevated to a higher level of consciousness, where joy and peace are your natural state of being.

The True You desires expression.

At some point, all strategies do the opposite of what they were intended to do. When the cost is perpetually greater than the gain, crisis or chaos may manifest in order to wake us up. Once we are conscious, and aware of the hidden agenda that controls our lives, we have the power to transform.

Chapter 15

Energy Deprivation - Energy Conservation

If we are always trying to prove worth or protect worth, we likely live in an unconscious state of stress. Just like a fish cannot identify water because he is always in it, we don't have the ability to identify the stress caused by the Worthiness Program – at least until we become conscious.

In the short-term, all "motors" require a great deal of energy to run, and they are all ultimately draining. Mid-day and/or end-of-day fatigue and exhaustion are big indicators that "motors" are running and maybe even running our lives, and, in fact, we may need one "motor" to compensate for the energy lost from another "motor," and then another to compensate for that one. We may even go through our days using one type of "motor" after another. In the morning, we may use the "motor" of arguing with our kids, driving to work we may use frustration at bad drivers, at work competition, comparison or stress, after work mentally replaying mistakes and regrets and at night the "motor" might be social media, an addiction, self-judgment, complaining or blaming. Even a good night's sleep may not be enough to recoup, and we wake up feeling like we never went to sleep, and it starts all over again.

Indeed, it is possible to live on artificially-generated energy for many, many years, but in the long-term, the "motors" that once provided energy begin to deteriorate, and it takes more energy to stay in dysfunctional dynamics than the energy generated by them.

When we rely on artificial energy sources, inevitably, we reach a threshold where it takes more energy to keep our "motors" running than the "motors" give back, and, consequently, we become drained and depleted. For instance, if you have been keeping up an identity or fulfilling a role in order to prove worth, at some point, it will cost more energy to maintain the identity or role than the energy it generates.

Any way you look at it, EGO-driven energy is unsustainable.

When a "motor" costs more energy to operate than it generates, the EGO will conclude that the "motor" is a bad investment and turn it off; for example, if you are motor-vated by the hope of attaining success in some way, but you keep failing, the EGO will eventually conclude that the hope of success is a bad investment of energy and it will stop the motor-vation for success - you might still dream of success but you will lack the necessary motor-vation to do much about it. Or, if you rely on motor-vation from self-judgment to improve yourself in some way, eventually the energetic cost of stress-related self-judgment will outweigh the motor-vation produced by self-judgment. When this happens, the "motor" fails, and there is no motor-vation left for following through on your self-improvement goals. This can cycle over and over many times – and explains why we may be super motor-vated to begin a self-improvement routine, but we lose steam before ever reaching our goals.

When all our "motors" cost more energy to operate than they produce, the result is energy deprivation, and when we do not receive adequate energy to live, the EGO goes into "code red" survival mode and must strategize to conserve energy in order to keep us alive. First, energy will go to vital organs, the brain and essential systems in the body, while energy will be restricted from non-essential needs, with motor-vation often being the first to go.

Your body needs energy in order to survive, and, if it does not get adequate energy, it begins to suffer and break down. Just like oxygen deprivation or extreme dehydration causes severe health issues, so does the lack of energy in the body. When any part of the body is deprived of energy, that body part may show signs of deprivation in the form of disease, disorder or weakness that makes that body part susceptible to injury.

In addition, the ongoing stress of EGO generated energy takes a toll on our bodies. Energy generated through fear, fighting, judging, competing, proving and negative emotions adversely impacts the body, year after year.

The bottom line is, every "motor" that we use for energy eventually burns-out, and when this occurs, "motors" do the opposite of what they were intended to do, ultimately depleting more energy than they generate. When our "motors" fail, we may experience fatigue, exhaustion, overwhelm or depression.

Depression ensures that vital energy does not go to unnecessary functions.

Depression is a survival program that shuts down non-essential functions in order to make sure that energy is conserved. This is why depressed people almost always complain about severe fatigue and having no energy to do the things they once enjoyed; when this is the case, the body needs every ounce of energy to survive and has no extra energy for hobbies, interests or socializing.

Depression may allow us a time out, but under the surface, the worthiness meter is still calculating – worthy or unworthy?

Free Energy

In the quest for life energy, we can sure make a simple process complex, convoluted and problematic.

Isn't it astounding that we fight and compete over something to which we each have unlimited access? Despite the fact that we all have the innate ability to tap into unlimited Life Force Energy, we still give our power away in exchange for it - depleting our bodies, minds and spirits due to the perpetual stress and distress associated with all the "motors" we run in order to generate energy.

Life Force Energy is free for everyone and the only reason we don't experience an abundance of it is because we are not plugged into the source. The time and energy that it takes to artificially generate energy could be more effectively used in learning how to embody our True-Selves so that we are permanently plugged in and able to access as much energy as we will ever need or desire.

The Air Factory

No one has to make air because it is a natural manifestation of natural forces, so there is no cost to creating or using air, but, imagine that there wasn't enough air for everyone, and our scientists and inventors had to figure out a way to manufacture huge amounts of air.

In the process of artificially manufacturing air, large polluting factories would have to be built and certain chemicals and devices would be necessary for mass production. This all sounds doable, but when we need polluting factories, possibly harmful chemicals and devices to manufacture anything, we compromise that which we artificially create, and the unfortunate byproduct is usually detrimental to the health and wellbeing of the human being, as well as the Earth.

Maybe these artificial air machines also use up natural air in the production of artificially-generated air, further increasing the lack of natural air.

We might be able to artificially manufacture air, but there would be an accumulative cost, until one day it outweighed the gain. Wouldn't it make more sense to figure out why there is a scarcity of natural air, in the first place, and do whatever it takes to fix the cause?

We can apply this same philosophy to Life Force Energy. Yes, our EGO's can and do manufacture artificially-generated energy, but, over time, the operation of energy generation causes all sorts of problems, issues and dysfunctions, and eventually the cost of generating energy outweighs the gains.

Let's Recap

- At some point, all "motors" cost more energy to run than they produce, and when this occurs, they burn out.
- When you are not getting enough energy to live, the EGO goes into a state of "red alert" where it conserves energy.
- During times of severe energy deprivation, energy is delivered only to vital organs and bodily functions necessary to keep you alive.
- Unlike Life Force Energy, artificially-generated energy has a cost to our lives, often resulting in various issues.

What happens when all your "motors" stop working?

To best answer this question, I have included a bonus chapter at the very end of this book.

Chapter 16

Power in Exchange for Worth

Inside you is the power of unlimited possibility. This power allows you to consciously create the life you most desire. Your power belongs to you alone, and no one can take this power from you or use it against you. Only you have the ability to access your own power, and, if you use it consciously, no dream or possibility is out of reach.

Your power lies in your ability and willingness to express your real self; think your own thoughts, speak your own mind, create your own dream, love with an open heart and consciously choose how to live your life. Your power is expressed through the unique expression of you.

- When you express yourself, you activate your power, and the more you confidently express yourself without inhibition, the greater your power grows.

> *Signpost on the path*
> *For increased power go within!*

- Just as self-expression activates your power, self-suppression deactivates your power.
- When you suppress expression, you suppress power.

You may be thinking, *if power is accessed through expression, why would we ever suppress ourselves?*

If you look carefully, you will see that the Worthiness Program keeps us from self-expression. If you need the approval of others in order to feel worthy, you must behave in acceptable ways that guarantee approval, requiring you to hide any expression that could be judged negatively. Self-expression opens us up to judgment and disapproval, thereby triggering feelings of unworthiness. If we need others to find us worthy, we must suppress ourselves in all ways that might be judged unfavorably.

The high price of worthiness is the suppression of self, and, in fact, every time we choose approval, acceptance, appreciation, etc... over self-expression, we give our power away in exchange for worth.

Self-expression increases/decreases in direct proportion to how much you know and own your unconditional worth, while, at the same time, your power increases/decreases in direct proportion to self-expression/suppression.

Unconditional Worth – Expression – Power

Unconditional worth manifests in self-expression and self-expression manifests as your intrinsic power; when you know your unconditional worth, you can express your real self, and, in doing so, you access your power. Self-expression results in self-empowerment.

Conditional Worth – Suppression – Powerlessness

When you must prove your worth, the fear of disapproval causes you to suppress expression, and, in so doing, you inadvertently inhibit your power. Self-suppression results in disempowerment.

It is true that when others approve and we feel worthy, the EGO gets a boost and we get an energy charge, but, if we are hiding our true expression, the cost of this energy is our intrinsic power.

The more power we give away in exchange for a temporary EGO boost, the more we disconnect from Life Force Energy, and the more the EGO will motor-vate us to do whatever it takes to generate more energy, including giving up more power in exchange for energy – a vicious cycle ensues.

Powerlessness Program

The act of self-suppression tells your subconscious mind that you believe that you are powerless, and your belief in powerlessness activates the Powerlessness Program.

Belief is the "on and off" switch for subconscious programs.

The Powerlessness Program is designed to artificially generate a sense of power (albeit false power), so that we feel powerful and others perceive us as powerful. The primary way in which it makes us seem powerful is through motor-vating us to control. According to the program, control equals power, so we must prove that we are powerful through the use of control.

In other words, in order to compensate for perceived disempowerment, the program motor-vates us to control - the more control, the more power. But, in order to be controlling, we need things to control, thereby creating the drive for material possessions, money and all sorts of dysfunctional dynamics. This is the hidden cause of control issues and why so many of us are obsessively controlling.

If the "better than" version of the Worthiness Program is running, we generally express ourselves without inhibition, and, therefore, we access a sense of power, but since this power is based on being "better than," we might need to be even more controlling of circumstances, events and other people in order to stay on top.

Regardless of the version of the Worthiness Program, the EGO motor-vates us to control just about everything, including the future, everyday details, the lives of other people and uncountable situations and events.

When we truly own our intrinsic power, we don't need others to act in ways that make us feel powerful, and we don't need to control anything because we are empowered at the very core of our being.

Let's Recap

- You are an intrinsically powerful being!
- You tap into this power whenever you express your authentic self.

- If you are playing the Worthiness Game, it is very likely that you unconsciously suppress expression in order to gain approval, acceptance, etc….
- In suppressing expression you give away your power.
- The Powerlessness Program activates as a result of believing you are powerless.
- The program is designed to make you feel and look powerful by means of control, therefore, it motor-vates you to control.
- In the attempt at controlling anything, you give your power and energy to the subject of your control, inhibiting energy that could be used for expression.

Chapter 17

THE DYNAMICS OF DISEMPOWERMENT

As you now know, if we do not own our unconditional worth, the EGO initiates a dynamic designed to prove our worth. However, this dynamic sets us up for disempowerment, because in trying to prove our worth to others, we must behave in ways they find worthy, causing us to suppress our authentic selves. As this manifests in how we act, the choices we make and in speaking our truth, we inhibit our power.

Without the expression of free-will and freedom of speech we are disempowered.

When we subject ourselves to the whims, wishes, opinions, judgments and conditions of others so that they approve of us or meet our primary emotional need, we make ourselves powerless, and, if we are willing to compromise our values and sacrifice our needs in order to prove worth, we subject ourselves to victimhood. Once we believe that we are a victim or could be a victim, the Victimhood Program activates, as the belief in victimhood activates the program.

THIS THING CALLED "NEGGING"

To fully understand the dynamics of disempowerment and how the Worthiness Program sets the stage for disempowerment, let's look at something called "negging.

When my teenage son was trying to figure out how to meet girls, he stumbled upon a website for pick-up artists. Because he thought it was fascinating and he believed it could help him, he began to study pickup artistry. After many months, he concluded that there were much healthier ways of meeting girls, but in the interim, he learned all sorts of tools, tricks and techniques which he openly shared with me so that we could discuss the underlying dynamics of manipulation. He learned that some pick-up artists use a process called "negging" where they intentionally insult a very attractive woman in order to get her to bed.

How does it work?

In a bar, club, mall or coffee shop, the pick-up artist finds an attractive woman, considerably out of his league; he knows that she would not be interested in him because he is "less worthy" according to dating standards so he must re-balance the measurement of worth. Once he approaches her, he casts insults at her, intended to put her down in some way, thereby lowering her worth, and, simultaneously increasing his – the shift in worth is perceived by the pickup artist and the woman.

Suddenly feeling less worthy, the woman instinctually attempts to regain her sense of worth by trying to elicit the man's interest and approval, but he continues to make her doubt her worth. Many women, not knowing that they are the subject of this negging game, end up compromising their values, often engaging in sexual encounters with men they would never consider otherwise - because they are trying to regain their worth, women who are negged may cross their own boundaries, undermine their own values and possibly even risk safety.

Is the "negged woman"a victim? By normal standards, you might say yes, but not if we look at the bigger picture.

Firstly, if a woman knows and owns her unconditional worth, negging would never work; the fact that a random man insults her would mean nothing to her. She would probably set a strong boundary that insulated her from his disrespect or she would walk away. Either way, she would put a stop to the improper behavior, and it would not go any further. With a strong foundation of worth, there is no possibility of becoming a victim.

Since worth is often conditioned upon a strength or gift, many attractive women associate their worth with their appearance and depend on appreciation or admiration in order to feel worthy. If a woman does not know her unconditional worth, and her worth is conditioned upon others finding her attractive, or treating her in special ways, she stands on a weak foundation where victimhood is possible.

So, when a pickup artist "negs" a beautiful woman whose worth depends on her appearance, his insults have the potential to make her feel unworthy, and, if this is the case, her EGO might be triggered to protect her worth – motor-vating her to prove to the man that she is worthy (exactly what the pickup artist is counting on). As she gives up her power in exchange for worth, she sets herself up for manipulation and possibly mistreatment.

If we were watching this scene in a movie, we would probably be yelling at the woman on the screen, "Don't do it! You're being conned!"

It is easy to recognize that this woman is giving up her power and allowing herself to be vulnerable to victimhood, but, the thing is, most people do this every day in their own particular way; doing jobs they hate, pretending to be someone they're not or staying in relationships that aren't good for them - just to meet the conditions of their worth and prove to others that they are worthy.

When you don't know your worth, you can be "negged" without even knowing it.

We make ourselves powerless anytime we sacrifice our values, integrity or free-will in order to gain approval or prove to others that we are worthy. Every time we compromise, suppress or sacrifice ourselves in order gain acceptance, appreciation, respect, etc…, we give our power away in exchange for the illusion of worth.

Your power is expressed in your ability to make conscious choices that support you, speak your truth, express your authentic self, follow your inner guidance and do what you love to do.

- Power of Choice –the power to make conscious choices that support free-will.
- Power of Expression - the power to express your unique style and creative spirit.
- Power of Speech – the power to speak your truth.
- Power of Intuition – the power to follow your inner guidance.

Once we are willing to give up our power (in anyway) in order to prove our worth to others, we make ourselves vulnerable to unwanted experiences. Without the power to consciously choose, we become victims to the whims and wishes (good or bad) of everyone to whom we must prove our worth – strangers and friends alike.

If we are willing to compromise ourselves in order to prove our worth to others, or we are afraid to say no because we fear disapproval or judgment, we subject ourselves to disempowerment and even victimhood.

The good news is, no one is ever doing anything to us because we are responsible for setting ourselves up for empowerment or disempowerment.

If you own your unconditional worth, your foundation is built on solid rock and you are aligned with empowerment. If you doubt your worth, your foundation is built on quicksand, and you open yourself up to powerlessness and possible victimhood. This all means that you can only be a victim when you believe that you are unworthy or your worth is conditioned upon others finding you worthy.

To overcome victimhood, you must take back your power by owning your worth and not making it subject to the opinions of anyone for any reason, and because you own your power, you are not vulnerable to disempowerment. The moment you choose to own your unconditional worth, you can never be a victim again.

Let's Recap

- When you don't know your unconditional worth and you suppress expression in exchange for acceptance, approval, etc…, you set yourself up for disempowerment, and possibly even victimhood.
- The key to empowerment is knowing and owning your worth, courageously expressing your real self and making conscious choices that support wellbeing.

Chapter 18

The Worthiness Game of Love

The Hidden Truth about Romantic Relationships

Have you ever wondered why so many relationships end in heartache? Even relationships that begin with incredible love, faithful promises and the best of intentions often come to a bitter end. If love is all you need, why does it all go so wrong?

In this section, we will explore the hidden dynamics that cause relationships to fail, or that might even keep us from finding love in the first place. These insights will awaken your consciousness, empowering you to recognize and overcome many previously unknown relationship snags.

No matter how wise or careful you may be, it is virtually impossible to avoid relationship pitfalls that you can't see or recognize, but once you know they exist and how to recognize them, suddenly those hidden pitfalls are easy to avoid or overcome!

Why Falling in Love Goes So Wrong

When we first fall in love with someone, we are actually letting go rather than falling. As we let go to the feeling of being in love with another, we naturally become conscious, making it possible for our True-Selves to be embodied. In fact, True-Self embodiment is often experienced when we fall in love.

Being in love feels so good because we embody our True-Selves and we are plugged into Life Force Energy, resulting in feelings of bliss and a sense that anything is possible. This explains why we have so much energy and inspiration when we are in love.

This divine experience of being in love can last for days, weeks, months and sometimes even years, but then something unexpected occurs and we "lose the feeling."

The beginning of the end happens when we associate our partner with these "feel good feelings," and on some level, we create an expectation that he/she is the source of our positive and abundant energy and will perpetually provide this high-flying energy.

As long as our lover's attention is on us, there doesn't seem to be a problem, but, as soon as our partner is distracted, or withholds love for any reason, we suffer because we believe that without him/her our energy source is cut off. Maybe we feel betrayed, hurt or angry, and, in response, we withhold our love - unknowingly depleting our energy even more, because you cannot withhold love from another, without also withholding it from yourself. The unconditional love we once felt for our partner becomes conditioned on him/her meeting our needs and providing energy in the way we have come to expect.

Maybe we change our behavior, or alter ourselves in some way in order to regain love and attention, but, even if it works, the cost is great, because, in doing so, we unknowingly give away our power – ultimately displacing our True-Selves and further impeding Life Force Energy.

Once the love has died, and we are no longer receiving energy from the relationship, we may choose to move on and find someone else to fall in love with, seeking a new source of energy and beginning the cycle over again.

If you stay in the relationship, but you are no longer embodying your True-Self, you are likely to unconsciously develop artificial ways of generating energy. If you are not getting energy through unconditional love, anger, resentment and arguing with your mate will do the trick. One or both partners may also gain energy in passive aggressive ways, and when people generate energy through complaining, nagging, fighting and passively manipulating, they may stay in problematic relationships indefinitely. This type of relationship is a Negative Energy Relationship, and it can keep a "motor" running for a long time.

In a Negative Energy Relationship partners do not know and own their worth. They often use each other to artificially generate energy, thereby giving their power away to each other in exchange for energy. As time goes by, the relationship generates less and less energy, and the cost of energy (to argue, complain and nag) becomes greater than the energetic payoff. As partners fight for energy, sooner or later, they each become drained, and, at this point, they often stop looking to each other for energy, and the relationship comes to an end.

Sometimes, however, after the relationship is done and finished, the breakup instigates more feelings of hurt and betrayal, resulting in the energy generating emotion of anger or even rage. When ex-partners hold onto anger and hostility, they are still using each other as a source of artificially-generated energy, which may be why some people refuse to forgive and forget; to let go and forgive means losing an energy generator.

The overall cost of holding onto a relationship that is over may include physical issues, financial challenges, lost time, aging and negative impacts on other relationships.

In Positive Energy Relationships both people love themselves – they know their unconditional worth and they are each connected to Source through their True-Selves. Because they are not dependent on each other for energy, Life Force Energy flows and is shared freely and without conditions. Partners are able to grow and expand individually and together.

Looking for Love in All the Wrong Places?

The Worthiness Game is the single core issue responsible for almost every break up and break down, and, not just in our romantic relationships, but in all our relationships.

Until we awaken, *Conditional Worthiness* is the foundational belief for almost every human being on the planet, and the core belief that every other disempowering belief is based upon. If you believe that you are fundamentally unworthy of love unless you meet certain conditions, you will construct a reality built on this false premise, and, as a result, you will embark on this game of life seeking love outside yourself, and building unsustainable relationships upon that search.

Most people spend their entire lives trying to prove that they are worthy of love, never considering that the quest for worthiness is impossible to fulfill, nor understanding that this impossible quest covertly sabotages virtually every loving relationship.

As previously discussed, the EGO copes with the emotional wound of unworthiness by selecting a primary emotional need that when met, temporarily fills this wound; the most common emotional needs include: appreciation, approval, acceptance, understanding, respect and being heard, but there are many more. This means that if your primary emotional need is appreciation, you must somehow get others to appreciate you, again and again, in order to feel worthy of love.

Although we are usually unaware of this primary emotional need, there is a part of us who is constantly tracking for its fulfillment, and, consequently, altering our behavior in order to get it met.

Romantic Chemistry - a trick in disguise?

In an unconscious attempt to heal this wound, many of us search for that one special person who can love us enough to make us whole, but we fail to take into account that the wise Universe has another plan.

A substantial component of what we call romantic chemistry is the unconscious pull towards someone who will ***not*** meet our primary emotional need, and, as a result, trigger our emotional issues. In fact, oftentimes, we are unconsciously drawn to people who remind us of the pivotal parent who did not meet our primary emotional need as a child. For instance, if you felt rejected by your mom, you might be attracted to people who have similar qualities, because the EGO reasons that this person represents your mom, and, if you can get him/her to give you what you didn't get as a child, you will finally feel worthy. But, remember, there are hidden rules to this tricky game. Namely, you are attracted to people who will not meet this need, just like your parent, so that you have to prove that you are worthy before getting him/her to deem you worthy, evidenced by fulfilling this need. In other words, if you felt rejected by your mom, you will work very hard to get your (potential) partner's approval because, according to your Worthiness Program agenda, approval is proof that you are worthy.

Needless to say, this rarely, if ever, happens. In most cases, we chase the very people who will never give us what we most need emotionally. Of course, when we are first attracted to a potential partner, we usually believe that he/she will provide us with what we need emotionally, even if we are not sure what that is - which is generally the case.

So, we open our hearts and we let this person in, totally expecting the relationship to grow and flourish, but within days, weeks, months or years, we recognize that we feel hurt and unloved because our partner is not giving us what we need emotionally, and then we blame him/her for withholding love. Our love language is really a *language of emotional needs.* No matter how much your partner says, or does, the "right" things, if he/she doesn't meet your primary emotional need, you will likely feel unloved and unsatisfied.

This is the cause of dysfunction in virtually every problematic relationship. When our partner is not meeting our primary emotional need, we might do whatever it takes in order to get our partner to love us in the way that we desire, be that through appreciation, approval or understanding, etc..., and, if our partner still does not meet this emotional need, we defend ourselves with anger, resentment, resistance or we just shut down. We withhold love from our partner by denying him or her their primary emotional need in return. Of course, this is all orchestrated unconsciously; we just feel hurt and unloved, and, so, we try to defend ourselves.

Your Love Receptors

If you unconsciously believe that you are only worthy of love when your primary emotional need is met, your love receptors will only turn on when you perceive that this condition is satisfied, but, as soon as the condition is no longer satisfied, the receptors turn off. Your condition must also be met by a certain type of person or a specific person. You might also have self-imposed conditions, for example, if you don't feel attractive, even if your partner is meeting your primary emotional need, you won't feel loved because your love receptors are turned off. This means that even a "bad hair day" can negatively impact a relationship.

The bottom line is, even if someone truly loves us, if our conditions are not met, we unconsciously block love. Conditions don't bring us love – conditions reject love.

On the surface, challenging relationships that are based on the Worthiness Game might seem like a waste of time, but, by no small means, this dynamic is *by Divine Design.* On a higher level, our True-Selves are playing the healing game. No matter the facts, details or history, the greater part of us is conspiring for our awakening. We don't attract people who will meet our emotional needs because if those needs were met by others, we would remain oblivious to the deeper wound of unworthiness, and that wound would go forever unhealed, keeping us out of alignment with our true spiritual nature. We need someone (important to us) who will withhold the very thing we believe we need most, so that the pain and suffering associated with not getting this need met will alert us to this wound, in such a way, we cannot ignore.

- ***Relationships are meant to trigger issues so that we know that they exist within us, and we have the opportunity to heal, and free ourselves.***

  Many years ago, I found myself in a long term relationship where I felt completely unappreciated. I bent over backward and even sacrificed my own integrity in order to receive morsels of appreciation, but no matter what I did, I still felt unappreciated. I requested, I demanded, I whined – still, less than nothing. As I grew resentful that my partner withheld appreciation, I began to withhold understanding. The key nuggets of our frequent arguments were, "You don't appreciate me" versus "You don't understand me." As I felt unappreciated, I also felt unworthy of love, and as the pain grew with the passing of time, I arrived at the point where I was done seeking appreciation because it was just too painful.

- ***The true purpose of emotional pain is to wake us up, and make us pay attention to the false belief(s) that is causing the pain in the first place.***

  Of course, you can ignore this pain through methods of distraction, addiction, rationalization, etc..., but pain is designed to grow stronger the longer you ignore it, requiring greater and greater methods of avoidance. Depending on your ability to tolerate emotional pain, eventually there will come the point, where the only way to be free of this pain is to uncover its true source and pull it up from the roots.

Finally, I stopped looking outside myself and I looked within. I began to see a hidden history revolving around my need for appreciation that began with my mother in childhood. I could see that my need for appreciation was a symptom of trying to prove that I was worthy of love. I could also see that there was an empty space inside me where my own self-love was missing. It became perfectly clear that in this unconscious game of trying to prove my worth, the cards were stacked against me.

Relationships cannot prove or provide worth. Relationships can only demonstrate if you believe that you are worthy or not.

Until we are fully awake in our lives, the purpose of relationships, and especially intimate ones, is to alert us to our disempowering beliefs, so that we can heal and wake up. Other people, we call family, lovers and friends unknowingly act out our false beliefs and trigger our issues so that we have the opportunity to recognize and release these false beliefs and heal our wounds. Therefore, if I believe that my worth is conditional and I must prove that I am worthy, my partner can only reflect this belief by unconsciously offering behavior (withholding my primary emotional need) that activates my feelings of unworthiness.

If you don't love yourself, you will need others to behave certain ways so that you feel worthy of love, but others can only demonstrate your belief that you don't feel worthy of love.

In addition, because worth is intrinsic and unconditional, it cannot be proven or disproven. The mere act of trying to prove that you are worthy or getting others to treat you in certain ways, so that you feel worthy, comes from a belief that you are not worthy. If you know that you are unconditionally worthy of love, you don't need proof.

As long as you expect others to meet your emotional needs so that you feel worthy of love, you remain imprisoned by your own hands. No one can give you what you need, if you don't first give it to yourself. If you are not respecting yourself, for example, no matter what your partner does, or doesn't do, you will never feel respected. You free yourself when you stop looking outside, and you meet your own emotional needs. *No one is keeping love from you but you.* When you know that you are unconditionally worthy of love, you generously give yourself an abundance of appreciation, approval, understanding and acceptance, etc... You withhold nothing from yourself, and you withhold nothing from those you love.

Worth by Proxy

When the Worthiness Program is running, we perceive the entire world through the filter of worthiness; seamlessly scanning everything and everyone in terms of how the person, place or thing will influence our worth. We don't usually realize that we are operating in this manner because it is automatic, and, oftentimes, we don't know any other way of perceiving the world so it seems completely natural - especially since everyone else is doing the same.

Until we are fully conscious, the EGO may motor-vate us to seek out people with higher worth, because our worth can be positively or negatively affected by the worth of a partner. *I call this "Worth by Proxy."*

Needless to say, we are often attracted to people who will increase our Worth by Proxy, so that the relationship generates energy for us. In order to determine a potential partner's worth, we must make an assessment based on our standards of measurement. Specific criteria may include: physical attractiveness, intelligence, education, cultural or religious background and popularity (how worthy others find this person).

If we assess that a possible new partner has more worth than us, the relationship could boost our worth, but, if we judge him/her less worthy, the relationship has no potential to boost our worth, and, in fact, it may actually lower it. This is one of the reasons why we may reject someone who we judge as less worthy, especially if they are using our worth to boost their own. This dynamic is common in high school, but it doesn't end there – we just become more secretive about it as we get older, and maybe more unconscious.

We might also form relationships with people we perceive as "inferior," so that we feel superior, but these are usually not people we fall in love with, or feel sexually drawn to, and when one person feels superior to another, there is the risk of mistreatment.

Solving a Dating Riddle

Does the following dynamic ring a bell? Either you are attracted to someone who is not attracted to you or you are not attracted to someone who is attracted to you.

Have you ever asked, *"Why do all the men/women I like, not like me, and why do I not like any the men/women who like me?"* Or, maybe you experience a mutual attraction but you lose interest in a short period of time. Have you ever wondered why?

Most single people are playing the Worthiness Game of Love and don't even know it. On a not-so-conscious level, we might only be attracted to people who are "better than us" (according to our worthiness meter) because the relationship can improve our worth, providing an EGO boost.

If someone more worthy finds us attractive, we feel more worthy, but there are a few problems with this dynamic:

1. If the person we are attracted to is playing the Worthiness Game, he/she will not find us attractive if we come across less worthy, or if he/she is using the same measurement of worth. Therefore, our love will go un-received and we will feel rejected. This is why the people we are attracted to don't find us attractive.
2. If someone with higher worth finds us worthy, we get an initial EGO boost, but it doesn't usually last long, due to the fact that if they find us attractive and worthy of attention, their value (in our eyes) decreases – we may secretly fear that if this amazing person is interested in us, there must be something wrong with him/her.
3. If someone with higher worth finds us worthy, we get an initial EGO boost, but once we get to know him/her and see his/her faults, we lose interest because their worth decreases.

We may also be addicted to "what we can't have" because only in the conquest do we experience an EGO boost; once a highly valued person chooses us and we get a boost, we may quickly lose interest because we can no longer increase our worth and generate energy from the anticipation and realization of the conquest.

Some other factors to consider:

- **Jealousy**

  We may not find a person attractive until someone with perceived higher worth finds this person desirable, and we suddenly experience jealousy. Our jealousy is an indication that this person's worth has increased in our discernment, offering the potential to increase our worth.

- **Playing hard to get**

  It is quite common to judge another's worth based on their availability, which may be why chasing a potential partner is devaluing, why people who play "hard to get" are perceived as having more worth and why we are attracted to potential romantic partners who offer a challenge.

- **Confidence**

  When we lack confidence in a potential relationship, it says to the other person that we rate our worth lower in comparison, and when we are confident, it says that we rate our worth equally high (superiority may manifest as arrogance, which is least attractive). When someone is confident, we interpret it as worthiness. Confidence increases perceived worth because a person must feel worthy in order to exude confidence. From this perspective, a woman's or man's sense of worth is what makes her/him most attractive. Also, keep in mind, if you don't know your worth, it might be common for others to treat you as if you are less worthy.

Worth by Proxy may explain many dead-end relationships.

The people we try to get energy from, are often the same people who try to get energy from us, but, like us, they don't have it to give. Those who are tapped into Life Force Energy naturally, don't play games where they give their power away in exchange for energy - they do not want or need your energy because they have more than enough of their own.

When you are a channel for Life Force Energy, others can feel this energy, but they cannot take this energy from you because you don't need anything from them - you are not willing to compromise your connection to your True-Self for anyone or anything.

Let's Recap:

- Falling in love allows you to be your True-Self, and this is why it feels so wonderful.
- But, if you or your partner depend on each other for the good feelings that come with True-Self embodiment, sooner or later, there will be relationship issues.

- Oftentimes, discord ensues, with you and your partner fighting to get your primary emotional needs met – so that you will feel worthy.
- Most relationships fail due to the fact that couples are unknowingly playing the Worthiness Game.
- You might be attracted to someone who will increase your worth, but, at the same time, you might be attracted to potential partners who will not meet your primary emotional need. When this need is not met, it is probable that you will be emotionally triggered.
- The higher purpose of emotional triggers is to alert you to an issue so that you can heal it.
- Challenges in relationships can turn into "motors" that continue to generate energy even after a break up.

Chapter 19

The Unconscious Path of Self-Sabotage

The hidden cost of getting your primary emotional need met may be sabotaging your life, and your most valued relationships.

Getting others to meet your primary emotional need is so vital that it may result in self-sabotaging behaviors and even attracting unnecessary problems. To understand this dynamic, let's consider the primary emotional need to be right.

The Need to be Right

The need to "be right" can be so self-sabotaging that we might dig our heels into problems or focus on negativity just so others will agree that we are right? No matter how you look at it, being right is never worth the cost.

The need to be right often, but not always, comes from the "better than" version of the Worthiness Program because it creates the feeling of superiority which boosts the EGO.

Most people who want to be right really don't want to hurt anyone, but, in fighting to be right, you must make someone wrong, and the cost can be sabotaging a potentially loving relationship. When you always need to be right, it pushes the other person to take a stand against you, even if being right isn't his primary emotional need. If you win, the other person is diminished, and likely shuts down to protect himself from future emotional hurt, or if he takes a righteous stand, it results in distance and disconnection.

Even if it is never stated, making yourself *more* worthy makes others feel *less* worthy, and it never feels good to those who must play inferior parts. This dynamic is often a common way in which relationships are damaged. You might ask yourself, "Do I need to be right more than I desire love and connection?"

You cannot be right and in love at the same time.

Not by any means does this mean that you need to be wrong and accept defeat - it is really about creating a large space for each person to express their perspectives, even if they are completely opposing. Experience shows that the truth, of any situation, usually lies between the extremes, and only by considering each version can the full picture come into focus. *Living in love often means living in the paradox.* Who knows what is even possible when there is room for contrast to co-exist and even collaborate?

If being right is a condition upon your worth, the EGO will not allow you to be wrong because being wrong is equated with being unworthy, and, as such, letting go of the need to be right requires that you own your unconditional worth, so that your worth does not depend on being right, or others agreeing that you are right.

The Need to be Understood

Let's look at another example of how we might self-sabotage ourselves in order to get others to meet an emotional need.

If your primary emotional need is to be understood, and no one understands you, it is possible that you unconsciously attract issues so that someone important in your life finally understands just how difficult it is to be you. But, this is a terrible strategy because in order to get others to "pay attention," you must self-sabotage yourself in the process, and probably sabotage one or more relationships, as well; just for a little understanding - it's not worth it.

The thing is, no one can ever really understand what it's like to be you because that is your job; no one has had your experiences, lived your ups and downs and developed your unique views of life. Even those who love you can never know what it is like to be you, and because they want the best for you, they will offer their own version of "the best" - their best solutions, advice and opinions are what they know and believe in, and when people believe in something, they have a tendency to believe that it is right for everyone, but, of course, it never is. When others seem to misunderstand you or "not get you," it is not that they don't want to understand, it is only because they don't know how.

We just examined how the need to be right and the need to be understood can lead to self-sabotaging behavior and sabotaging relationships, but all primary emotional needs run the same risk.

- The EGO will go to great lengths to get your primary need met, often resulting in less than empowering behavior.

What is your primary emotional need, and how does it influence your behavior?

- Do you over-compensate to get respect?
- Are you a people pleaser to get appreciation?
- Do you seek permission to get approval?

In exchange for getting your primary emotional need met, how might you be giving away your power by compromising values or sabotaging wellbeing?

Instead of digging yourself into a deeper ditch in order to get an emotional need met, what would happen if you stopped applying meaning to the way in which others treat you?

Let's Recap

- The unconscious desire to get your primary emotional need met is so strong that in order to get it met, you may unknowingly sabotage your life and relationships.
- Freeing yourself from self-sabotaging behavior requires that you make the unconscious conscious, by identifying your primary emotional need, and understanding how you may be compromising yourself or sacrificing values in order to get it met.

Part 2 will deal more extensively with this issue.

Chapter 20

Real Life Zombies

In an attempt to prove worth, we are unconsciously motor-vated to avoid judgment by overriding personal desires, inner guidance and even following our dreams.

If you fear that others will not approve of something you want to do, be or experience, you will naturally suppress any dreams or desires that others might find unacceptable. This inevitably means that you must hide your real self, not speak your truth and possibly even repress your gifts and talents - and only do what others think you should do.

The end result might be a career that pleases your father but you hate, a spouse that pleases your mother but you don't really love, hobbies that please your friends but bore you to death and a lifestyle that pleases everyone but you.

> *Signpost on the path*
> *Warning, beware of becoming a zombie!*

If all your major life choices were based on gaining approval, status or acceptance, you are probably experiencing symptoms of being out of alignment with the authentic expression of your True-Self and the natural flow of life.

Staying in relationships, environments and experiences that don't support your real dreams and desires ultimately manifests as issues that represent your dissatisfaction and misalignment with that area of your life, including problematic relationships, missed opportunities, dysfunctional patterns, money issues, health issues, miscommunication, overwhelm and stress - and even if you succeed, according to the expectations of others, you will never truly feel successful because it is not your idea of success. *There is a huge cost for not being your real self.*

Don't Be Fooled by Money

Oftentimes, we make important life choices, such as choosing a life-long career based on potential income. Because the majority of people make career choices this way, it seems perfectly normal, but consider for a moment that it actually sets us up for an unfulfilling life.

There appears to be a great deal of proof that indicates, if we want to be financially well-off, we must pursue certain careers; doctors are paid better than writers and lawyers are paid better than artists, but there is so much more to the story. If you are a gifted writer who chooses to practice medicine for the paycheck, the cost of betraying your soul may be immensely greater than all the money you could ever make as a doctor. If you are an inspired artist but you have repressed your gift in exchange for a law degree, the cost of burying your inspiration may be infinitely greater than all the wealth a lawyer could ever accumulate. If your dream is medicine or law, or any other profession, following your dream will likely bring fulfillment, but, if money is your motivator, you might have set yourself up for an unfulfilling way of life.

We only make career choices based on money when we believe that the Universe won't support us if we follow our true dreams.

If you believe that you must do certain things or perform certain roles in order to be worthy of abundance, the Worthiness Program is likely operating.

When it comes to financial abundance, I know that it seems as if there are no other choices but to follow the herd, but your life's work should be something that you love to do, and when you do it, you should feel inspired, joyful, fulfilled and grateful - isn't this the foundation of abundance? When you feel great about yourself and your life, abundance flows, including money.

Maybe you think that if everyone did what they love to do, no one would do the "yucky jobs" like picking up garbage or washing dishes. The Universe, and everyone in it, is Self-Adjusting so that the whole Universe is in sync - if there is a role to fulfill, there is a person inspired to fulfill it, and in the fulfillment joy will overflow.

We are each directed to our life's work or mission through our dreams and desires.

Your dreams and desires come from the Universe, which means that the Universe communicates with you by offering you a dream, idea or desire and then draws you to it through inspiration. In fact, the only reason we feel drawn to something is because the Universe gives us the inspiration and the energy to follow that inspiration - this is why we always have energy for the things we truly enjoy.

We are meant to do the things we love to do!

Only a cruel Universe would give us dreams, along with the perfect gifts required to fulfill those dreams, yet only provide financial rewards if we ignore those dreams, and do something we don't really want to do. This is ***not*** what the Universe has in mind for any of us!

Do you see that this dynamic is all part of the Worthiness Game?

By not knowing your worth, the EGO makes your life choices, and since it will always choose in the direction of survival, it will choose money over anything that deeply matters. Chasing dollars is powerful EGO-driven motor-vation, which cannot change as long as the EGO is in charge.

No matter how big the sacrifice of our dreams in exchange for money, there is no guarantee that we will even be financially well-off, and, in fact, if you hate your job, you cut off the flow of Life Force Energy, thereby inhibiting dollars.

Let's Recap

- In an attempt to gain approval, acceptance, etc... the EGO persuades you to compromise your dreams, desires and inner guidance.

- When you suppress yourself for extended periods of time, it results in issues related to the ways in which you are compromising yourself.
- Not owning your worth may cause you to make choices based on fear and survival, allowing money to have the final say.

To fully comprehend the dynamics of unconscious self-repression, we cannot forget one additional factor - The fear of self-expression.

Chapter 21

Afraid to Be Your Real Self?

Are you secretly afraid of self-expression?

If you are like most, your deepest dream is to express your hidden gifts, speak your truth and create something of unique value for humanity, yet, at the same time, this might also be your deepest fear.

Having both the desire and fear of expression is like living between two worlds, wanting to live in one, while allowing yourself to be tormented by the other; preventing yourself from the very thing you crave most often leads to anxiety, hopelessness and depression. But, if your deepest desire is to be your real self, why are you so willing to suppress creativity and sacrifice unique expression?

Self-expression would be very easy, if it were not for the Worthiness Program, as well as an unconscious fear that runs our lives.

Although we might not think about it, most of us worry about fitting-in, or more precisely, we fear that not fitting-in could lead to shame, rejection or abandonment. This causes us to struggle between the overwhelming desire to express our real selves and the compulsive fear of judgment, or worse. *But, where does this debilitating fear come from?*

The Fitting-in Program

The Fitting-in Program is a subconscious program designed to ensure the survival of the human race. It is specifically designed to motor-vate us to behave in ways that allow us to fit-in with our "tribe" and it operates by motor-vating us to fit-in through the use of fear.

The Fitting-in Program originated during humanity's most primitive era when survival was uncertain; unforgiving wilderness, non-accessible natural resources, fierce enemies, plague and natural disasters threatened to wipe out the entire human race.

Our primitive ancestors understood that every member of the tribe played an important role, and if the whole tribe was to survive, everyone had to play their parts, making it mandatory to stick together, work together and abide by the tribe's rules, laws and beliefs.

Tribes controlled their members with the use of shame, so, if you were not fulfilling your part within the tribe, you broke a tribal law or crossed a boundary, you would be shamed by the entire tribe. This might also result in physical rejection or abandonment, which likely meant death because it was extremely dangerous to be on your own, but, believe it or not, most tribe members feared shame more than death because the collective judgment of your tribe automatically deemed you worthless, casting irremovable shame upon you, in this world and the next.

The thing is, the Fitting-in Program was successful for our ancestors! They fit-in, they worked together and the human race made it! The program served its purpose beautifully, as it was a crucial component in the development and preservation of our entire species.

The problem is that human survival is no longer dependent upon fitting-in, yet, the Fitting-in Program is still operating subconsciously, controlling humanity's current behavior by making us fear self-expression, as if it could actually kill us if we dared to be different, speak our truth or express creativity. It makes us believe that if we express ourselves or do things differently than our modern day tribes, we will be shamed and shunned, just like our primitive ancestors. If that's not enough, inherent in the program is the fear of death associated with being judged and consequently rejected by one's tribe. This fear was rational for our primitive ancestors, but irrationally debilitating for us.

The Fitting-in Program is why so many people stay in unfulfilling jobs and unhappy relationships, as well as religions, organizations and groups that constrict rather than support. This is the reason we may experience overwhelming fear for even thinking about doing something that goes against the ideals of family, culture, community, etc..., and this also explains why we worry about what others think and say about us, and why they worry too!

Current day, the Fitting-in Program is not only obsolete, it is also counter-productive. Like any strategy or program that has lived past its necessity, it now opposes the original intent; it is hurting us rather than helping us.

The worst part about the Fitting-in Program is that it makes you reject your dreams and desires, or not even have the capacity to access them in the first place, and because the program makes you abandon your True-Self, you must do to yourself, what you fear others doing to you.

We might not even realize that the program was still operating in our lives, if it were not for the fact that the drive and desire for individual expression has more recently become active in the collective consciousness of humanity. We have reached a remarkable point in evolution where the auspicious future of human-kind depends on authentic, individual expression, but, in order to do so, it must be without fear, resistance or trepidation.

Beyond a shadow of a doubt, the Fitting-in Program must be turned off, but, unfortunately, the program wasn't on an "off-timer," and the only way to turn it off is to do it ourselves. Part 2 will show you how!

Underneath the Mask

When we deny our dreams, repress our heart's desires and suppress our true expression, we restrict the natural flow of life, and the flow of Life Force Energy through our bodies. Living, year after year, like this may result in scarcity, physical challenges and a deterioration of our natural abilities.

When we suppress, repress and depress ourselves for so long, we forget our dreams and desires, and we cut ourselves off from any sense of what might bring joy and fulfillment.

Unconscious programs can turn a bright and gifted soul into a real life zombie.

Without unconscious programming, we would never sacrifice our lives for anything or anyone. We wouldn't make choices based on the need for approval, and we wouldn't give our entire lives to unfulfilling work, while ignoring the dreams that could make our hearts sing with delight.

The good news is that underneath the mask of illusion, the True You is alive and well - and it is never too late to claim your intrinsic worth and remember *who you really are*!

We are each given gifts along with the inspiration and energy to follow our dreams, and when we do, we experience True-Self embodiment and the flow of Life Force Energy, which can manifest in an abundance of real life dollars, wonderful experiences, great relationships or virtually anything that we desire.

Let's Recap

- The purpose of the Fitting-in Program is to suppress expression that could result in being shamed or shunned by your tribe.
- This program ensured the survival of our primitive ancestors, and has been passed down through the generations, but, currently, it is hurting us rather than helping us - due to the fact that our survival no longer depends on fitting-in.
- This program is vastly responsible for the need to be liked, and, as a result, it may be causing you to suppress your individual expression, while possibly keeping you in a job or relationship that is not right for you.
- The Fitting-in Program operates by invoking fear anytime you consider doing anything that your family, friends, co-workers or community might judge.
- According to the program, you must avoid judgment because it can result in abandonment or rejection, and, therefore, it is life-threatening.
- Whenever you suppress expression, you inhibit Life Force Energy, and, along with it, the joy and fulfillment that you seek.
- At this time in history, the drive and desire for individual expression has become active in the collective consciousness of humanity.
- When the drive for expression hits up against the Fitting-in Program, strong feelings of frustration and lack of fulfillment are triggered.

Chapter 22

Conspiring for Your Awakening

Challenges, issues, problems or anything that "pushes our buttons" are all wake-up calls which we can pay attention to and use to wake-up, or we can push the snooze button and remain asleep until the next alarm sounds, or the one after that.

We humans can tolerate a great deal of disharmony in our lives, but, sooner or later, we experience a crisis that we cannot tolerate. The experiences that cause us the most emotional pain also hold the most potential for breaking free of limitation.

A crisis can be almost anything: the end of a long term relationship, a career that goes by the wayside, the loss of our home/community or a serious health issue. Although we might have spent a lifetime tolerating low grade issues, when the crisis hits, we can't just *tolerate our way through it* and hope for smooth waters on the other side. We must face our real or imagined demons and find the strength within - strength and *courage* we didn't know we had. If we are going to survive, we have to choose life over death, and, if we are going to thrive, we must choose ourselves for the starring roles of our lives.

> *Signpost on the path*
>
> *All challenges are opportunities in disguise.*
>
> ---
>
> Despite how it may seem, the Universe is conspiring to wake us all up. Although many challenges are the result of the EGO's quest to prove worth, these same challenges also offer invitations for awakening.

This means that we can no longer live our lives according to the opinions of others.

If you look closely, and you know how to look, you may see that a real crisis or challenge shakes loose a major source of worth. Oftentimes, we lose the person, relationship, place, role, identity or material thing(s) that we most depend on for our worth, and we experience crisis because our sense of worth has been shattered, but that is exactly what must happen in order to wake-up.

If your worth is conditioned upon something that you refuse to let go, the Universe may remove that condition so that you have no choice but to let go.

At this point, you might transfer your worth onto something else, either similar or not so similar; for instance, the loss of one partner for another, or replacing the lost partner with a new identity or business, but that only delays the inevitable. As long as your worth is conditioned on anything or anyone, your life is still built on quicksand. If you are ready to wake-up, or, if you are simply done playing the Worthiness Game, crisis opens the door to awakening.

Crisis or a series of losses may result in feelings of victimhood, causing us to close down and go inside to protect ourselves, and, in order to prevent more emotional pain, we let go and detach from the world. Nothing feels worse, but this is exactly the higher purpose of victimhood because in letting go, we are propelled toward awakening.

Of course, you don't need crisis or loss in order to wake up – you can just wake up, but it requires that you let go.

Many people want to awaken because they have tried everything to stop the emotional pain and have discovered that nothing works for very long, as the pain always returns. The only thing left is to wake-up - out of misery. However, there is a disclaimer on the Door to Awakening that says, "*In order to pass through this door, you cannot take anything with you.*" This doesn't refer to personal belongings, material things or other people – it precisely means that you cannot awaken as long as you possess guilt, regret, fear, frustration, shame or any emotions induced by disempowering beliefs, or disempowering beliefs themselves.

Certainly, this means that unworthiness or conditional worthiness prevent awakening. You can see the door, you can open the door and maybe you can even poke a toe across the threshold, but no matter how hard you try, you cannot cross through while carrying the heavy burden of unworthiness.

It is time to finally release the quest for worth so that you can wake-up and be who you really are!

The pivotal feature of awakening is being free of all programming so that you are conscious, and, consequently, all your choices are made consciously - transforming the quality of your life, and, as such, being fully awake means being conscious in all areas of your life.

Living as your True-Self is the ultimate realization of spiritual awakening, and, in fact, self-actualization and self-realization are actually other ways to describe the awakening of your True-Self. The "self" that they are each referring to is the True-Self.

Your intention does not have to be spiritual awakening in order for this book to transform your life, but, if this is your intention, it may be used as a *handbook for awakening*.

The Humbling

At any given moment, the entire Universe is showing up for you, so when you struggle with this moment, you struggle with the entire Universe.

When your True-Self has a vision that cannot be achieved by EGO-driven motor-vation, the EGO must be turned off. This naturally happens as our "motors" wear out, but, if the EGO is strong and successful, how do you turn it off?

The only way for the EGO to be overcome is through an unconscious process of Humbling orchestrated by higher powers. This may result in the loss of everything we have associated with our worth and power.

> *Signpost on the path*
>
> *Release struggle now - burdens gain weight*

The Humbling can happen with anyone but is often common when the "better than motor" is running.

The "better than motor" can run for years and decades, but, like all "motors," sooner or later, it begins to fail. The onset of failure might be the first time you cannot overcome a challenge and you begin to doubt yourself on the inside, while on the outside you fight for victory - but like dominos, one big challenge may create a chain of events, manifesting as one struggle after another. At some point, you may ask for help, but, since you have trained the people in your life to see you as strong and independent, your pleas may be met with resistance – causing you to feel resentment, due to the fact that when you finally swallow your pride and ask for help, it doesn't come.

No matter what "motor" is running, the key is always letting go.

Even if you lose everything, but you are still holding on to regrets, resentment, guilt, shame, judgment, blame or anything else, you have not let go. Any of these emotions or states of mind will keep the EGO inflated and "motors" running. A complete letting go frees you to be *who you really are*. Undoubtedly, you will discover yourself to be so much greater than the EGO could ever imagine or create.

Once the "motors" turn off and the EGO is deflated,
your True-Self is free to be fully embodied.

Let's Recap

- The Universe is conspiring to wake us up!
- Challenges, issues, problems or anything that "pushes your buttons" are all wake-up calls.
- Free-will allows you to either pay attention and wake -up, or ignore the call.
- If you keep ignoring wake-up calls, the severity of issues will increase until you are faced with a crisis of some sort.
- Oftentimes, the crisis involves losing a primary source of worth, such as a partner, job or money.
- When this occurs, the Universe is attempting to help you disentangle your sense of worth from externals, but, free-will allows you to replace the loss of worth with another external source, thereby prolonging awakening.
- If the Worthiness Program is running in any area of your life, your actions, reactions and behavior are programmed to prove worth, and, therefore, you are unconscious in exactly those same areas.
- You cannot fully awaken as long as subconscious programs are operating your life.
- Very strong EGOs often experience the Humbling where one thing after another is lost – until you let go.
- Despite crisis or loss, if you are still holding on via regrets, resentment, guilt, shame, judgment, blame, etc…, you are no closer to liberating the True You.
- Letting go is a pivotal key to transcending the EGO and waking up as your True-Self.

The journey from EGO to True-Self is literally a journey of awakening, but, ironically, when we are in the process of awakening, we may feel more lost and asleep than ever. With only glimpses of understanding, we may not have the clarity to discern the process or follow the path, yet, all the while, the intrinsic wisdom of the journey pushes us and the path unfolds, moving us in the direction of awakening whether we want to go or not.

Wouldn't it be nice to have a road map so that you know where you are and you know what to expect?

Your wish is my command!

The following chapter will unlock the mystery, providing a detailed road map for each stage of awakening.

Chapter 23

The 5 Stages of Awakening

What does it really mean to awaken? It is fair to say that awakening is a journey from limitation to freedom - from unconscious to conscious. It is a sacred journey that takes you from the programmed constraints of the EGO to the full embodiment of your True-Self.

Whether you intentionally choose to take this journey or an unexpected experience propels you onto the path, once you start, there is no turning back. It is true that the journey might be quite arduous at times, but no matter how long or challenging, the extraordinary destination far exceeds any bumps and bruises along the way.

The end result of Full Awakening is freedom from personal suffering, clarity of mind, boundless joy, inner peace and the ability to live an incredibly fulfilling life. The awakened state holds everything we have ever desired, and so much more.

There are 5 Stages of Awakening, and when you understand each stage, and where you are on the journey, you can recognize the signposts along the way, and the possible pitfalls to avoid.

Please use the following guide as a way to navigate the stages of awakening, but keep in mind that everyone's experience is different. There is no right or wrong way to wake up. Like art, it is all beautiful and perfect.

Stage 1 of Awakening: The Stage of the False-self

Subtle awareness of "something more" begins to grow.

In Stage 1 of Awakening, we are most asleep, and we do not even know that we are asleep. With the EGO fully in charge, we are entrenched in mass consciousness and going through the motions of life, generally following the rules of culture and laws of the land.

We don't usually question reality or seek answers beyond what is necessary for survival and maintenance of a lifestyle.

Our identities define us and we live within the construct of religion, culture and/or society.

We may even play the part of victim or perpetrator.

Unconscious programming runs us, and, as a result, we see the world in black and white - good and bad. We likely process a rigid model of the world according to our specific programming.

Because there is a great desire to fit-in and be accepted, in this stage, it is common to sacrifice our needs and compromise our values in order to receive approval and be included in our desired community, be that family, culture, business, religion, etc...

Self-worth is likely conditional and attached to identity or the roles we play, or there may be other means of proving that we are worthy.

Because the EGO generally runs the show, we likely believe we are the EGO, with little or no awareness that there is a greater part of us.

In stage one, happiness is based on externals, therefore, in order to feel happy, we try to control reality; other people, places and experiences.

Although we attempt to control our lives, for both happiness and security, it is more than likely that our emotions rule, and our actions and reactions are based on our moment to moment feelings.

We make no connection between our thoughts/beliefs and our experiences in reality, and, therefore, we have no direct ability to consciously create our reality.

Despite our unconscious nature, the first signs of awakening happen during this stage; a "flash feeling" that there is something more, or an inkling of doubt that makes us uncertain about life or reality.

Stage 2 of Awakening – The Stage of Questioning

The doubts experienced in stage one begin to turn into meaningful questions. The first signs of movement from unconscious to conscious are experienced.

In Stage 2 of Awakening, we experience a growing discomfort in our lives. There is a feeling that something is wrong or missing. We begin to question mass consciousness and the validity of rules, beliefs and laws. Things that once brought us comfort, like religion or traditions, are no longer satisfying and the places that we once found answers no longer provide relief.

We question our identity but we still hold on to it because we must continue to prove our worth, and we don't yet know ourselves outside of our human identity. As we question the roles we play, we may feel lost, and even betrayed by others or life in general.

We may even blame religion, family, culture, government, karma, astrology or the world for our problems, or maybe we blame specific people for our dysfunctions. As we shift responsibility onto others, we feel powerless over our lives; not yet realizing that in order to take back our power, we must take responsibility. In this stage, we might move from victim to survivor, but we are likely still blaming others and feeling powerless.

We begin to ask, *"Who am I? Why am I here?"*

Although we are searching for answers, we still hold on to certain limiting beliefs that keep us enslaved in the reality we have known. When we attempt to challenge these beliefs, fear brings us back, keeping us asleep a little longer.

In our discomfort with reality, and our search for answers, we may experience a great deal of confusion, overwhelm, anxiety and even depression. We "keep up" with our lives but we are secretly just "going through the motions."

As we experience a variety of challenges designed to help us wake up, tolerable discomfort turns into pain and suffering. As our disempowering beliefs are demonstrated in real life situations and relationships, we get our first glimpse of the unconscious programs running our lives, but our desire to fit-in and be accepted is likely stronger than any desires to free ourselves. Although this is the beginning of our internal programs breaking down, we are still trying to prove our worth by demonstrating our importance and seeking approval for our efforts.

We begin to understand that happiness cannot be found in the outside world, but we are still playing the game - seeking happiness in other people, places and experiences.

In this stage, there can be a great deal of emotional triggers. We may even experience trauma or remember past trauma. Emotions are generally very strong, and we may feel most fragile or vulnerable. What we do not yet realize is that our issues are coming to the surface to be healed and released.

Even though we are beginning to see the world in a whole new light, we may still possess black and white thinking – maybe more than ever. We are not ready to take responsibility for our lives and, therefore, we make little or no connection between our thoughts and our experiences in reality.

As the outside world no longer satisfies our hunger, the shell of the EGO begins to crack and the journey inward is about to begin.

Stage 3 of Awakening – The Stage of Introspection

Immense personal/spiritual growth and the start of conscious evolution through self-discovery.

In Stage 3 of Awakening, we begin a journey of introspection. In Stage 2, we rebelled against the external world with little or no success in relieving our pain, suffering or discomfort, so now we retreat as we begin to seek answers inside ourselves.

We start to disentangle from mass consciousness, releasing many limiting beliefs that were programmed into us by asleep parents, teachers, culture, society, religion and media. As we release these beliefs, we may experience both grief and relief. If we spent a lifetime imprisoned in beliefs that caused emotional suffering, physical hardship and lost happiness, we may grieve for the life we never had, and at the same time, we may feel great relief as we break free from limitation.

As we recognize how asleep we have been, we can clearly see that most people we know are still asleep. We try to wake them up, but our attempts are seen as judgmental and, therefore, met with deaf ears.

Not surprisingly, with our eyes wide open, it is common to experience greater judgment of other people (friends and strangers alike), society and the world. Others may feel our judgment and defensively respond with their own judgment of us. We are seen as different, weird and maybe even crazy. Sooner or later, we decide to keep our growing awareness to ourselves; maybe rationalizing that it's better to be silent than be judged. At this point, we don't have a lot of hope that others will wake up.

We are still focused on everything that is wrong in our lives, and in the world, but, at the same time, we have resistance to letting go. The process of letting go is often "the work" in this stage, and, as we learn to let go, Stage 3 is where we may leave unsatisfying jobs, intimate relationships, families, friendships, religions, organizations and any disempowering ways of life. We may disentangle from roles we played, reject our past identity, and there may even be a total withdrawal from society.

Our former model of the world is failing and we no longer see the world in black and white or good and bad. There may be a growing sense that we are all connected, but at the same time we may feel completely disconnected from every other human being. In many ways, we are faced with the dichotomy of life and existence.

The most common attribute of stage three is loneliness. In a sea of billions of people, you may feel like you are the only one awake; no one understands you, and there is no one with whom to connect. At this point, you might begin to question "the questioning" - why did you ever begin this journey? What's the point of waking up, if you must be alone and lonely? After all, you might have been unhappy when you were asleep but at least you had friends, family and people who cared about you. Now, there is no one. You consider "going back." You wish you could forget about everything you now know just so you can be part of a family or community. You yearn for "normalcy" in order to fit-in with others, but you also know that it is too late. You cannot forget what you have remembered, and despite your loneliness and your desire to fit-in, you wouldn't go back or undo your path even if you could.

Issues of worthiness often surface in this stage, due to the fact that the ways in which we once proved worth no longer work or are no longer available because we left the job or situation that once made us feel worthy. We may still try to seek approval, acceptance or appreciation or get other emotional needs met by those still in our lives, but it doesn't fulfill us, as it once did, and we are left feeling empty – forced to deal with feelings of unworthiness on our own.

Our desire to fit-in and be accepted is slowly being drowned out by our desire to be free and awake.

In the quest for answers and relief from emotional pain, we may embark on some sort of spiritual practice such as meditation, yoga or mindfulness. If we are not using the practice to avoid something, its purpose is likely to get us somewhere, accomplish something or wake up.

In stage three, we may experience the first real sense of power, but, if the EGO claims this power, we may have challenging and humbling experiences. We are now living more as our True-Selves than ever before, but, at the same time, the EGO may be stronger than ever – fighting to stay in control. This stage may be marked by frequent and huge shifts between the EGO and your True-Self.

By now, we may be able to see the connection between our thoughts/beliefs and the creation of our reality, and, as a result, we try to control our thoughts, but it is a difficult process because old programs are still running.

We no longer look outside ourselves for happiness, but maybe we don't yet know how to find it within. Peace and freedom may also take precedence over happiness.

Stage three is often the longest stage and almost always the most challenging, but it is also the most important in terms of awakening.

This stage is marked by the swing between resistance and letting go, with moments of clarity and enlightenment, but they don't last. It is very common to have multiple experiences of awakening in this stage and even to believe that each one is the final awakening; only to find yourself back in "reality", hours, days or weeks later. With each experience of awakening, the sense of your True-Self grows stronger. You are unknowingly making room for this real self to emerge in your consciousness and integrate into your life.

In stage three, it is common to experience a fear of losing oneself, and you may struggle to maintain a sense of self, but ultimately, toward the end of this stage, an "EGO-death" is inevitable. The EGO doesn't exactly die because it is not real to begin with, but many people experience it this way. When the EGO loses hold, there is often a realization that there is no absolute point to life. This can be liberating, like a breath of fresh air, or it can be devastating, resulting in hopelessness and despair. Without a grandiose point, we no longer know how to live our lives, and nothing is ever the same.

There is a foreboding sense that awakening will cost you everything, yet, at the same time, there is a greater sense that something inside you is waking up.

Stage 4 of Awakening – The Stage of Resolution

Spiritual awakening is effortlessly experienced in everyday life.

Stage 4 of Awakening is the stage of resolution where your True-Self has finally overshadowed the EGO. The struggle that you experienced during the first three stages is over and you now experience a deep peace and knowing of *who you really are,* and you are no longer seeking answers. This is fondly known as the Eckart Tolle Stage.

All your beliefs have been overhauled in the past two stages, and the beliefs that remain support harmony and balance. You have mastered the art of letting go, and surrendering to a higher power. You also experience and have access to your inner power, without EGO control.

Doubt has been replaced with faith and trust. You are able to see and understand your life in such a way that your past and present all makes sense. You have forgiven everyone for everything, including yourself.

Unconscious programming has been replaced with consciousness, and there are no emotional or mental prisons holding you captive.

You take responsibility for your entire life, no longer blaming anyone for anything. As you have freed yourself, you have also freed all the people who have ever been affected by your judgment and expectations.

You are no longer trying to prove your worth. You now know and own your intrinsic worth, and, as a result, you experience unconditional self-love.

Although you might still be alone on your journey, you experience a deep and profound connection to all of life and the sense of loneliness has likely faded into all oneness. The need and desire for the old paradigm of relationships have shifted and you no longer yearn to fit-in or be "normal." You allow yourself to be exactly who you are, without needing approval or acceptance from anyone. You no longer have a need to change anyone or help those you love wake up, and you are pleasantly surprised that some people you know are actually awakening. All your relationships improve, and the new people who come into your life are better aligned with who you are.

In this stage, you integrate your insights and develop greater understanding for the journey you have been on. You may teach, mentor or share, but not because you feel you have to, or because you need to, but only because it brings you joy, and you are guided to do so. You may have a compelling desire to support others on their journey or you may have no inclination whatsoever. If you take the role of teacher, mentor, healer or coach, you do not take responsibility for others, but rather, you empower them to empower themselves. You don't take anything personally, and another's behavior has little, or no, effect on you.

During stage four, it is common to have some sort of spiritual practice, such as meditation, yoga or mindfulness, but not because you are trying to get somewhere or accomplish something (as in the previous stage), but rather because it feels good to you, and it is a natural expression of your life.

You may also experience increased intuition and the ability to access infinite intelligence, as if, you have a direct line to unlimited information.

This stage is marked by living in the moment.

You have made peace with the realization that there is no definitive point to life, and, as a result, it is effortless to live in the present moment. Your love for life and all living beings overflows unconditionally with gratitude and appreciation as a common state of being.

The concepts of good and bad have dissolved, and, yet, you have the full knowing that inside everyone and everything is love.

You take stock of yourself, realizing that you are still you. You are free from EGO-control, and no "authentic parts" have been lost in the journey to awakening. Your personality may be quite the same, but you are likely more easy-going and light-hearted.

Either you have found a livelihood that is aligned with who you are, or you have made peace with your present day livelihood.

There is really no thought of happiness because you no longer need anything to make you happy. You have realized that the secret to happiness is living in the moment and it is now easy to be present at all times.

You have learned how to master your thoughts and beliefs, but, surprisingly, you may have no desire to change anything in your life.

Although you likely experience a full range of emotions, they no longer rule you or control your choices or your relationships.

Your True-Self has integrated in your body, and you live your life as this real self.

You are finally conscious and awake, and grateful that your past "asleep-self" had the courage and tenacity to make this journey. It was worth it - a million times over.

Stage 5 of Awakening – The Stage of Conscious Creation

The ability to consciously create one's life from the awake state.

Many people arrive at stage four and mistakenly believe it is the final stage of awakening, but it is actually a bridge to an even greater experience of awakening.

In Stage 5 of awakening, you experience, and deepen, all the attributes of stage four, but you also step into your power as a conscious creator.

You realize that life can be anything that you choose, and you integrate this understanding by consciously choosing the path of your life. Work and play merge into one, and you experience peace and fulfillment equally in both.

You no longer do anything out of obligation or need, but, instead, you are guided through inspiration and pure desire.

You experience a direct connection to all of life, and you are inspired to create in a whole new manner. Through "intuitive connection" with Infinite Intelligence, you might develop new paradigms of community building, teaching or leadership.

At this stage, you have the ability to attract relationships and form communities that support the betterment of humanity.

Since you have mastered your thoughts and beliefs, you can now consciously create the life you desire; living in the moment, while also creating for the future.

In pure connection with Prime Creator, you are a channel of expression in all you do.

Whatever stage you might now be experiencing, you cannot get it wrong and there are no tests to pass. Awakening is simply a natural process, just like the caterpillar that awakens as the butterfly.

A common question is, how long does each stage take? The time we spend in each stage is not predetermined, but we can move through a stage quicker and easier when we utilize a mindfulness practice of letting go. *Letting go is truly the secret of awakening.*

As more and more people awaken, a threshold of awakening will be experienced, and the masses will awaken in a much a different paradigm than those of us who have already awakened or who are awakening now. The stages of awakening will be less defined and maybe even disappear altogether.

No matter where you are on your journey to awakening,
you are exactly where you need to be.

Part 2
The Awakening of True-Self

Making the Shift from EGO to True-Self

Welcome to Part 2!

Now that you understand how the EGO operates and the hidden dynamics that keep us asleep, let's take a journey that will show you the clearest path to awakening as your True-Self.

In Part 2, you will learn how to:

- Identify and turn off "motors"
- Perform an energy analysis of your life
- Identify the conditions of your worth
- Deactivate the Worthiness Program
- Activate unconditional worth
- Deactivate the Powerlessness Program
- Activate your power
- Discern the EGO from your True-Self
- Shift disempowering beliefs
- Overcome negative thinking
- Avoid EGO hijacking
- Reprogram the EGO
- Channel Life Force Energy
- Explore a day in the life of your True-Self
- Preview True-Self Relationships and raising True-Self Children
- Your True-Self Purpose and Mission will also be revealed
- You will also learn how to avoid over 20 EGO Pitfalls!

Part 2 is intentionally designed to support the shift from EGO to True-Self, but in order for this process to work, you must do all the exercises provided, and you may need to do some of them multiple times until you experience a shift in consciousness. The processes offered are the same ones that I personally used for my own awakening and the ones I share with clients and friends, so I know that they work. Some of them might seem silly or illogical to you, and that's okay - do them anyway. If you are going to deactivate disempowering programs and reclaim your life, the process must be a method that transcends the logic of the EGO, as well as the programming of the subconscious mind.

The shift from EGO to True-Self invites you to move beyond your comfort zone, and, if you accept this invitation, there is a whole new world of possibilities awaiting your exploration.

Chapter 24

More of Who You Really Are

I've heard many people express concern that if they disengage from energy generating behaviors, roles and relationships, their lives will be empty and boring, but nothing can be further from the truth. Freeing yourself from an EGO-driven lifestyle allows you to be *more of who you really are*; no longer limited by the opinions of others or needing to prove anything to anyone, you are free to live your life as only you can do.

If you want adventure, you can have adventure. If you want romance, you can have romance. If you want to create, invent or innovate, you can do all that too! Nothing is out of reach when you embody your True-Self and you are tapped into Life Force Energy.

Imagine living your life without inhibition, limitation or fear.

You may still do the same things, but they will not be the same when you no longer rely on them to prove your worth or generate energy. As you follow your joy and the magnetic flow of inspiration, you will feel energized when partaking in roles, behaviors and activities, because you don't depend on any of them to prove your worth or generate energy. When you live as the True You, your source of energy is a direct connection to Source, and because you are purely connected, Source works through you - directing you through ideas and inspiration in ways that offer joyous energy and fulfillment, and, at the same time, your unique experiences and creative expression contribute to serving those around you.

Your life does not get smaller or more limited as you make the shift from EGO to True-Self, and, in fact, your life expands exponentially with many more positive possibilities showing up.

You can still experience success, win a race, be the best at something, enjoy the finer things in life, have lots of money or accomplish the impossible. In fact, when you are not depending on external things for worth or needing anything to generate energy, you can actually experience, manifest and attract a great deal more of what you desire.

As your True-Self, you are tapped into an abundance of Life Force Energy, which can be utilized to manifest your grandest dreams and sweetest desires.

The nature of one's True-Self has an innate curiosity to experience the finest of human potential - so, as you fearlessly follow your inspiration, your life will unfold as a brilliant journey of unimaginable joy, creativity and adventure.

Knowing your unconditional worth allows you to follow your dreams, desires and inner guidance without the need for emotional, physical or financial guarantees or the need for permission - because your worth is not conditioned on any outcome, there is no risk of unworthiness. From the knowing of your worth, you can easily trust that wherever your dreams and desires take you, the Universe, and all its representatives, will support you abundantly in every way.

When you follow your heart and express your gifts, you are aligned with infinite and unlimited Life Force Energy which can manifest as anything and everything that you need or want, or even just fancy for pure delight.

What about Personality?

Be careful not to confuse the traits of the EGO with your individual personality. Oftentimes, we are afraid to transcend the EGO because we falsely believe that the EGO provides our unique personality, and without the EGO we would melt into non-distinctness. Indeed, the EGO does influence personality, but the characteristics that describe the True You go well beyond the construct of EGO.

Without the EGO in control, you are still you, but it is much easier to be you.

Transcending the EGO transforms...

- Struggle into Ease
- Scarcity into Prosperity
- Confusion into Clarity
- Distraction into Presence
- Challenges into Opportunities
- Unrealized Dreams into Reality

Chapter 25

Worth the Wait

If you are going to manifest big dreams or sweet desires, your True-Self must inhabit the commander's seat full time. Your positive experience of life, your best choices and your most empowering behavior is directly dependent on your True-Self.

Because the EGO experiences the world through the filter of worth, and bases decisions on survival, the result is often disempowering behavior and living an inauthentic life, but, with inauthenticity comes emptiness, lack of fulfillment and an inner hunger that can never be satisfied through the EGO or any of its "motors." The truth is that you can only be authentic when you know and own your unconditional worth, and your behavior is free of EGO controls.

Authenticity is the byproduct of living as your True-Self.

Your True-Self experiences life through the eyes of love without distorted filters. It inspires you to express your most authentic self, always resulting in empowering behavior. Not only is life profoundly different when lived as your True-Self, your True-Self allows you to manifest every experience, relationship and possibility as an evolved version, ultimately resulting in higher outcomes, more joy and greater fulfillment.

The EGO and True-Self may partake in very different actions, but even the same actions result in contrasting outcomes, because the action is coming from a completely different intention. *So, why do anything important unless your True-Self is in command?*

Imagine that you are about to take a small plane to another country, and your pilot gets delayed, making you potentially late for a very important meeting. One of the passengers volunteers to fly the plane, but when you ask if he is a licensed pilot, he says no, although he plays video games where he pilots planes. Even though you need to make your meeting on time, would you consider allowing the "video pilot" to fly the plane? Of course not, you would wait for the real pilot because a "video pilot" doesn't compare to an experienced and licensed pilot.

When you allow the EGO to operate your life, instead of waiting for your True-Self to make choices and take actions, it is very much like allowing a "pretend pilot" to fly your plane. Yes, you might need to invest some time and energy in order to call forth your True-Self, but the results of True-Self Living far outweighs the cost of investment.

Let's Recap

- Without the EGO in control, you can be *more of who you really are.*
- No longer limited by the opinions of others or needing to prove anything to anyone, you are free to live your life.
- The EGO experiences the world through the filter of worth, and, therefore, bases all decisions on how it will influence your worth.

- EGO-driven choices result in disempowering behavior and inauthentic living.
- Authenticity is the byproduct of living as your True-Self.
- Your True-Self allows you to manifest every experience, relationship and possibility as an evolved version, resulting in more joy and greater fulfillment.
- The EGO and True-Self may partake in very different actions, but even the same actions result in contrasting outcomes, because the action is coming from a completely different intention.
- Living life as your True-Self aligns you with your best possible destiny, which is the one you intended to live!

If you are ready for your True-Self to slide into the pilot's seat of your life, it is essential to identify all your "motors" and begin a process of disengaging from each and every one.

Chapter 26

WHAT IS YOUR MOTOR?

The first step to aligning with your True-Self and connecting to Life Force Energy is understanding how you are currently generating energy and also identifying all the "motors" you have operating. The more "motors" you have running, the more time and attention needed to maintain them, and the less time and attention you will have to consciously create your life.

To get the most out of this book, please complete the following processes and answer all the questions, as your responses will be used in upcoming chapters.

IDENTIFYING "MOTORS" VIA ENERGY ANALYSIS

In order to understand where the EGO is generating energy it is important to do an Energy Analysis of your life. Let's begin by looking at Areas of Worth.

Areas of Worth

Since your "motors" for energy often have to do with worth, determining all the ways in which you gain a sense of worth can help you pinpoint many "motors."

> *Signpost on the path*
> *"Motors" wear-out, but*
> *Source Energy lasts forever*

In what ways do you boost your sense of worth?

Give each of the following a rating from 1 to 5:

- Number 1 representing not at all.
- Number 2 representing occasionally.
- Number 3 representing sometimes.
- Number 4 representing most of the time.
- Number 5 representing all the time.

Being the Best

__1__ Winning a game or contest
__3__ Being the best, fastest, smartest, etc…
__4__ Perfectionist
__4__ Being a "know it all"
__5__ Survivor

Success

__2__ Accomplishments or success
__2__ Material things – fancy cars, big house, etc….

__2__ Wealth

Extrovert

__2__ Being popular (or the chosen one)

__4__ Being liked (others speaking highly of you)

__2__ Fame – community, national or worldwide

__3__ Center of attention

Status

__2__ Job/career

__3__ Position of authority

__1__ Education, degrees or awards

__5__ Intelligence

__1__ Awards

Appearance

__3__ Physical appearance

__3__ Receiving compliments

__3__ Attention, looks of admiration

Entertaining

__4__ Telling stories

__4__ Life of the party

Pleasing Others

__3__ People pleasing

__4__ Dependability

__4__ Being a nice or good person

Roles

__2__ Any roles you play; teacher, parent, preacher, authority role, etc..

__4__ Playing the part of fixer, healer, helper, mediator, etc…

Relationships

__1__ Relationships with "inferior" people to feel superior

__3__ Relationships with powerful, smart or super attractive people

"Negative" roles/identities

__4__ Playing the victim

__3__ Any physical challenges

__4__ Co-dependency

5 Lack or loss of Money

Is it possible that you get a sense of worth from something not on this list?
Add it here ______________________

- Anything that scored 4-5 is likely a major "motor" for energy in your life.
- Anything that scored 3 is a medium "motor."
- Anything that scored 1-2 is a low "motor" or not a "motor" at all.

Keep in mind that your "motors" may change depending on circumstances and other conditions.

Identifying Behavior "Motors"

Since the EGO often generates energy through behavior, it is helpful to consider that anything which boosts the EGO, or motor-vates you, may be a "motor" for energy generation. Behavior "motors" most often coincide with "motors" that increase worth.

Please use the following questions in order to gain insight:

What are the conditions upon your worth? For each item of worth that scored 3 and above, what do you have to do/prove in order to be worthy?

Look good be fit act "younger" be the smart one be good at whatever I do earn money be a "good person" go to church (ugh)

What identity or role are you most attached? How is it generating energy?

being cute, smart & funny "needing" help to survive financially

How do you use/need situations, relationships or experiences in order to gain energy?

to feel wanted, attractive, to make ends meet, sometimes

What types of experiences and relationships generally boost your EGO?

When people say how smart & funny I am.

What do you frequently talk about? Think about?

my horrible abusive poorly paid job
How in the HELL will I live
manag to payall my bills and even survive

Do you feel a negative energetic charge in your body when you think about certain things or do certain things? List them here:

when I do something that is out of
integrity. lie, cheat steal ignore boundaries

Have you felt negative emotions about the same person, place or thing for an extended period of time? If yes, describe:

Job. everyone there. one neighbor. the
State I live in.

Do you keep replaying a past situation, experience or relationship over and over in your mind? If so, what?

all the ways I failed my son as
I raised him. How I have only rarely
managed to fully support myself financially

Do you have difficulty letting go of a relationship, job or situation even though you know letting go is in your best interest? If so, describe:

Job. I'm a failure loser useless person
worthless piece of shit without a job.
wholelly devalued.

Do you often feel stressed, overwhelmed, frustrated, angry or depressed? If so, describe:

only at work. or when I am terribley
lonely & isolated at home.

Do you experience compulsive thoughts? If so, describe:

yes I call myself terrible things.
Sometimes I punch myself & slap my
head & face very hard.

Are you overly attached to anyone or anything? If so, describe:

my son. he is literally the only human being I have ever trusted to Love me.

Are you driven to get things done or control things? If so, describe:

no so much I love a clean house though. and my yard & indoor plants MUST be thoroughly cared for they depend on me.

Do you live more in the past or future than the present? If so, describe:

past. no future, really. I just live in fear & shame & regret.

If you are completely honest with yourself, the answers to these questions should provide profound insight into many of the "motors" operating your life. You don't have to do anything to turn off them off just yet. For now, you only need to notice how they operate so that you can understand the mechanism at deeper levels. It is very helpful to keep a journal that focuses solely on this dynamic so that you can track unconscious motor-driven behavior. *Making the unconscious "conscious" is the first step in awakening as your True-Self.*

Challenges Reveal

Our 'motors' are often revealed in our most common or chronic challenges, therefore, observing your ongoing life challenges is quite helpful.

Energy generating "motors" are often hidden within life challenges for two reasons:

1. In the attempt to generate energy, behavior often becomes distorted, resulting in various issues.
2. Challenges are often created by the EGO in order to generate energy through emotional reactions, such as frustration, worry, fear, anger, resentment, jealousy, etc....

Make a list of everything that challenges you (use a separate piece of paper if necessary):

my recent poor health, both mental & physical
my lack of financial security
my need for time with my son & the ache it causes when its not possible.
needing a pet/companion but not trusting I can take adequate care of it.

when I fall, people have to take care of me. If people take care of me it means they love me.

For each challenge on your list, ask yourself: **How am I getting energy from this…?**

Joy to be the helpless abused victim who has to be taken care of to survive.

A big key to uncovering this answer is to be aware of your normal emotional reaction to each challenge.

As an example of this process, let's say your list includes: facial acne, a neighbor's dog that barks all night and a challenging relationship with a co-worker. Your responses might go something like this:

> **Facial acne** – every time I wake up with a break-out I feel out of control. I get energy from feeling out of control and frustrated, as well as obsessively focusing on it.
>
> **Noisy dog** – the barking dog keeps me up all night, and I feel angry at my neighbor. I get a charge of energy every time I think of my inconsiderate neighbor and I get fueled by imagining revenge.
>
> **Challenging co-worker** – we don't agree on most things and this causes arguments. I often feel resentful that I have to work with someone incompetent. I get an energy charge every time I have to deal with him because I am so frustrated, and then I go home and complain about him to my spouse, which generates more energy every time I tell the story.

Can you see that each of these challenges generates an emotional charge, thereby producing energy? The acne, dog and co-worker are all energy generators.

As long as something is being used to generate energy, it is very difficult to change, which explains why we often experience ongoing challenges. In addition, emotional reactions feed into situations and perpetuate them.

Once you identify the ways in which you are artificially generating energy, the next step is to disentangle, which means that you must consciously and intentionally stop getting energy from these sources. In other words, withdraw your emotional reaction. Instead of getting angry about the barking dog, let it go. Instead of feeling out of control about the acne, let it go. Instead of feeling frustrated about the co-worker, let it go. You know when you have let something go because you no longer get energy from it.

You might still have certain reactions, but, as soon as you recognize them, do your best to take a deep breath and let go. Because sometimes it is difficult to let go, a back door approach to letting go is to ask yourself one of these questions:

- How would it feel to let go?
- How would I feel if I let go?
- What would it be like to let go?

These questions invite your subconscious to let go without the EGO resisting.

As you drop emotional reactions, you no longer need these challenges to generate energy, and when they stop being sources of energy, the EGO no longer has a need for them, and it can let them go, as well. Once we disengage, challenges often resolve on their own; the skin clears up, the neighbor moves and a promotion ends the problem with the co-worker.

Lying to Yourself?

Other clues in identifying your "motors" include areas of your life where you are not telling yourself the truth; shame, embarrassment, hiding, secrecy, rationalizing, justifying or any form of defense may be an indication that there is a "motor" running.

List the areas, situations or relationships where you may be deceiving yourself.

I hide my depression deflect it with humor & caretaking people who I know won't be there if I

When you have no energy, you feel down and powerless, but, if you were to suddenly get a shot of energy, you would feel on top of the world. Nothing in your life has to change – just increased energy.

My Energy Analysis

It is extremely helpful to review all the sources of energy that you have relied upon throughout your life. As an example of this process, and how to identify your personal "motors" for energy, I offer my own life-long energy analysis.

As a child, I received attention from my very busy mom only when sick or hurt. Sickness and accidents became my first "motors" for energy. *Motors: sickness, accidents.*

I became interested in performing arts in order to gain the approval and attention of my equally busy father. *Motor: being the center of attention.*

At fourteen years old, I developed a sexy woman's body; I immediately received a great deal of attention and appreciation from others. As a result, my worth became conditioned on my physical appearance and others appreciating me. I focused on getting energy this way by working out, wearing sexy clothes, and emphasizing my sensuality. *Motors: appearance, sexuality, attention, appreciation.*

I received a sense of worth by being the only woman participating in male dominant activities. I was also very different in many other ways, and I got energy from standing out among the crowd. *Motor: being different/better.*

At seventeen years old, I experienced, and escaped, a violent relationship, and for the following eight years, I received energy for overcoming victimhood, and being a survivor of domestic violence. *Motors: victimhood, survivor.*

In my teens and twenties, my focus was on acting, modeling, teaching and public presentations. I desired to be famous and make a difference. I received energy from being the center of attention, and I desired even more. The more special I could be, the more worthy and the more energy. *Motors: fame, popularity.*

I also gained a great deal of energy from story-telling. I had a lot of stories to tell, and I was constantly accumulating more as I frequently found myself in unusual challenges that were story-worthy. *Motor: story-telling.*

In my twenties, I suffered from chronic fatigue syndrome and didn't know why. I can now easily see that my "motors" for energy were burning out, and the cost to keep them running was greater than the gains. As a result, I had no choice but to pull my energy back from nonessential roles, behaviors and relationships. At the time, I didn't yet understand the hidden dynamics that I share in this book, but hindsight, I can clearly see that I reclaimed my energy from every area of my life, particularly where the EGO was attempting to generate energy through proving worth. But, the EGO is tricky, and I can now see that I unconsciously replaced one "motor" with another. I transferred my sense of worth from my physical appearance and performance to being a healer, counselor and teacher. It seemed like an upgrade, but hindsight, I can see that I still depended on roles and identifications in order to prove worth.

I should also mention that I spent many years healing worthiness issues and powerlessness issues, and each turning point on the journey granted me greater insight. It was a process of finding that space inside me where I knew my intrinsic worth and I owned my power. When I realized that my worth was dependent on something, I let it go, and I turned within to know my true worth - independent of everyone and everything.

At some point, I realized that I was attached to being a nice person. I questioned if this was really me or if I was just people pleasing in order to get appreciation (my primary emotional need). I made the conscious choice to let go of "being nice." I stopped doing things for others, and I stopped being a helper or healer. I actually became rather selfish, and one of my best friends even described me as being mean. "*So be it*," I thought, "*Let me find out who I really am*." I remember thinking that I might never be a nice person again, and I was fine with it. I no longer identified my worth with being nice or pleasing others. I was free from this life-long bind. Time passed, and I discovered that something greater than me desired to work through me by helping others, and I openly welcomed it, but this time, it was no longer about worth. It was about being a channel for Source. Since my actions were no longer dependent on outcomes or appreciation, it felt inspiring and empowering to be of service.

In this time period, I experienced a complete shedding of the false-self which was accelerated exponentially after visiting the Amazonian Jungle in Peru and drinking the sacred tea, Ayahuasca, for the first time.

Whatever issues remained hidden within me were exposed, enlightened and released. It was an extremely challenging time in my life, but I now believe that it allowed me to emerge decades beyond my previous awareness, fully empowered, conscious and awake.

During this lengthy purification process, pre and post Peru, I released my identification with my roles, relationships, accomplishments, personal identity, gifts, talents and life dreams. I made a conscious choice not to talk about myself and I no longer defined myself according to any titles; in fact, upon meeting new people, I would intentionally say little more than my name.

The more I knew my worth and expressed my power, the less I needed "motors" to generate energy. I disentangled my sense of self from everyone and everything, until my worth was no longer conditional – and I was finally free. As I plugged into Source more and more as the years unfolded, my True-Self embodied my life on a regular and consistent basis until fully integrated.

Then, for about two years, I had no idea how to live my life because I no longer needed to be, do or have in order to prove my worth or generate energy. All I could do was live in the moment, and it was enough and much more than enough.

I went back to Peru years later and I hiked up to Huayna Picchu; I sat perched on a small cliff overlooking Machu Picchu, speaking with God (what I personally call Source) for hours. I asked, "*How am I to live my life now*?" The answer was clear and concise...

"Do whatever brings you joy for the sake of joy alone. Do what you love to do."

Two years previously, I had surrendered my dreams and desires to Source, and now I was surprised to discover that Source gave them back to me, but this time, however, the path of manifesting was not cluttered by my own personal needs and issues.

Now, with an enlightened vision, I continue to find myself creating, writing and channeling in ways that offer profound wisdom and guidance. I still do many of the things that I did before, but it comes from an entirely different space. I don't do any of these things to generate energy, but in doing them I experience tremendous energy that supports my creative journey, which is the creative journey of Source through me. I fully understand that the best I can ever do is get out of the way, providing the clearest channel possible.

I share my process only as a guide. You have all your own answers inside you. ***You, and only you, know what is best for you.***

Chapter 27

TURNING OFF "MOTORS"

Clearly, all "motors" are controlled by subconscious programs, so without inner awareness, you have no power to turn them off. Conversely, once you are conscious of your specific "motors," and you understand how (and when) they operate in your life, you have the power to flip the off switch.

THE 6 STEP MOTOR PROCESS

There are 6 Steps required to turn off the EGO's energy generating "motors."

1. **Identify "motors:"**
   - Recognize all the dynamics in your life that generate energy for you; using the list you made in the previous chapter and your personal assessment, take ***one at a time*** and perform the following process.
2. **Take a good long look at the dynamic:**
   - How long has it been going on?
   - How much time/energy is required to keep it going?
   - What are all the costs (emotional, mental, financial, relationship, health, etc...)?
   - What are the ripple effects?
3. **What beliefs perpetuate this dynamic?**
   - What must you believe in order to keep this behavior operating? List all possible beliefs, and break them down to the core belief.
4. **What might you gain, heal or improve once you turn off this motor?**
5. **Release the core belief that runs the motor.**
6. **Stop engaging in the dynamic:**
   - Consciously choose to stop engaging in the behaviors, actions, thoughts and reactions in order to break the dynamic.

To help exemplify this process, let's play with the example that one of your major "motors" is fighting with your ex-partner.

1. **What is the Motor?** Arguing with ex-partner triggers the emotional reaction of anger which is an energy source.
2. **Take a good long look at the dynamic:**
   - How long has it been going on? 2 years.
   - How much time/energy does it require to perpetuate? Many hours each week.

- What are the all the costs (emotional, mental, financial, relationship, health, etc…)? It has affected every area of life; constantly stressed, can't focus, not eating properly, feel emotionally and physically drained, possible health related issues.
- What is the ripple effect? Affects the ability to attract a new relationship and start a new business.

3. **What beliefs perpetuate this dynamic?**

- List them all, and break them down to the core belief.

What must you believe in order to fight with your ex? Maybe you believe that he abandoned you in some way, he didn't accept you and you were never enough.

What must you believe in order to feel abandoned, not accepted and not enough? In order to feel these emotions you must believe that you are not worthy of his love (the EGO interprets this as you are not worthy of love in general). The core belief is "I am unworthy of love."

The purpose of arguing is an ongoing, yet unconscious, attempt at proving your worth to your ex; as long as you need him to believe you are worthy, you remain powerless to heal and you will stay entangled in the relationship dynamics. In order to turn off the motor (fighting with your ex), you must release the need/desire that he finds you worthy, and instead you must claim your unconditional worth.

4. **What might you gain, heal or improve once you turn off this motor?** Emotional wellbeing, healing, improved relationship(s), more time, etc…

5. **Release the core belief that runs the motor:** The core belief is, "I am unworthy of love." In order to release this belief as it relates to your ex, you must let go of the need that your ex finds you worthy. After all, you are no longer together and whether or not he thinks you are worthy of his love has no bearing on your life. As you let him off the hook, you free yourself from a dysfunctional dynamic and you turn off the "motor." Instead of needing him, or anyone, to find you worthy of love, you only need to remember that you are unconditionally worthy and you must love yourself. This is the healing - whatever you believe you need from another, you must give to yourself. (An additional process of disentangling worth is included below.)

6. **Stop engaging in the dynamic:** Make the choice not to see your ex, and if you must be in contact, consciously choose not to be triggered. Also, make it your intention to release all thoughts and beliefs about your ex and the past relationship.

Most internal shifts require a tangible demonstration; this means that in order to turn off a "motor" you must take the appropriate actions that demonstrate your choice and intention – not as a one-time process but as a consistent way of life.

Disentangling Worth

Trying to prove your worth is a waste of time, so instead of wasting your time playing the Worthiness Game of Misfortune, just claim your worth once and for all!

The key to turning off your "motors" and freeing yourself is disentangling your worth from any and all conditions. If you haven't yet, go back to the previous chapter and do a self-assessment to determine the conditions upon your worth.

Once you have a good understanding of the conditions you have placed upon your worth, you can begin the process of disentanglement.

Disentangling Worth Process

1. Take full responsibility - if you blame someone for imposing conditions upon your worth you give away your power; no matter how it seems, you are responsible for adopting all conditions, and, therefore, you can let them go.
2. Non-judgmentally observe when and how these conditions are showing up.
3. Notice how you behave in order to feel worthy; what do you do and say in order to prove worth? How does it make you feel?
4. Practice disengaging from these behaviors; if you get worth from behaving a certain way, consciously choose to override the behavior on a consistent basis - for as long as it takes to end the behavior.
5. This is the most important part; as you disengage from worth generating behaviors, reaffirm your unconditional worth on a daily basis, "I am unconditionally worthy. My worth does not depend on .... (fill in the blank)."
6. Commit to a daily meditation or mindfulness practice where you can experience your unconditional worth in an altered state of consciousness; speaking directly to your subconscious mind. I offer a free guided process at *www.Nanice.com/worth*

Upcoming chapters will address more about the process of releasing unworthiness and turning off the Worthiness Program.

Now, let's look at turning off many of the most common "motors."

Turning off the "Money Motor"

When you believe that future abundance will make you worthy, money that you don't yet have provides the potential for worth, and, therefore, the EGO motor-vates you in the pursuit.

The following section focuses on the use of scarcity as an energy generator, however, if money is an energy generator for you, but you have an abundance of money, you may not see this "motor" as a problem. Keep in mind that all "motors" eventually wear down and create chaos in one way or another. Even if a "motor" results in positive outcomes, thereby boosting the EGO, it is still an artificial energy generator and a symptom of conditional worthiness. It might make sense to heal this false belief before the "motor" burns-out.

The lack of money, or quest for money, is often a major "motor" for energy generation; as we discussed previously, money can generate energy through many dynamics, such as: worrying about money, trying to get money, complaining about not having enough money, feelings of jealousy/resentment of others who have more money, fighting with your partner/family over money, stress, overwhelm and frustration caused by scarcity, relief or gratitude when you finally get money.

If the lack of money is a "motor" that generates energy for you, and you suddenly won the lottery (eliminating all your money issues), a huge source of artificially-generated energy would no longer be accessible. The EGO knows this, and, therefore, is invested in keeping you in scarcity. According to the EGO, energy generation is tremendously more important than money, so it will perpetuate a scarcity dynamic as long as scarcity generates energy. This may be one of the main reasons why it is so difficult to attain wealth and keep it.

Whatever your current financial experience, if you want more abundance, it is important to disentangle *energy generation* from anything that has to do with lack of money. If you are no longer relying on scarcity for the generation of energy, the EGO will no longer be invested in maintaining scarcity.

How do you disentangle energy generation from scarcity?

- Stop worrying about money
- Stop talking/thinking about lack of money
- Stop complaining about not having enough money
- Stop reacting to scarcity or the fear of scarcity
- Relax around money
- Imagine abundance
- Feel joy for others who are abundant
- And say to yourself, '*That's for me too!*"

Once again, as long as you are receiving energy from something you desire to heal or change (no matter how negative or uncomfortable), it cannot heal or change because the EGO will not allow you to lose a means of energy.

If you desire to heal an issue, solve a problem or overcome a challenge, you must break the dynamic of energy generation; you must consciously withdraw your attention from the issue, problem or challenge, you must stop telling the story and you must stop seeking and receiving energy from the dynamics in anyway.

When you stop giving a dynamic your power, the EGO cannot generate energy from it, and when there is no energy to be generated, the EGO will let it go.

As with turning off all "motors," you must replace the lost energy with Life Force Energy - no doubt, this requires True-Self embodiment and the knowing of your unconditional worth.

Let's be clear, turning off the "Money Motor" does not mean you are giving up money. In fact, just the opposite, when you no longer use money to generate energy or need it to prove your worth, you have a greater ability to manifest more abundance with less effort, especially when using the manifesting powers of your True-Self. For an intense exploration of True-Self Manifesting, please read, "Seducing the Field."

Turning off the Most Common "Motors"

To get the most out of the following section, please refer to your responses from the previous chapter. Also, remember that a core element of turning off any "motor" is practicing unconditional worth.

Roles We Play Motor

As you now know, the roles you play in life do not make you worthy, and, in fact, believing that they do keeps you from knowing and owning your intrinsic worth.

Once you identify the roles you play and how you depend on them for your sense of worth, you have the insight and power to disentangle your worth. This may result in letting go of certain roles and identities, while you may also discover that you can enjoy a particular role a great deal more without using it to prove your worth.

One of the hardest concepts to comprehend is that you really do not have to do anything in life. Indeed, it seems otherwise, but there is really nothing you absolutely have to do. Since this includes the roles you play, imagine giving yourself permission to drop every role and identity, and from a blank canvas, carefully consider what you really want to do, and how you want to do it. Maybe you really do enjoy certain roles but you don't enjoy the way in which you do them. What would it look like to change the way you perform these roles so that they better suit you? How might you show up differently and how might it transform the role?

Story-Telling Motor

Because you may not even realize that you use your stories to gain worth or generate energy, it is helpful to be conscious of the things you share and how often you are telling the same story. Notice if you are trying to invoke sympathy for a hardship or praise for success. Either way, when you notice that you seek a payoff for story-telling, do your best to disengage your worth from the behavior, and maybe even disengage the behavior. Just for one day, consciously decide to do without story-telling and see what happens. If it is difficult not to share your story, chances are the Story-Telling Motor is operating.

Stress Motor

Stress and pressure can often be insidious "motors" because we don't realize that stress is optional. Many of the things that cause us stress are "motors" themselves. Therefore, to turn off the Stress Motor, it is important to analyze all the things that cause you stress, and first turn off those "motors" - this likely means disengaging your worth from the things you do.

Consider that there is nothing that you have to do in order to be worthy; this means that you can likely let go of many of the items on your "to do" list. In order to turn off the Stress Motor, it is essential to let go of the needless pressure that you put upon yourself to be who you think you have to be in order to be worthy. The truth is, you don't have to be anyone because at the very core of your being, you are worthy.

People Pleasing Motor

When you really look at it, "people pleasing" is actually quite self-serving because we only do it in order to get our emotional needs met, and so that others will see us as worthy. To break this dynamic, stop automatically doing things to be nice or kind, and get real with yourself; do you really want to do the things you do or are you only doing them for the payoff - to be seen a certain way, feel needed or because you feel obligated or guilty if you don't. Once you make this discernment, start cleaning up your life by eliminating all actions that are tied to your worth, and give yourself permission to please yourself, first and foremost, and, at the same time, meet your own primary emotional need.

Complaining Motor

Next time you complain, nag or argue, pay attention to the energetic payoff and notice how you might be using this negative dynamic (focusing on the negative) to generate instant energy. If you feel an emotional "charge," the behavior is most certainly generating energy. The thing is, every time we complain, nag or argue it may immediately generate energy but it is ultimately quite depleting. Making the connection between your behavior and the longer term effects will help you to withdraw your attention from negativity. From a manifestation standpoint, focusing on the negative aligns you with more of what you do not want, and then you have to deal with it - problems may give us a burst of adrenaline initially, but overall they are energy depleting.

Since there is no good reason to complain, nag or argue, one of the best things you can do for yourself is eliminate negative thinking altogether and consciously focus on the positive. In a later chapter, we will discuss overcoming negative thought patterns.

Judging and Competition Motors

Judging others may provide an instant EGO boost by making you feel better about yourself, but the energy generated has a big price to pay because you cannot judge another without going unconscious and misaligning even further with your True-Self.

You don't need to judge others in order to feel good about yourself and you don't need to be better by comparison to be worthy. In order to turn off this "motor" you must own your worth independent of all others and you must consciously choose not to be the judge. Whenever you find yourself in judgment, stop and replace the thought with something positive about the subject of your judgment.

You don't need to compare yourself to anyone, compete in anyway or win in order to be worthy. Instead of wasting your time competing for worth, practice seeing yourself, *and others,* independently worthy - without conditions.

Self-Judgment Motor

You might not even realize the ongoing dynamic of self-judgment because most of us judge ourselves relentlessly and we don't even know we are doing it. So, the first step to turn off this "motor" is to realize that it exists in the first place, and to what degree. Of course, try your best to do this process without judging yourself for judging yourself; in other words, don't judge the judgment, and, if you do, instead of judging the judging of the judging (are you following me?), arrive at some level of self-allowance in order to break the cycle. Therefore, instead of judging yourself for judging yourself, you actually allow yourself to judge the judging. The more allowing you are of yourself, the more you will align with unconditional worth.

Once you choose to turn off this "motor," consider setting a boundary with yourself that says, "I am no longer motor-vated by self-judgment." This means that you stop giving your power to self-judgment and you stop permitting it to dictate your actions and behavior. If self-judgment no longer motor-vates you to take action or behave in certain ways, the "motor" will lose steam. At the same time, it is important to practice thinking supportive and empowering thoughts - about yourself. A daily practice of positive affirmations can do wonders. If you are looking for a New Year's Resolution, the absolute best thing to give up is self-judgment - and you can start a resolution any day of the year.

Perfectionism is just another word for self-judgment so all of the above applies, with one addition. Consider that you are already perfect and everything that you do is already perfect. Instead of looking for what is wrong or noticing imperfections, make it your intention to see the perfect beauty in yourself and all things.

Rushing Motor

If you often find yourself running late or being behind schedule, you may be using rushing as a "motor" for energy. If this is the case, set an intention to give up the rush; don't schedule as much in a day, space out appointments, give yourself more time to travel, etc... Incidentally, the less you rush, the more time will expand.

Problem Solving Motor

When problem solving (or fixing things) is your "motor," it is best to disentangle your worth from the solution. Otherwise, the EGO will relentlessly attract and create problems for you to solve in order to prove worth. You can discover more effective solutions when your worth is not attached to the outcome. Since your True-Self has a direct line to all answers, it pays to embody True-Self before seeking solutions.

Fighting Against Motor

How often do you fight against something, or take a stand for a cause, in the name of righteousness? Whether your fights are personal or global, if you experience an emotional "charge" or an EGO boost because you believe you are right and you want justice, validation or some other proof that you know best, this "motor" is likely running.

When the EGO depends on this "motor," you might unknowingly be feeding your power into the very issues you are fighting to resolve. It is true that if you win, the EGO gets a boost but once the issue is resolved, the potential for more energy is lost. Consider that you place yourself in a no-win situation whenever the EGO uses the *fight against anything* to generate energy. Since there is often greater energy potential in an ongoing fight than in winning, the EGO might perpetuate the fight or sabotage the win.

Of course, this depends on the person, issue and other related factors. Some EGO's are only invested in the win, with the fight merely being the means to the end. If this is the case, the EGO motor-vates you to win at all costs, which, of course, creates problems of its own.

Just understanding these hidden dynamics may be enough to turn off this "motor." When behavior is seen for what it really is, the foundation of the behavior could naturally collapse, turning off the "motor" with it. If you recognize that you are using a public cause for a private gain (worth/energy), you may simply lose interest in the fight, or, if the cause is truly important to you, this awareness may result in a shift in consciousness that automatically turns off the "motor" so that your actions originate from Pure Desire opposed to EGO gratification.

However, if your participation in a cause keeps the "motor" running, you must disentangle your worth from the ongoing fight and desired resolution, and you must also be aware of the energy that is generated through your emotional reactions so that you can consciously release emotional triggers associated with the issue. You don't need to be angry or enraged in order to expose a truth or reach an enlightened resolution. In fact, the more grounded you are, and the more your worth is unaffected, whether you win or lose, you align with the highest and best outcome.

The Scar Motor

If you experience an emotional "charge," such as regret or self-pity every time you look at a scar or something else you judge about yourself, the Scar Motor may be running. This "motor" might also show up when a scar is associated with a past event that triggers any positive or negative emotions; anything from shame to pride. With awareness, you can disengage the "motor" by choosing not to use your scar or other physical irregularity negatively or positively. It is possible to neutralize your beliefs by consciously choosing to see something in a different light.

PTSD Disorder Motor

Post-traumatic stress disorder is most commonly a deeply embedded response to past life-threatening trauma, often requiring the support of a professional with expertise in releasing trauma. Having said this, many of us develop "low grade" PTSD associated with emotional trauma.

When PTSD is triggered, there is often a fight or flight response designed to protect us in times of danger. If PTSD is in response to emotional trauma, we may experience an emotional reaction intended to protect us.

Nonetheless, all types of triggers motor-vate us to react so that we can protect ourselves accordingly, which is good news in case we really do need to protect ourselves in a hurry, but usually that is not the case. The sneaky, but clever, EGO sees PTSD as a source of energy, so it has no reason to release this disorder, but that doesn't mean you can't.

When PTSD is the result of emotional trauma, it indicates that we have adopted certain beliefs in order to "make sense" of the trauma, and these beliefs always funnel down to the core belief of unworthiness. Since all emotional trauma has its origin in unworthiness, healing always involves releasing the false belief of unworthiness and remembering that you are unconditionally worthy. More on emotions and emotional healing in a later chapter.

Extra Weight Motor

If you experience an emotional charge every time you get near a scale or a mirror, this "motor" may be running. Disentangling your worth from your weight is key for turning off this "motor," but it also helps to make peace with your body by *getting in your body* and befriending your body. In other words, stop treating your body like it is the enemy. An essential component to True-Self embodiment is loving your body as it is, and consciously inhabiting your body. Ultimately, learning to use it as the sacred temple it was intended to be.

Drama/Chaos Motor

If you want to turn off the Drama Motor or the Chaos Motor, you must first let go of the belief that life will be boring without drama or chaos. Nothing could be further from the truth. While it is true, without drama/chaos, life would not be so dramatic, it is also true that ongoing drama/chaos in your life, and the care and handling of that drama/chaos takes up so much time and energy that there is nothing left for conscious creation. Wouldn't you rather live the life of your dreams? To turn off this "motor" you must emotionally disengage from the drama and chaos playing out. Observe it, and deal with it when necessary, but do not react emotionally. If you are no longer generating energy via emotional reactions, the EGO will release the need for drama and chaos.

It also helps to embrace peace and presence by consciously dropping into the present moment. The more you can access Life Force Energy (available only by being present), the less you will need artificially generated energy, brought to you by chaos, drama or another "motor."

Abuser Motor

Abuse is the result of feeling powerless, and the EGO's way to reclaim a sense of power, but it never works because in abusing another, we accentuate our feelings of powerlessness. We only abuse others when we shift responsibility, believing we are powerless, and, if we didn't feel powerless, there would be no reason for abuse. Putting an end to abuse requires taking full responsibly for one's own life. It is essential for someone partaking in the "motor of abuse," to dig deep inside, release the lies and false beliefs that have formed an internal prison, and do whatever it takes to remember your unconditional worth and intrinsic power.

Victimhood Motor

Turning off this "motor" requires that you notice all the ways in which victimhood plays out, and how you use it to experience an identity. Just like the Abuse Motor, turning off this "motor" requires you to take full responsibility for your life. As long as you believe that someone has power over you, this "motor" will operate. The Victimhood Motor turns off the moment you stop believing you are a victim and you stop making others believe that you are a victim. The more you know your unconditional worth, the more empowered you will be, and when you are fully empowered, there is no chance for victimhood.

Survivor Motor

To turn off the Survivor Motor, you must see yourself beyond the identity of survivor, and you must stop getting energy from telling other people your story. Yes, you can still share your story and help others on their journey to empowerment, but it will be a very different experience for you and them, when your worth is not dependent on the role or identity. *When your worth depends on any identity, you imprison yourself in limitation.*

Lying or Deceit Motor

The path to turning off this "motor" is first recognizing that it exists, noticing the pain associated with it (for you and others), and finally being willing to let it go. You might discover that truth, openness and transparency align you with the flow of abundant Life Force Energy.

Relationship Motor

This "motor" turns off when you stop seeing everyone in terms of worth; using the inferiority or superiority of others to feel better about yourself. As you begin to know and own your unconditional worth, you have the ability to see others unconditionally worthy, as well. This "motor" cannot operate when you view everyone equally as worthy without conditions or exceptions.

Being Defensive Motor

How often are you defensive? You might say that your defense is justified, but also consider that being defensive perpetuates situations and relationships where defense is necessary. Turning off this "motor" requires you to stand in your power and communicate in ways that are empowering but not defensive. We defend ourselves only when we feel powerless. Being fully empowered and confident allows us to speak up and stand up without offense or resistance.

Believe it or not, the state of allowing provides immensely more energy than the state of defense. It is in defense, offense and resistance that we inhibit the flow of everything. When we allow life to unfold naturally and others to be, do and act as they wish, the power of the Universe naturally flows through us - bringing with it an abundance of Life Force Energy.

Unconscious Sex Motor

This "motor" can be turned off by replacing it with conscious sex. In Tantric sex and other conscious sexual practices, the sexual outcome is secondary to the experience of connectedness, intimacy and oneness. Conscious sex requires each partner to be fully present and responsible with their own energy, which means that partners are not using each other for gratification or to boost their EGOs. Conscious sex requires you to show up as your True-Self, and, as a result, the sexual relationship allows both partners to channel increased Life Force Energy that is experienced as ecstasy.

Grudge Motor

Turning off the Grudge Motor requires you to take full responsibility for all grudge-related experiences. Having a grudge indicates that you believe that someone did something to you, and you are a victim who needs protection. Holding a grudge acts like an invisible wall that protects you.

Forgiveness turns off this "motor" but in order to forgive, you must know your worth and own your power as the creator of your life, because if you don't, you may be vulnerable to getting hurt again - especially if you allow others to decide your worth. *Keep in mind, if your worth is not dependent on anyone, no one can hurt you - and there is nothing to forgive.*

Shopping Motor

The journey to unconditional worth requires a disentanglement from everything of which you depend on for your sense of worth. Until you completely own your worth, consider not going shopping on days that you feel unworthy or powerless. Simply, save your shopping for days when you feel aligned with *who you really are*, and you might even experience more fun while exploring possibilities.

Social Media

To turn off the Social Media Motor it is important to be aware of why you are sharing or commenting. Notice if your worth is attached to how others respond; are you seeking attention, approval, compliments, sympathy, etc…? If the answer is yes to any of these, imagine how you would feel if you didn't share. If you still decide to share or comment, affirm to yourself, "I am unconditionally worthy and my worth does not depend on anyone or anything." Even if you don't believe it yet, the more you say it, the closer you will get to believing it.

If you engage in forums where opinions are fiery, consider that a Battle of Belief may ignite energy in the moment but the long-term energetic cost is never worth it - keep your power and energy by not engaging.

Control Motor

It helps to turn this "motor" off by understanding that no matter how much we try to control anything, it is really an illusion. If we get energy from control, we lose even more when we are unsuccessful. The only control that we ever have access to is the control of our thoughts. If you can control your thoughts, you can control your life. So, instead of trying to control circumstances or other people, focus on controlling your own thoughts about the situation at hand.

Usually, when we try to control external events, we are really focusing on the undesired outcome which only fuels what we don't want. Instead, stop focusing on what you don't want and practice focusing on what you do want. The more you control your own inner imagination, the more power you will access.

Teasing/Bully Motor

If you get energy from teasing, simply notice the hidden dynamic that may be running this behavior, and if teasing does make you feel better about yourself, imagine yourself on the receiving end and see if that loosens this dynamic. The core cause of bullying is feeling unworthy and powerless, therefore, once again, the cure is doing the inner work required to discover your unconditional worth and intrinsic power.

Fame Motor

Like most "motors" nothing is wrong with fame or popularity, but when it is a "motor," it induces a tremendous amount of stress in order to keep energy generated. To turn off this "motor" it is important to disentangle attention and admiration from fame and/or popularity. Without this payoff, you may simply lose interest in the dynamic of fame or popularity, but, if the dynamic still ensues, disentangling worth will completely change the experience, releasing the burden of unnecessary pressure, and possibly making it a great deal more fun and enjoyable.

Illness Motor

As we have discussed previously, we often don't heal because we unconsciously use our physical issues to generate energy, and the EGO learns to depend on these issues for energy. While healing requires us to turn off all related "motors" associated with the issue, turning off this "motor" requires that you stop using the illness, disability or injury to elicit sympathy or attention, nor use it as an excuse for any reason. As you release your identification with the physical issue, it is important to stop talking about it and focusing on it. To counteract the dynamic of a physical challenge, it is essential to focus on health and wellness, so, instead of seeing yourself sick and/or weak in anyway, imagine yourself whole and perfect in every way.

Co-dependency

Taking care of a partner who is dependent on a dysfunctional lifestyle can improve our sense of worth by making us feel needed, but the ongoing issues in a co-dependent relationship are also energy generating. Turning off this "motor" requires a process of disentanglement that focuses on discovering *who you really are* – independent and separate from the relationship. It is important to rediscover yourself and make choices that support your own inner and outer exploration. Since the People Pleasing Motor often accompanies this "motor," it important to discern this dynamic, as well, and not shift from enabling one person to pleasing another.

Being a "Know It All"

Like all "motors," it is necessary to identify the behavior associated with this "motor" and consciously disengage from the behavior. Even if you are completely right, refrain from saying, "I told you so." If you can't make the shift immediately or consistently, don't beat yourself up (another "motor"). Instead, non-judgmentally observe the behavior and notice where it comes from without trying to change it. The simple act of observation over a period of time often loosens a "motor" making it easier to transcend.

Spiritual Seeking Motor

The search for peace, wisdom or enlightenment motor-vates us and generates energy, but what are we searching for? We are searching for ourselves - for the embodiment of our True-Selves which brings to us a sense of wholeness and the absolute knowing of *who we really are.* If you don't know your unconditional worth, the search will never be complete and it will run your life, but once you remember your worth and you own your worth, the "motor" that runs the search can turn off. Ultimately, finding yourself awake and conscious in this moment, exactly as it is now. *Nothing needs to change - you don't need to add something, become someone or accomplish anything - you are already there, just as you are now.*

Religion Motor

Although many turn off the Religion Motor by leaving religion, this is not always necessary. However, it is necessary to take your power back. Instead of allowing a religion to decide your worth or depending upon that religion to feel worthy, you must find your worth within, separate from doctrine and dogma. You can keep your spiritual beliefs and practices while also reclaiming your power. *Above all else, learn to trust your inner guidance.*

Credit Score Motor

Even if you can't recall your school grades, do bad grades really decrease worth? Do good grades increase worth? Are you more or less worthy right now as a result of that A or F that you received in fifth grade math? If a part of you can see the truth and accept the idea that your school grades had no bearing on your worth, then or now, ask that same part of you to see that this truth extends to the numbers on your credit score. In fact, your worth is not dependent on any numbers at anytime - not the numbers on the scale, not the numbers in your check book and not the numbers on your birth certificate. Imagine disentangling your worth from all numbers and all types of measurement.

Proving You Can Do It Motor

Oftentimes, when this "motor" operates, we are trying to prove our worth to one or two pivotal people. This dynamic may have begun so long ago that we don't even remember that we are doing it. In order to finally feel worthy, we need these naysayers to show signs that they see us worthy, but this rarely, if ever, happens, because these same people are often very critical and they are programmed to judge us. Even if they offer positive acknowledgment, it is often followed by more criticism, leaving us feeling like we will never be enough. The only way to turn off this "motor" is by taking your power back and letting these perpetual critics off the hook. Your worth is not dependent upon anyone finding you worthy, and as long as you wait for others to agree on your worth, you will be trapped in an unfulfilling dynamic of your own making.

Self-Importance Motor

The Self-Importance Motor is often one of the more pervasive "motors" due to the fact that it is a "core motor" that precipitates the operation of many other "motors." In an upcoming chapter, we will take a deeper look at disarming self-importance, but, in preparation, it pays to pinpoint all the ways in which self-importance may be operating in your life. You might even want to keep a journal and record every incident of self-importance.

Image Motors

Image Motors include status, career, position, material possessions and accomplishments, but also includes anything that might improve image or prove worth through image. Image Motors require a great deal of time and energy to keep running, and there is always the background fear that you might lose status, position, accomplishments or material things. The key is to free yourself from all conditions upon your worth, and surprisingly, when you own your worth, you possess greater power to succeed and attract all that you desire. Notice how you depend on certain things to improve or prove worth, and do your best to disentangle your sense of worth from each one, reminding yourself that your worth is intrinsic and never dependent upon anything external or transient.

Being Special Motors

Being Special Motors include above average intelligence, gifts or physical appearance or being different in some way. In our attempt at proving worth, it makes sense that we would identify and cling to that which "makes us better" – especially if other people give us feedback that indicates we are worthy because of being special.

The biggest problem is that if your worth is dependent upon anything, you will miss the crucial fact that your worth is inherently unconditional. Not even a profound gift, incredible beauty or a genius mind can make you more worthy than you intrinsically are. If you believe that your worth depends on anything (even a wonderful thing), you will never experience the freedom that comes from knowing your unconditional worth. Notice how, and in what ways, your worth may be attached to being special or better. Also notice how there may be some fear around losing this aspect of you. To turn off this "motor" do your best to release ownership of your specialness, and recognize that it is actually an expression of the Divine in you. Practice seeing your gifts as a pure and exquisite expression of Source.

Helping and Healing Motors

If helping or healing others is a "motor" for energy, does that mean you should never help?

If you are not using the act of helping or healing others in order to prove your worth or generate energy, it is not a "motor," and, therefore, you are not motor-vated to participate in EGO-driven ways.

The same dynamics that the EGO uses to generate energy, such as healing, helping, teaching, fixing, etc…, your True-Self can use for expression, but the action comes from a completely different space. Instead of focusing on "what is wrong" you see beauty and perfection, and from a state of "nothing is wrong" you are aligned with a higher version of helper, healer, teacher, etc....

- Lower version of any role/behavior:

  EGO-driven to prove worth and generate energy.

- Higher version of any role/behavior:

  True-Self inspires you to be of service.

When you are unconscious and the EGO is in charge, you may be motor-vated to help or heal others in order to boost the EGO, but when you are conscious and your True-Self is in alignment, you are a channel for Source and you are guided.

When you embody your True-Self, being of service to others doesn't boost the EGO, and you don't rely on it for a sense of worth or to generate energy, but it does bring you joy and fulfillment because you are in the flow of Source energy and nothing feels better than flowing with Source and allowing Source to work through you.

> *Signpost on the path*
>
> *Do not substitute one "motor" for another*
>
> It can be very empowering to turn off a "motor," but be careful not to substitute one "motor" for another.

The EGO Flip

The EGO is tricky so you have to be conscious and aware. An EGO Flip happens when you let go of one source of worth and unconsciously replace it with another - you are still playing the Worthiness Game, only with different components. The point is to withdraw your dependence on everyone and everything, and to know your unconditional worth without the need for proof.

The key to sustainable energy is disengaging from all artificial energy sources and connecting with Life Force Energy.

What Happens without Motor-vation?

Some might wonder, if we are not motor-vated by the EGO to get things done, what happens? Do we just sit around all day and meditate?

When the EGO stops running the show, we are no longer doing things in order to prove worth, and when we are not motor-vated to perform, we are free to live our lives as we truly desire and dream. When the "motors" turn off, issues clear up, relationships harmonize and abundance flows, allowing us time, space and energy to consciously create.

Since we are no longer playing the Worthiness Game, life takes on a flowing quality, where it is effortless to manifest our dreams, experience fulfilling relationships and embark on adventurous journeys.

As our True-Selves, we are clearly connected to Source and Source moves us to create and inspires us to fully live our lives.

Without the need to prove, gain, fix or accomplish, we are open channels for divine expression - now able to explore human potential and innovate new ways of living.

Imagine collaborating with our fellow travelers to manifest collective ideas based on universal principles of love, co-creation and wholeness.

As our True-Selves, we have the ability to create Heaven on Earth – not because there is anything wrong that has to be fixed, changed or improved, but, rather, because the experience of Heaven on Earth inspires us to discover un-manifested possibilities.

Let's Recap

Turning off the "motors" in your life requires you to first identify each of them, and then appropriately disentangle your worth.

This means withdrawing your dependence on everyone and everything, and owning your unconditional worth without the need for proof.

An EGO Flip occurs when you substitute one "motor" for another, thereby transferring your worth from one to the other.

When the EGO is no longer in control, you will not do things to prove worth.

You are free to live your life authentically, when you are not motor-vated to perform.

As "motors" turn off, issues clear up, relationships harmonize and abundance flows, allowing you time, space and energy to consciously create.

By no longer playing the Worthiness Game, life effortlessly flows with ease and grace, making it possible to manifest your dreams, experience fulfilling relationships and embark on adventurous journeys.

The following chapters are designed to support True-Self alignment, embodiment and integration.

Chapter 28

True-Self or EGO?

In order to make the journey from EGO to True-Self, it is essential to recognize your current "location." Are you located in the "land of EGO" or in the "Utopia of True-Self"? With conscious awareness, it won't take long before you can easily identify your current location, but, until then, here are some questions that will help you make the discernment.

These questions are intended to assess your current state of being so answer each one as it applies to you in the present moment.

EGO Assessment

If you answer yes to any of the following questions, the EGO is likely dominant at this moment.

- Are you angry or annoyed at someone or something?
- Do you feel like a victim or do you feel powerless?
- Are you questioning your worth or value?
- Are you comparing yourself to others and feeling "less than" or "better than"?
- Are you jealous, envious or resentful?
- Do you feel fragile or unprotected?
- Are you hiding or do you have a fear of being seen?
- Are you changing your behavior in order to gain approval, acceptance, appreciation, etc...?
- Are you seeking permission to express yourself in some way?
- Do you feel threatened, unsafe or unstable?
- Are you looking for compliments or admiration?
- Are you judging others or gossiping?
- Are you thinking about negative outcomes or anything you don't want?
- Are you trying to control circumstance or other people?
- Do you feel "on edge"?
- Are you living in the past or future?
- Do you feel shame or embarrassment?
- Are you blaming others?
- Is someone's behavior negatively affecting you?
- Are you judging yourself?

Signpost on the path

Follow the signs for True-Self

The ability to discern the EGO from your True-Self is pivotal on the path to being who you really are.

Do any of the following emotions describe your current experience?

> Worried, afraid, anxious, overwhelmed, stressed, confused, hopeless, depressed, frustrated, impatient, etc…

Additionally, if you are not in your body, your True-Self is most certainly displaced. Signs include; not being grounded, often feeling cold, confused, disoriented, frequent mishaps, accident prone, distracted, reactive and defensive.

If the EGO is, in fact, dominant at this moment, simply observe without judgment or resistance, as judging the EGO only feeds it. In a later chapter we will explore the conscious shift to True-Self.

True-Self Assessment

If you answer yes to several of the following, you are likely embodying your True-Self.

- Do you feel as if anything is possible?
- Are you able to intuitively access knowledge, answers or information?
- Is there a sense of timelessness, or are you experiencing more done in less time?
- Are you experiencing stress-free productivity?
- Are you living in the moment?
- Is there a sense that everything is okay and/or will be okay?
- Do you feel safe and protected by something greater than you?
- Are you in the flow, experiencing synchronicity?
- Is your creativity flowing?
- Are you experiencing fun/laughter?
- Do you feel love, loving or loved?
- Is there a sense of expansion?

Do any of the following describe your current experience? Joyful, peaceful, confident, empowered, full, connected, clear, playful, exhilarated, enthusiastic, blissful, etc…

Whereas, the EGO is limited to constricted programming and subject to stress, anxiety and overwhelm, living as your True-Self allows you to be almost limitless, living in peace and joy.

What if you experience attributes of the EGO and True-Self at the same time?

Simultaneous signs of the EGO and True-Self indicate that you are teetering from one to the other. If this is the case, focusing on the attributes of your True-Self will help to tip the scale in this direction. Choosing to embrace the attributes of your True-Self doesn't automatically result in True-Self embodiment, but it does help alignment - making embodiment more possible.

Chapter 29

Spiritual Schizophrenia

On this journey of awakening, we all experience a process of "spiritual schizophrenia" where we frequently shift between the EGO and our True-Selves.

When you live mostly from the EGO, you may not notice how uncomfortable it really is because it is what you consider normal, but the more you live as your True-Self, the greater the discomfort when you are not.

In fact, once you know what it feels like to be the Real True You, anything less causes pain and suffering. When we are accustomed to living as our True-Selves, any misalignment that triggers the EGO results in immediate feedback that makes us take notice and do whatever it takes to re-align. Even the slightest misalignment of our True-Selves can feel intolerable.

Indeed, it would be nice to just one day wake-up as your True-Self and be done with it, but this is simply not the natural process. It takes conscious intention to transcend the EGO, reclaim your power and ultimately live as your True-Self.

It is impossible to know how long the process will take or how many times we may flip back and forth between the EGO and True-Self, but, inevitably, the day will come when we finally experience True-Self integration.

The following chapters are designed to help you bridge the gap from unconscious EGO programming to consciously living as your True-Self.

There are 4 Essential Elements that set the stage for embodiment, and must be mastered for True-Self integration:

- Unconditional Worth
- Intrinsic Power
- Emotional Healing
- Self-Love

Now, let's explore each one…

Chapter 30

Essential Element # 1 - Unconditional Worth

The trick to True-Self embodiment is no trick at all. There is nothing to do, nothing to become and nothing to prove. True-Self embodiment is an undoing - a peeling away of who you thought you were, or had to be, in order to reveal who you really are.

You might think that your True-Self is a better version of you, but your True-Self is not a better version – *your True-Self is you!* It might also make sense that you must improve yourself in order to embody your True-Self, but this is simply not the case, and, in fact, the very act of trying to improve, prove or fix misaligns your True-Self.

There is nothing that you must do or become in order to live life as your most authentic self.

> ৯Signpost on the path৩
> *Since there is nothing to prove, just be who you really are!*

The one core thing that displaces your True-Self is disempowering beliefs, and, especially the false belief that you are not enough as you are, and you must become more in order to be worthy, but this is simply not true, and, in fact, the quest for worth is what displaced your True-Self in the first place.

The key element of True-Self embodiment is letting go of unworthiness, but this requires turning off the Worthiness Program once and for all.

Turning Off the Worthiness Program

Since the moment the Worthiness Program was activated, your entire life has been lived through the mechanism of this disempowering program, affecting every aspect of life, and keeping your True-Self displaced. It's time to deactivate this program, but exactly how can this program be turned off? What is the magic off switch that will take you from limited to limitless?

Inherent in every internal program is the key to deactivate that program.

The key is the specific "required condition" that must be met in order to flip the off switch.

Only when the "required condition" of worth is realized does the Worthiness Program terminate.

> ৯Signpost on the path৩
> *The only way to win the Worthiness Game is to stop playing it!*
>
> The quest for external proof of worth completely fails at some point. No matter what we do or how we do it, even if we attain the greatest of success, there is always someone who will disapprove, judge or reject. Sooner or later, we are worn out and exhausted by relentlessly losing at the Worthiness Game, but we can't stop playing, because as long as the program is running, it is running us.

The "required condition" is not external. No matter what you do to prove your worth, it will never be enough – the entire world could see you as worthy, you could be the greatest leader that ever lived, you could be the most loved and respected being of all times, but, if this one condition is not met, it would still not be enough to turn off the Worthiness Program. In order to understand how to turn it off, you must first understand how it was turned on and by whom.

You turned on the Worthiness Program on the day you first believed that you were unworthy.

According to the EGO, your survival depends on being worthy of life, so when you first believed that you were not worthy or you questioned your worth, the EGO needed a way to ascertain your worth in order to ensure survival. The purpose of the Worthiness Program is to unconsciously motor-vate you to prove your worth to others so that you won't be abandoned and left to die.

In addition, once you believe that you are unworthy, your True-Self is displaced and Life Force Energy is inhibited, and, therefore, the EGO must generate energy for you - its primary method is motor-vating you to prove that you are worthy via the Worthiness Program.

So, now that you know the Worthiness Program was turned on by believing you were unworthy, how do you turn it off?

Belief is the key!

Your belief is the one and only key to turning on and off internal programs.

Believing you were unworthy turned on the Worthiness Program.
Believing that you are unconditionally worthy turns it off.

The program turns off when you believe that you are unconditionally worthy because your survival is no longer at risk. In believing that you are worthy to live, your belief ensures your survival, and there is no longer a need for the program to operate.

You may be wondering why the EGO motor-vates you to prove your worth to others, when the required condition (that turns off the program) is to believe it yourself.

Think about it, if you don't believe that you are worthy, how would you know that you are worthy without getting feedback from other people? Doubting your worth causes you to doubt yourself, therefore, you need others to believe that you are worthy before you can ever believe it yourself. In other words, you develop an unconscious strategy that says, *"Before I can believe that I am worthy, others must first believe it."* Hmmm, there are at least three problems with this strategy.

The first problem with this strategy is that in order to make others believe we are worthy, we must gain their approval, but, to do so, we probably have to change our behavior and suppress our authentic expression. So, even if they do find us worthy, it is not really us they are finding worthy because we are playing a part or hiding behind a mask. When we pretend to be someone we are not, we instinctually discard any forthcoming approval because the real us is hiding in the shadows of unworthiness

- believing that true self-expression would be met with rejection, thereby proving unworthiness. So, even if we do receive approval, it means nothing to us in terms of self-perceived worth.

The second problem with this strategy is that it doesn't have an ending pointing. How many people have to find us worthy in order for us to believe that we are really worthy? Suppose ten people find us worthy but another ten find us unworthy - are we worthy or unworthy? The EGO solves this problem by making it necessary for everyone to find us worthy, or at least the people we consider most important and pivotal, but usually it's everyone. This may be why we want the whole world to like us, even people we will never see again. Since it is impossible to get approval (proof of worth) from everyone at all times, we never really feel fully worthy.

The third problem with this strategy is that the "required condition" to turn off the Worthiness Program is believing that we are unconditionally worthy, but, if we need others to believe we are worthy before we can believe it, our worth is not unconditional.

So, how do you meet the one "required condition" that turns off the Worthiness Program?

The Worthiness Program is installed in your subconscious mind so you must *convince* your subconscious that you are worthy. Your subconscious will believe whatever you tell it, but you must communicate in a way that it can "hear." The main way in which you communicate to your subconscious is through your beliefs. Remember, that is how the program got activated in the first place. This means that you must first believe that you are unconditionally worthy in order for your subconscious mind to accept it as truth. But, there's a catch....

Only the highest degree of belief turns off the Worthiness Program. What is the highest degree of belief? **Absolute Knowing.**

The power of your intrinsic knowing turns off the Worthiness Program permanently.

This means that you must know your unconditional worth beyond a shadow of a doubt, because even a shadow of doubt can contaminate a belief, making it void of any real power. Additionally, when you really know you are unconditionally worthy, you will support your knowing with tangible proof via your behavior and actions, as discussed below. This means that you must demonstrate (to your subconscious mind) that you know and own your unconditional worth.

The bottom line is, for your subconscious mind to deactivate the Worthiness Program, you must absolutely KNOW that you are unconditionally worthy, and your actions and behavior must support this knowing!

Stop Playing the Worthiness Game

You have been playing a game that began the day you forgot that you are unconditionally worthy, but it is only a game. As long as you play this game of unworthiness, the program will keep running because your attempts at proving worth demonstrate that you don't believe that you are unconditionally worthy. If your subconscious is going to know that you are unconditionally worthy, you must stop acting like you're not.

You cannot win this game, but you can stop playing, and, in fact, this is exactly what you must do in order to satisfy the "required condition" that turns off the Worthiness Program once and for all.

There is a proven formula that will enable you to meet the "required condition." By consistently following this formula, you will inevitably convince your subconscious mind that ***you know you are unconditionally worthy***, and the Worthiness Program will automatically turn off.

The Formula

- ***Step 1 - Stop trying to prove your worth!***

  Consciously disengage from doing anything in order to prove your worth.

- ***Step 2 - Release conditions!***

  Disentangle your worth from what you do, how you look, where you live, status, accomplishments, diplomas, roles you play, being a certain way or whatever your conditions of worth might be. All those things are temporary and transient. Your worth is permanent and not dependent on anyone or anything. This chapter also includes a process that is designed to help you release the conditions upon your worth.

- ***Step 3 - Claim your worth!***

  Even if you don't fully believe it yet, claim it,

  "I Am Unconditionally Worthy."

  Whatever you say after "I am" is a command to the subconscious mind, but, in order to be a re-programming command, you must believe it. You may have to affirm this command thousands of times before you believe it, but keep doing it until you do. Eventually, you will reach an energetic threshold where it will take.

- ***Step 4 - Release the jury that decides your worth!***

  Stop allowing others to decide your worth. This means that you must stop seeing yourself through eyes that are not your own. Let everyone off the hook and take your power back - no one gets to decide your worth ever again. *It's none of your business what anyone even thinks about you.*

- ***Step 5 - Demonstrate your worth!***

  No matter how hard you try, you cannot fool your subconscious - you either believe something or you don't. When you do believe, your thoughts, actions and behavior consistently demonstrate what you believe. This means that if you believe that you are worthy, you will treat yourself as someone who is worthy, and, therefore, your thoughts, actions and behavior will consistently demonstrate your worth.

- If you believe that you are worthy, what thoughts would you think, and what thoughts would you not think?
- If you believe that you are worthy, how would you show up in the world?

- How would it impact the choices you make, your relationships and all the ways you live your life?

Ask yourself:

- If I knew my unconditional worth, what choices would I make?
- If I knew my unconditional worth, how would I dress, communicate and act?
- If I knew my unconditional worth, would any of my relationships change and how?

When met with a challenging situation, ask yourself, if I knew my unconditional worth, how would I respond?

In knowing and owning your unconditional worth, your life will reflect self-love in every way.

On the path to knowing and owning your unconditional worth, it is essential to develop your own **Worthiness Practice;** in conjunction with the formula above, your practice should ideally include:

- Think empowering thoughts
- Say no to self-judgment
- Care for your body as a sacred temple
- Set boundaries that teach others how to treat you
- Enforce your boundaries
- Protect your energy
- Not allow others to bring you down
- Respect your time
- Do what you love to do
- Don't do anything you don't want to do
- Say "no" when you want to say "no"
- Share your gifts and talents
- Speak your truth
- Stand in your power
- Love who you really are
- Treat yourself as a treasure
- Honor every aspect of your life

Not only does this list create a powerful Worthiness Practice, this list also compiles many of the most essential True-Self behaviors, and it may seem like a big list to master, but healthy and abundant people fulfill all the elements listed - on a consistent basis. Each item that is overlooked and not lived, results in corresponding issues and dysfunctions. It is true that it may take time and energy to master your Worthiness Practice, and fully live as your True-Self, but, once you do, that time and energy will return exponentially. In fact, there is no greater investment! *As this book unfolds, we will address many of these elements.*

Change doesn't usually happen overnight. If you've been practicing unworthiness for a very long time, be kind and patient with yourself as you develop a new practice of unconditional worthiness. The key point is choosing to believe that you are unconditionally worthy, and doing your best to act, think and behave as someone who knows and owns their worth. It is a step by step, moment to moment process, until you reach a threshold where you really do believe in your unconditional worth, and, once you do, your subconscious will too, and the Worthiness Program will deactivate.

The Conditions of Worth Process

(supports step 2 in the formula above)

Your subconscious mind will not believe that you are worthy as long as your worth is entangled with external conditions: relationships, roles, accomplishments, identity, etc… Therefore, it is essential to disentangle your worth from all conditions. The following process will assist you in this manner. Please refer to your personal assessment of worth that you completed in a previous chapter.

For each condition upon your worth perform this 8 step process:

1. Spend a few moments moving into a relaxed, mindful or meditative state where you can sense your intrinsic worth. If you need help, I offer a guided meditation at ***www.Nanice.com/worth***

2. Choose ***one*** condition of your worth to work with during this process.

3. Imagine yourself experiencing this condition. For example, if your worth depends on money, imagine yourself with an abundance of money and notice how you feel. If your worth depends on a role that you play (teacher, parent, professional) imagine yourself in the role and notice how you feel.

4. Now, imagine yourself ***without*** the condition and notice how you feel in regards to worthiness - when the condition is lost, how does it influence your sense of worth? Be honest with yourself and just notice what there is to notice without judgment.

5. With your mind's intention reactivate the part of you who knows your intrinsic worth. Notice how it feels to be unconditionally worthy and breathe deeply into this sensation to anchor it in your body, and, once again, notice how you feel without the condition of your worth (the same one you were working on in this process).

6. Still connected to your intrinsic worth, imagine yourself with the condition as you did in step 3 and notice how you feel.

7. Release the condition and imagine yourself without the condition - make sure that you are still connected to your intrinsic worth.

8. Flip back and forth - still staying connected to your intrinsic worth, imagine yourself with the condition and then without the condition. Do this several times or until you feel the same with, or without, the condition.

Preferably, do this process with every condition on your list. The point is to develop unconditional worth so that you feel intrinsically worthy void of any condition. When you feel the same with, or without, a condition, it is no longer a condition.

In order to reprogram your subconscious mind, and turn off the Worthiness Program, you cannot ignore your primary emotional need.

Primary Emotional Need (PEN)

There is no way that your subconscious mind will ever believe that you are worthy if you don't stop depending on others to meet your primary emotional need. This doesn't mean that you have to leave a career or a partner – that is not the point, but you must let everyone off the hook.

Equally as important, if you are going to convince your subconscious mind that you are worthy, you must not only meet your own primary emotional need, *you must fulfill it.*

In virtually all cases, we unknowingly withhold from ourselves the very thing we desire from another. If we seek appreciation, we take ourselves for granted, if we seek approval, we judge ourselves, if we seek acceptance, we reject ourselves.

Why would we withhold the one thing that would make us feel worthy?

Instinctually, we will not meet our own primary emotional need, if we don't believe we are worthy. It's a catch 22 because without knowing our unconditional worth, we have lost the power to believe in ourselves, and, if we don't believe in ourselves, we cannot deem ourselves worthy.

We withhold our primary emotional need because we unconsciously believe that we must ***first prove*** that we are worthy before the need can be met. *In other words, meeting your primary emotional need is the reward for being worthy.*

When others give you approval, acceptance, understanding, appreciation, respect, admiration etc… you receive it as proof that they believe you are worthy, for the brief moment it is being met. However, it doesn't matter how many people meet this need, if you don't meet it yourself. As long as you withhold your primary emotional need from yourself, you perpetuate the Worthiness Program because, in withholding the need, you are literally saying to your subconscious mind, "I am not worthy."

This also means that by judging yourself, taking yourself for granted, disrespecting yourself, not listening to yourself, rejecting yourself and so on, you are telling your subconscious mind that you are unworthy, and, as a result, the Worthiness Program must continue to operate in order to prove your worth.

There is no way around it - in order to turn off the Worthiness Program you must give yourself the emotional need that you most associate with being worthy.

What is your Primary Emotional Need? ________________________________

How do you withhold this need from yourself? Please consider your thoughts, behaviors and actions, and write your detailed answer on a separate piece of paper.

For example:

- If your P-E-N is approval, how do you judge yourself?
- If your P-E-N is acceptance, how do you reject yourself?
- If your P-E-N is respect, how do you disrespect yourself?
- If your P-E-N is being right, how do you make yourself wrong?
- If your P-E-N is to be heard, how are you not listening to yourself?
- If your P-E-N is appreciation, how do you take yourself for granted?
- If your P-E-N is to be understood, how are you not being compassionate with yourself?

It is essential to create a plan that will meet and fulfill your primary emotional need, so, therefore, what are the necessary thoughts, behaviors and actions that will fully satisfy your P-E-N? The best way to answer this question is to consider how you want others to think about you, talk to you and relate to you, and then treat yourself this same way.

- If you appreciate yourself, how do you think, act and behave?
- If you respect yourself, how do you think, act and behave?
- If you accept yourself, how do you think, act and behave?
- If you validate yourself, how do you think, act and behave?
- If you understand yourself, how do you think, act and behave?

Just to clarify, meeting and exceeding your primary emotional need is not a temporary process that has a stopping point, but, rather, it is meant to be a permanent way of life, and that's the point.

Let Them All Off the Hook

As you practice meeting your own primary emotional need, it is also important to release the belief that others have to meet this need – *unquestionably, this means letting everyone off the hook forever!*

No one can ever give you what you need if you first don't give it to yourself. If you are not respecting yourself, no matter what your partner does, or doesn't do, you will never feel respected. If you are not appreciating yourself, no matter what your friends and family do, or don't do, you will never feel appreciated. Even if others try to meet your primary emotional need, it will never be enough to fill the bottomless pit of unworthiness. As long as you expect others to meet this need, you will remain imprisoned by your own hands. You literally *free yourself* by letting everyone off the hook.

> *Signpost on the path*
>
> *For more love, drop conditions*
>
> *When you drop all your conditions, and you no longer need people to act in certain ways, your love receptors open up, so that you can actually receive and experience more love in all relationships.*

Here's how to begin:

Take a moment to think about the one person whose *approval, acceptance, understanding, respect, appreciation, etc...,* you need in order to feel worthy (hint: it might also feel like you need this person's permission). It could be a parent, partner, sibling, teacher, friend, co-worker or even someone you haven't seen in a long time. If there is more than one person, choose one for the following process, and then you can repeat the process for the other(s).

Once you identify this person, imagine him/her standing before you, and imagine that you can see and hear each other.

Then say the following words:

> *"I am letting you off the hook. I am now letting you go. I am freeing you. I no longer need your _______ (fill in your P-E-N) in order to be worthy, and I no longer need your permission to live my life. As I now take my power back, you no longer get to decide my worth, and I now stop judging you for judging me."*

If it feels good to you, and you don't have to force it, imagine offering this person unconditional love. *You free yourself when you stop seeking love, and also when you stop withholding it from others.*

You may need to do this process with several people in your life, and you may need to do it more than once with each person, but, each time you go through this process, you will consciously take more of your power back. The more power you reclaim, the more energy you will have to fulfill your primary emotional need.

Emotional Gifts

Ironically, when you no longer need others to meet your primary emotional need, because you have abundantly fulfilled it yourself, you will be pleasantly surprised to discover that it naturally flows from everyone, everywhere you go. Since you no longer need approval, appreciation, acceptance, etc… from others, when it comes, you receive it as a gift of love. Emotional needs transform into *Emotional Gifts.*

Your family and friends effortlessly reflect your self-love, and suddenly you are receiving an abundance of "emotional gifts" in all relationships, making you finally understand that you can only receive from others, what you are willing to give to yourself.

Whatever you desire, first give to yourself, and it will consequently flow abundantly from life.

Finally Free

Once the Worthiness Program is deactivated, and you fully know that you are unconditionally worthy, the entire world could hate you and you could fail at everything you try, but it wouldn't matter one bit. You would be no less worthy, and you would remain completely unbothered. From this conscious and awake state, there is no need for approval or acceptance, and, therefore, flattery and criticism play no bearing on your worth, nor influence your emotional wellbeing, whatsoever. When the fear of failure and rejection is a distant memory, *no dream or desire is out of reach.*

Firmly grounded in the absolute knowing of who you really are, you can fly high in your fullest glory.

Let's Recap

- You are unconditionally worthy, and there is nothing to prove.
- The Worthiness Program remained dormant in your subconscious mind until you first believed that you were unworthy.
- Your belief in unworthiness activated the program.

- Your True-Self is *who you really are*, but the quest for worthiness displaces your True-Self, and when your True-Self is displaced, the EGO takes control.
- The purpose of the Worthiness Program is to motor-vate you to prove your worth to others so that you are not shamed or shunned by your tribe, and your survival is ensured.
- The Worthiness Program is also used as a way to artificially generate energy by motor-vating you to prove your worth, and rewarding you with energy via an EGO boost when you do.
- Until the Worthiness Program is turned off, most of life is lived by trying to prove worth, which only perpetuates the program.
- In order to deactivate the Worthiness Program, you must meet the "required condition."
- The required condition is convincing your subconscious mind that you believe you are unconditionally worthy.
- The Formula that allows you to meet the "required condition" is: 1. Stop trying to prove your worth, 2. Release the conditions upon your worth, 3. Claim your worth, 4. Allow no one to decide your worth, 5. Demonstrate your worth through thoughts, beliefs and actions.
- Demonstrating your worth also requires that you develop a daily Worthiness Practice.
- You must also meet and fulfill your own primary emotional need, and stop looking to others.
- From a conscious and awake state, there is no need for approval or acceptance, and, therefore, flattery and criticism play no bearing on your worth, nor influence your emotional wellbeing, whatsoever.

True-Self integration requires that you know and own your unconditional worth, and it also requires that you know and own your intrinsic power.

Chapter 31

Essential Element # 2 - Intrinsic Power

The key that unlocks your power is Self-Expression!

Your power lies in your ability and willingness to express your real self; think your own thoughts, speak your own mind, create your own dream, love with an open heart and consciously choose how to live your life. Your power is activated through self-expression, and the more you confidently express yourself without inhibition, the greater your power grows.

Believing you are powerful, and manifesting that belief through expression activates the power of the Universe within you!

Your power is only as great as your demonstration.

- If you hide yourself, you are disempowered.
- If you come out of hiding, you are beginning to be empowered.
- If you express yourself, even if you are afraid, you are empowered.
- If you fearlessly express yourself, you are fully empowered.

The one thing that commonly stands between us and fully empowered self-expression is the EGO, and, in fact, if the Powerlessness Program is operating, the EGO will covertly sabotage self-expression, in order to protect us from tribal shame and rejection. This clearly indicates that if we are to embrace our intrinsic power, we must turn off the Powerlessness Program.

If the "better than" version of the Worthiness Program is running, self-expression is generally not suppressed, and, therefore, the Powerlessness Program does not operate. However, many "better thans" lack authenticity because their expression is based on the EGO demonstrating greater worth and power over others.

> *Signpost on the path*
>
> *Power lies dormant in non-manifested energy*

Turning Off the Powerlessness Program

Just to recapture the main points of this program, every time you choose approval, acceptance, etc… over self-expression, you give your power away in exchange for others finding you worthy, and, then, like a domino effect, the act of self-suppression tells your subconscious mind that you believe that you are powerless, thereby perpetuating the Powerlessness Program.

The "required condition" that turns off the Powerless Program is **believing** you are intrinsically powerful, and providing proof that backs up your belief; a belief without proof is empty of any real meaning or power. If you say that you believe you are powerful, but you demonstrate powerlessness by suppressing expression, hiding your real self or repressing your voice, you really don't believe you are powerful; behavior and actions always support beliefs, therefore, the way in which we act and behave are tell-tale signs of our beliefs. If you believe you are powerful, you will show up in the world as empowered. If you don't believe you are powerful, you will show up in the world as disempowered, and maybe even as a victim.

When we use Life Force Energy to express, create or innovate, we activate the dormant power in non-manifested energy.

Undoubtedly, power manifests in the demonstration, so, if you are to convince your subconscious that you ***know*** your intrinsic power, your demonstration must reflect empowerment.

The bottom line is, to deactivate the Powerlessness Program, the subconscious mind needs *proof of your knowing* and that proof is **realized** by demonstrating your power through the use of actions, choices and behaviors in each of four ways:

- Self-Expression
- Responsibility
- Reclaim Power
- Release Control

1. Self-Expression

Turning off the Powerlessness Program requires self-expression, but here's where it gets a little tricky - because you must do the one thing that the program prohibits you from doing - express your authentic self.

If you really know that you are powerful, it's very easy to express yourself, but, if you don't yet know it, even the thought of self-expression can invoke irrational fear that makes you want to protect yourself from being shamed or shunned. Turning off the program requires you to override the same demotivating fear that is produced by the program. Talk about needing courage, but maybe there is a way to reduce the fear?

Certainly, this fear is exacerbated by the Worthiness Program, so, what if the Worthiness Program was first deactivated or at least in the process of deactivation? If the EGO is not motor-vating you to prove or protect your worth, the fear of being shamed or shunned is greatly reduced or even non-existent. When you own your unconditional worth, you have no need to prove to others that you are worthy, and because you don't need anyone's approval or permission, you are free to be your authentic self, in whatever way makes your heart sing.

Oftentimes, we are empowered in one or more areas of our lives, but, not in others, and, therefore, turning off the Powerlessness Program requires us to express our power in the situations and relationships where it is the most difficult. If you look closely, you will see that the areas of life where we are empowered, are the same ones where we own our worth, while the areas of life where we are disempowered, are the same ones where we do not own our worth. Once again, the key to self-empowerment is owning your unconditional worth, so you literally don't care what anyone says or thinks and you can openly express *who you really are*.

Owning your worth allows you to freely express yourself by following your inner guidance, exploring your creativity, speaking your truth, setting boundaries, abiding by your own values and only doing those things that are in your highest good and support your integrity. When you consistently express yourself in this way, for as long as it takes to reach the threshold point, your subconscious mind receives the message that you know you are powerful, and the Powerlessness Program prepares to shut down, but not without first taking full responsibility for your life.

2. Responsibility

The EGO definitely wants you to take responsibility for anything that might prove or improve your worth, but it sure doesn't want you to take responsibility for anything that could diminish your worth. In fact, in order to avoid this risk, the EGO makes you shift responsibility, make excuses and blame others, but, the problem is, every time you avoid responsibility, you give your power away and you tell your subconscious mind that you believe that you are powerless, thus fueling the Powerlessness Program.

In lower states of consciousness, when the EGO is in charge, it appears that things are happening to us and taking our power away, so we react with anger or frustration in order to protect this power. However, it never works because as soon as we ***believe*** that someone or something has power over us, *we give our power to that person or situation* – ironically, we do the very thing that we are unconsciously trying to prevent. Instead of getting power back, this is really where we are giving it away.

In believing that the outside world has power over you,
you give your power to the outside world.

Anger, frustration, jealousy or any reactive emotion, all give your power away. You give your power away through any emotion that is the result of believing that someone has taken something from you or has control over something you need or want.

Habitually shifting responsibility can easily turn powerlessness into victimhood, thereby activating the Victimhood Program. If this is the case, turning off the Powerlessness Program requires us to release the false belief of victimhood and turn off the Victimhood Program, by taking complete responsibility for every experience that caused us to feel victimized, even if we don't understand how or why we created it.

As long as we believe that the outside world acts independently of us, we have no power, but once we remember that the outside world is a reflection of the inner world, we have unlimited power - because we know that in order to change the world, we must first and foremost change ourselves. *This is the grand mechanism for conscious creation.*

What does it look like to own your power?

Owning your power requires that you take responsibility for everything in your experience; this includes everything that directly happens in your life, as well as everything that you are even conscious of in the world. If you are aware of something, even if it is just what you see on TV, it is happening in your consciousness, and, therefore, it is a reflection of you. *Nothing is happening outside of you.* This means that there is no blaming others for anything – without blaming the world, anger, jealousy and a host of other low vibration emotions are no longer provoked.

You are never a victim to any person or situation because you are co-creating every experience.

Shifting responsibility or believing that someone or something is responsible for your life, in anyway, is like having a night time dream and blaming another person in your dream for hurting you. In your nighttime dream, there is no other person – it is just you pretending to be someone else. Just as it is silly to blame someone in our dreams for hurting us, it is just as silly to blame someone in our lives for hurting us.

Let's be really clear here, when you take responsibility, from a higher state of consciousness, it can only be without self-judgment, self-blame or self-criticism.

When you judge yourself for dis harmony in your life, or in the world, you are vibrating at a lower state of consciousness, and, as a result, you actually create more disharmony. Taking responsibility from a higher state of consciousness is empowering and freeing. Instead of self-blame, you simply find the corresponding "inner cause" of outer-trouble, and you shift it. If you don't like what is going on in reality, you pinpoint the inner cause (in your thoughts, beliefs and feelings) and you realign accordingly. The point is to find the dis-harmony in yourself and harmonize it.

The highest level of consciousness corresponds to owning your power – and not giving it away in exchange for anything!

Turning off the Powerlessness Program requires you to take full responsibility for every area of your life which invariably means that you must take back your power wherever you have given it away.

3. **Reclaim Your Power**

Turning off the Powerlessness Program requires that you reclaim your intrinsic power and not give it away in exchange for anything. Your power belongs to you alone, and no one can take this power from you or use it against you, unless you allow it by hiding your authentic self or suppressing expression in terms of not speaking or standing up for yourself.

Being fully empowered requires that you do not give your power away to anyone for any reason, and, if you have given it away, you must reclaim it!

In order to call back your power, and keep it, you must first understand how you are giving it away.

Some questions to ponder:

- Where, and with whom, are you hiding your real self?

- What are you not saying (in any area of your life)?
- What do you want to do that you are not doing?
- What are you doing that you don't want to be doing?
- Where are you compromising your personal integrity in order to fit-in or be accepted?
- How are you not listening to your inner guidance?
- How is life asking you to claim your power?
- Where in your life are you feeling powerless?
- What do you need to believe in order to reclaim your power?
- What actions must you take in order to be empowered?

The Power to Be Who You Really Are is the greatest power in the Universe, and when you give it up in order to be worthy in the eyes of others, you have given away the keys to your kingdom.

Stop giving your power away by ....

- Identifying with roles and identities - own your power by being your real self; express, reinvent and remove the limits of what is possible.
- Complaining, nagging or focusing on what is wrong - claim your power by focusing on what you desire.
- Aligning with illness, disability or injury - align your thoughts and actions with health and healing.
- Playing the victim - remember that you are a creator and you can consciously create!
- Living in the past or future - discover the power that lies in the present.
- Comparing, competing and judging - empower yourself through unique self-expression that cannot be compared or judged by normal standards nor downplayed by competition.
- Worrying about scarcity - empower yourself by imagining abundance.
- Allowing others to judge you or by needing acceptance/approval - own your worth and be free to discover *who you really are.*

You cannot know your intrinsic power, while, at the same time, compromise values, sacrifice needs or hide true expression, just so others might find you worthy to be who they want you to be.

You alone have direct access to your power, and when you use it consciously, you have the ability to create the life you most desire.

Inside you is the power of the Universe, making no dream unr

4. **Release Control**

No one can empower you - only you can empower yoursel whole point. If you wait for external proof of your powe your power, it will not come. The proof of your power d by you – proof of your power is realized by taking full your life, reclaiming the power you have falsely given *who you really are*, and, finally, the last bit of proof is release control.

werless Program, control equals power, thus it operates ɔ control your life and everything in it. The premise is ...re controlling, a sense of power is generated, and others see ...as powerful so they will not victimize you. For all intents and purposes, it is fair to say that control is a symptom of feeling powerless and believing you are powerless.

Controlling behavior is interpreted by the subconscious mind as inner powerlessness because we are simply not controlling when we own our power. Truly powerful people are not controlling due to the fact that they know how to access their intrinsic power and use it consciously. This means that controlling behavior perpetuates the Powerlessness Program, and, therefore, if we want to deactivate it, we must withdraw control.

The truth is, control is empty of any real power - to manifest, heal or create. For one thing, there is no way we can control everyone and everything in our lives at all times – with so many balls to juggle some of them are bound to fall. Then, of course, the people in our lives don't want to be controlled, and they don't want to act like we want them to act, even if it is in their best interest (according to us). It's fairly easy to see that control is a terrible strategy for any kind of lasting success.

Besides all the good reasons for giving up control, there is no way to turn off the Powerlessness Program without doing so. The subconscious mind equates control with powerlessness and releasing control with empowerment, and, as such, consciously releasing control tells it that you remember your power, and, if you remember your power, and you empower yourself through actions and behaviors, there is no need for the Powerlessness Program to generate artificial power for you.

But, what does it really mean to release control?

Letting go of control translates to *letting go to the Universe*, thereby trusting the intrinsic wisdom and power that exists within all of creation.

As you fully let go and trust the Universe, you don't become powerless, as many people fear - surprisingly, the exact opposite is experienced.

It is true that when you surrender control to the Universe, you do, in fact, relinquish your personal power, but there is no loss of power because letting go and trusting the Universe gives you access to the power of the whole Universe. In exchange for your itty-bitty personal power, you receive omnipotence – this means as you release the illusion of control, you are granted access to infinite and unlimited power.

Universal Power is accessed through the willingness to let go and the courage to trust.

This is not at all an easy task if the EGO is in charge because the EGO is clearly programmed to "hold on and control," and there is no way it will allow you to let go and trust, so don't waste your time trying to make the EGO surrender - it just won't happen. Plus, when the EGO is operating, your vibration is not aligned with the high vibration of Universal Power, and, as a result, the law of attraction will prevent you from accessing this power.

The exceptionally good news is that your intrinsic power is easily accessed as your True-Self, and, in fact, your True-Self is the channel for unlimited power. Living life as your True-Self aligns you with the power of the Universe, and this power flows through you and is experienced by you. Your ability to channel this powerful energy is determined solely by you, according to your thoughts and beliefs, personal expression and willingness to manifest your dreams and desires.

Power is Energy

By now, it won't surprise you to know that Universal Power is actually Life Force Energy (aka Source Energy). The power of the Universe is the power of energy, and, as such, accessing power is the same as channeling energy.

> ꕥ*Signpost on the path*ꕥ
> *To access unlimited Life Force Energy, claim your power!*

Power Channels Energy

As you express your True-Self, you activate the power of the Universe within you, and, as a result, Life Force Energy flows abundantly. Through the focus of your mind, this energy can be manifested as anything you intend. Life Force Energy is molded and shaped according to your mental instructions which are provided by thoughts, beliefs and intentions. A detailed exploration can be found in my book, "Seducing the Field."

If you have ever recovered from a debilitating illness, you might have experienced extreme fatigue and weakness - even the simplest things like brushing your teeth or walking to the bathroom are physically overwhelming. This is what it feels like to experience limited Life Force Energy. Conversely, have you ever had a day when you felt like you could fly or you had the world in the palm of your hand? This is what it feels like to experience an abundance of Life Force Energy.

We all have equal access to the same Life Force Energy, but we have free-will on how to use it, and how we use it determines how much we receive. Life Force Energy is inhibited when you hide yourself, suppress expression and close off to possibilities. Life Force Energy flows abundantly when you express your authentic self, share your gifts and open your mind to endless possibilities. It is a Universal Law that allows you to access as much Life Force Energy as you need for expression.

Your willingness to consciously use your energy for expression manifests as your power.

The more you express yourself, the more Life Force Energy you channel, and the greater your power. As you begin to you own your unconditional worth, you will be able to express yourself without fear of judgment, and as you express the real you, your power is activated.

As your True-Self you are eternally tapped into Life Force Energy.

Let's Recap

- True-Self Integration requires you to know and own your unconditional worth and intrinsic power.
- Your power is accessed through self-expression, with power increasing relative to expression.
- Self-suppression is the source of disempowerment.
- The Powerlessness Program suppresses and sabotages self-expression in order to protect worthiness.
- Choosing approval, acceptance, etc... over expression perpetuates the program, by giving your power away in exchange for getting your primary emotional need met.
- Self-suppression tells your subconscious mind that you believe that you are powerless, thereby perpetuating the Powerlessness Program.
- To deactivate the Powerlessness Program, you must know that you are powerful.
- The subconscious mind needs *proof of your knowing.*
- Proof is realized by demonstrating your power through the use of actions, choices and behaviors in each of four ways: Self-Expression, Responsibility, Reclaiming Power and Releasing Control.
- Universal Power is Life Force Energy.
- Your power is relative to the amount of Life Force Energy you channel.
- Self-expression regulates the flow of Life Force Energy – increased expression increases energy.
- Consciously using your energy for expression manifests as your power.

Chapter 32

Essential Element # 3 – Emotional Healing

On the path to emotional mastery, we must ultimately realize that we are not our feelings, and in rising up, we free ourselves from the emotional prison that once enslaved us.

The Awakening Path of Emotion

When we are slaves to our emotions, we frequently get stuck in emotional turmoil, retarding growth, healing and awakening - and misaligning our True-Selves.

As the EGO, emotions run our lives, influencing all our choices and impacting all our relationships, and, due to the fact that emotional reactions trigger the EGO, living as your True-Self requires healing emotional trauma, releasing emotional triggers and mastering your emotions.

No one ever tells us that the path to awakening involves learning how to feel our emotions without being overcome with emotional disability, nor, are we shown how to allow emotions to process through until they are released.

> *Signpost on the path*
> *Awakening the True You requires emotional mastery*

Many, well-meaning, spiritual seekers suffer from emotional wounds year after year, and never fully heal or awaken, because they bypass the emotional issues in their lives, and those issues are never released. We don't heal or awaken by ignoring our emotions or hiding our pain under a carpet of spiritual ideals; no matter how hard you pray, chant or sage, if you ignore your emotions, you will still be left spiritually asleep - in a home with a lumpy rug.

When we are awake and living as our True-Selves, we have the ability to feel the full spectrum of emotions, and we discover that emotions which we feel in response to present moment experiences are very different than emotions that are stored in the body and triggered as emotional reactions.

If we are to awaken fully, we must detox emotional wounds, while at the same time embrace the power and flow of emotion.

The Dark Mountain

There is a nearby mountain that I often hike just before sunset, so that when I arrive at the peak, I can sit on a big rock and watch vibrant colors fill the western sky as the sun melts behind the horizon. On one such occasion, I lost track of time, and before I knew it, the sun had completely set leaving me in complete darkness. As I started down the mountain, it occurred to me that I was walking blind and it would be very easy to unknowingly walk off a cliff. Oddly enough, I had no fear, which, on the surface, might sound like a good thing, but it actually wasn't. I realized that without fear keeping me alert and on my toes, so to speak, I had no hesitation, and I could easily find myself falling to my death.

At that moment, I got the full download of fear, and I understood that in order to make it down the mountain in one piece, I would need to manifest a healthy dose of it. I found this to be ironic since I spent a lifetime trying to overcome fear, and here I was trying to invoke it. I sat down on the ground and I consciously imagined what would happen, if I did indeed make a wrong turn and walk off a cliff. Once I intentionally conjured up just enough fear to keep me safe, I continued down the mountain without mishap. For the first time, I understood the gift and purpose of fear.

We tend to think of emotions as good or bad, but every emotion is a gift and every emotion has a purpose. Despite how it may sometimes feel, there are no bad or negative emotions. Emotions are like rides at the amusement park – they are all there for our enjoyment, and, in fact, if fear was a bad thing, no one would ever pay to go on frightening rides or to scary movies. Fear, like all emotions, can be fun and enjoyable.

Without emotions the experience of life would be dull and less meaningful. It is our emotions, from fear to love, and everything in between that creates the tapestry of life, and brings the dream alive. Yet, most of us are afraid of feeling. We fear that if we allow ourselves to feel certain emotions, we will experience suffering - so we rather not feel at all. *But, the truth about suffering can set you free.*

The Truth about Suffering

Suffering is not what most of us believe it to be. Even when we experience suffering, we often misinterpret the cause - what we call suffering is really the emotional manifestation of resistance.

It is not actual events that cause us to suffer, it is the resistance to those events.

We only suffer when we judge, reject, deny or argue with life – firmly believing things should be different, we deny or dissociate from consequent emotions, and, as a result, we stop the flow of Life Force Energy that would have naturally flowed with those emotions. Whenever we refuse to accept reality, we are in resistance, and, if we perpetuate resistance over time, it inevitably leads to suffering. *Resistance inhibits emotional energy, thereby creating stuck energy, and perpetually stuck energy results in suffering.*

> ꕥ*Signpost on the path* ꕥ
> *To end suffering*
> *release resistance*

Suffering can be immediately alleviated simply by releasing resistance, and allowing ourselves to feel whatever there is to feel. When we surrender to "what is" and we allow ourselves to experience sensation, intense emotions organically transform. All the energy that was pent up by resistance is suddenly released and when energy freely flows, it can manifest as positive sensation.

Emotions don't cause suffering - suffering is the result of resistance.

When I was about five years old, my dad and I were wrestling when suddenly his lung collapsed, leaving him desperately gasping for air. As he was rushed to the hospital, I was left believing that I had almost killed him. Of course, he had lung problems prior to his lung collapsing, and it was just "bad timing," but this experience left me feeling responsible for my father's life. I became hyper alert to any problems he might have and I spent my whole life dreading the day he would die.

I'm happy to say that he lived to the ripe old age of 81, but, even as I knew his time was coming, I feared the emotions that I would experience upon his departure.

When he finally passed, I did indeed feel heart-wrenching grief and sadness so intense that I thought it would kill me, but, instead of instinctually resisting emotions, as I had done so many times in the past, I courageously surrendered.

At first, I felt as if the emotions swallowed me up, and I would never recover, but the more I allowed myself to feel, the easier it became. As I completely let go, and allowed myself to be enveloped by intense emotion, I was shocked to find that joy was rising up to meet me, and, before I knew it, this extraordinary sensation of bliss was dancing with sadness, while alchemizing grief into gratitude. In the midst of my most feared emotional hurricane, I was greeted by grace, and healed.

Intrinsic in all emotion is joy and bliss, but you can only access this pure state by letting go, and allowing yourself to feel. When we fully surrender and allow ourselves to experience sensation, any emotion can dissolve into its prime source which is love, and is experienced as peace, joy and bliss.

As resistance causes suffering, surrender results in bliss.

The more willing we are to feel our emotions without resistance, the more we tap into Life Force Energy. Emotions flow to and from Source Energy, and, if we allow ourselves to go with that flow, freely experiencing and releasing emotions, we connect directly with this pure energy source and the sensation is blissful. Whereas resistance blocks Life Force Energy, going with the flow results in increased Life Force Energy

Only with the courage and willingness to feel our emotions,
can we flow with the river that leads us back to Source.

Few of us reach this pure state because we are afraid to feel. Instead, we spend all our energy in resistance, and in the suffering that results from it. What are we so afraid of? Despite how it might seem, there are no emotions that will kill us or even disable us. Conversely, it is the resistance to our emotions that causes us to become emotionally disabled, and dead inside, and when emotions are pushed down, stored and never released, they often become emotional wounds that can negatively impact our entire lives.

Freeing Stuck Energy

The "E" in emotion stands for energy, and the "motion" in emotion represents that energy in motion. The motion of energy in the body is what creates emotion. Our minds simply interpret this moving energy as a feeling, such as anger or happiness. Emotions are your mind's interpretation of moving energy in your body.

Your body naturally responds to life with a wide variety of emotions according to your thoughts and beliefs regarding situations, experiences and relationships.

Emotions are the way in which your body communicates with itself, allowing each and every cell to be informed of the current condition. Emotions, such as fear or stress, tell your body to be on guard for possible danger, while emotions, such as happiness and contentment, tell your body it is safe to relax.

Keep in mind, your emotions are not the result of any situation or experience, but, rather, your emotions are the result of your thoughts and beliefs about the situation or experience, and what it personally means to you. In other words, your story about anything is the emotional catalyst. Since emotions are in direct response to your personal assessment, two people can feel very different emotions during the same experience, completely dependent on individual beliefs.

Your body is equipped to systematically process this *energy in motion*, but only if you allow emotions to flow unrestricted for as long as it takes to process and release. Without resistance emotions are experienced and allowed to flow through us, with nothing getting stored as painful issues.

Even when emotions, such as sadness, are allowed to move freely in the body, they naturally clear, and without resistance pleasurable sensations may be experienced; this is due to the fact that the substance of energy is love, and when you allow love to flow in the body, the sensation is peace, joy or bliss. In fact, if we allow emotions to move and flow naturally without resistance, judgment or suppression in anyway, every emotion has the capacity to provide bliss.

Although your job is to feel emotion as it passes through your body, you have free-will to resist the feel of any emotion. Emotions that are tainted with shame, worthlessness, guilt, regret, betrayal, rejection, abandonment or fear are often too difficult to feel, and, as a result, our natural response is repression - pushing emotions down to where we cannot feel them.

What exactly occurs when we repress emotions?

Essentially, when we repress emotions, we override the automatic system of healing which would otherwise operate by processing emotional energy.

The body cannot process repressed emotional energy.

Anytime we repress emotion, we unknowingly remove the motion from emotion, and what remains is energy without motion, and this non-moving energy is then compacted and stored in the body, thereby creating stuck energy that becomes stagnant over time - this is how emotional wounds are formed.

Repression removes the motion from emotion, turning moving energy into non-moving energy.

Non-moving energy is commonly known as a block, and, therefore, when we say we have a block, we are referring to non-moving energy. Illness, disease and injury are all the result of energetic blocks, manifesting in the area of the body where the energy is stuck and stagnant.

This means that when we don't properly process emotions through to healing, those emotions get stored in the body, usually in the body part most associated with the trauma or crisis (no matter how big or small) that caused the emotional wound in the first place. For instance, if you were abandoned by a parent, lover or sibling, your broken heart may manifest as tangible heart issues. For more information on this subject, I suggest Louise Hay's book, "You Can Heal Your Life" or "Feelings Buried Alive Never Die" by Karol Kuhn Truman.

Most eastern health practitioners agree that physical issues in the body are caused by an energy imbalance. They believe that we get sick or disabled when we experience an energy block or deficiency in the area of the problem. Acupuncture, acupressure, Reiki and many other "energy modalities" are used for healing virtually every issue in the body. These modalities, and many others, recognize that you cannot heal the body without correcting the energetic cause of the problem needing to be healed.

Repression is the number one reason why emotions get stored in the body, but it is not the only one.

Emotional Overload

During a crisis, trauma or emotionally charged experience, your body produces large amounts of emotional energy, which it is well-equipped to handle, but there is a point of emotional overload, where energy is produced faster than it can be properly processed.

Fortunately, there is no such thing as being overloaded with joy or happiness because the nature of these emotions is self-regulating. This means that if there is too much energy circulating in the body, we naturally release extra energy without even being aware of the process. Unfortunately, it is the least desirable emotions that run the risk of overload.

Long-term challenges and experiences that we refuse to release, forgive or forget cause the body to continuously produce debilitating emotional energy. As massive amounts of emotional energy accumulate in the body, there is a threshold where it cannot process emotional energy as fast as it is being produced, and, if it doesn't process the energy, the body becomes overtaxed - too much energy in motion at one time could result in an emotional breakdown, but this rarely happens because there are safety mechanisms in place.

We may not have any idea that we are on the verge of an emotional breakdown, except for the fact that we may experience this pre-overload stage as feelings of overwhelm, anxiety or panic. These warning emotions indicate distress and are intended to interrupt the pattern of negative thinking by making us refocus on our distressed body.

Whether or not we heed the warning, in order to avoid an emotional breakdown the body immediately takes emergency measures by storing unprocessed energy; if energy cannot be processed, it must be stored. Mirroring repression, the body removes the motion from emotion, resulting in non-moving energy that can be compacted and stored. Because the body is programmed to bring all functions back to homeostasis, it will compact as much energy as necessary to get the job done. If our thoughts and beliefs continue to cause emotional overwhelm, the body will become proactive and store more energy than necessary - increasing the amount of stored energy.

In fact, as a strategic defense to prevent a future emotional breakdown, the body may overcompensate by automatically storing emotional energy; whenever the body senses this same type of emotion being triggered, it will automatically store this energy before we even recognize it as an emotion. This explains why we might feel numb to an experience that "should" normally trigger intense emotion.

Emotions are stored in the body for two reasons:

1. We repress painful emotions
2. To prevent an emotional breakdown

The human body can withstand a great deal of stored or stuck energy, so there may not be any initial signs of energetic blockage, or the signs may be subtle, such as a tolerable chronic issue. However, in most cases, blocked energy increases over time - frequently due to emotional reactions.

Emotional Reactions

Emotional reactions are the unavoidable consequence of unhealed emotional wounds stored in the body. When we are emotionally triggered in the same, or similar way, as the original trauma, the stored energy gets stimulated and begins to move, bringing up past emotional pain. For most people, the immediate and unconscious reaction is repression of this pain; this means that the stored energy is once again pushed down into the "storage area," but now it is also packaged with the current emotional reaction, thereby increasing the size and density of the storage area, and further inhibiting the flow of Life Force Energy.

The longer the energy is blocked and the more the blockage increases, the greater the chance of intolerable physical issues, such as disease, disorder or susceptibility to repeated injury.

Modern medicine attempts to heal symptoms without ever addressing the cause, which often explains chronic disorders or relapsing illnesses that refuse to heal. In order to successfully heal whatever ails us, it is essential to understand that the ***ailment is the symptom***, which means that we must stop treating the ailment as the cause, and we must get to the root issue.

Imagine that you are out at sea in a boat and suddenly that boat starts taking on water. You grab the nearest pail and use it to dump out water, but no matter how fast you work, it is not fast enough because the boat is continuously taking on more water than you can dump out, and before long, the boat is sinking. As you are going under, you notice a small hole in the boat. If only you had seen that earlier, you could have easily filled the hole and saved yourself and the boat. When we look at a situation like this,

it makes sense to locate the caus
modern medicine, and even som
water out of the boat without ever l

One day, mainstream medicine wi
energy issue, but you do not have
the power to heal yourself now. Ple
discard traditional or alternative m
play an important part in healing, but
expect medical practitioners to get t
Instead, understand that they are train
of stuck emotional energy. It is your jo
and clearing it.

Your Brilliant Body

The extraordinary intelligence of your bo
to breathe and your brain to think, and, at the ...ork in harmony to keep everything functioning, while hor... ...nd other internal signals maintain a perfect balance within a symbiotic re...tionship.

Part of this brilliance is the fact that your body is actually self-healing. That's right, it knows how to heal itself, and can heal practically anything under the proper conditions. We have all witnessed cuts and scrapes heal on their own, colds, flus and viruses overcome and even serious diseases and disorders triumphed. The body knows how to heal it all, but it needs a certain something in order to do the job.

You've guessed it – *healing requires Life Force Energy.*

When there is limited energy, your body goes into survival, conserving energy for vital organs and necessary bodily functions - leaving little or no energy for healing and rejuvenation. Even though your body has the ability to heal almost anything, if it does not have the necessary energy to provide healing, no healing can be done. Imagine that there are billions of "microscopic doctors" within your body and they are all trained specialists and excellent healers. They know just what to do and they know how to do it, but these doctors need energy in order to do their jobs. If they don't have adequate energy, they have no power to heal. Despite their advanced skills and the focused purpose to provide wellness in the body, without proper energy, all they can do is wait for the energy to arrive. What a waste to have an army of healers and no means for them to heal!

It is your job to provide them with the energy they need to heal you by:

1. Increasing Life Force Energy
2. Releasing stuck energy

Unquestionably, healing requires increased Life Force Energy, as well as the release of stuck energy that has become stagnant, thereby putting the motion back in emotion.

Let's put this all together…

- When Life Force Energy flows freely in the body, the body is healthy.
- Your perception of various experiences affects the flow of Life Force Energy, causing energy to move slower or faster.

energy flow as emotions,
preted as love or happiness,
nterpreted as fear or sadness.

ons, we literally inhibit the flow of
emoving the motion from emotion.

nergy getting stuck at, or near, the body
sociated with the emotional wound.

nergy remains stuck or stagnant for long periods of time, and/or
ows in size or density, the long-term inhibition of Life Force Energy
an result in physical issues that compromise health and wellbeing.

- In order to fully heal, the stuck energy must be released, and energy flow must properly resume to this area of the body.
- Health is synonymous with the flow of Life Force Energy and healing is the result of restoring Life Force Energy to the entire body.
- The bottom line is that in order to fully heal, you must address the core cause which is virtually always an energy flow issue caused by repressed emotions.

In a later chapter, we will explore how to increase the flow of Life Force Energy.

What makes emotions so painful?

We repress emotions only when they are too painful to feel, but what makes certain emotions so painful that we avoid them at all costs?

Remember, emotions are just moving energy in your body, interpreted by your brain as specific emotions. Energy in motion really doesn't have the capacity to cause emotional pain, so, in order to understand the real cause, we need to look deeper.

When we peel back the layers of emotion, we find disempowering beliefs to be the real cause of emotional pain.

It is not the actual events in our lives that cause emotional trauma or emotional pain, it is the beliefs that we adopt, in order to explain these experiences, which cause us pain and suffering. Emotional wounds are comprised of one or more of three disempowering beliefs; unworthiness, powerlessness and victimhood, with unworthiness virtually always being the core belief.

When we forget that we are unconditionally worthy, and we fail to prove our worth, or we experience proof that we are, in fact, worthless, shame is often the result, and, because shame is just too painful to experience, we bury it deep.

Until the disempowering belief(s) is released, the emotional trauma gets stored in the body as an emotional wound. An emotional wound is composed of the traumatic memory packaged with repressed emotions and held together with one or more disempowering beliefs.

Here's the thing, all disempowering beliefs are completely and absolutely can only "make believe" that we are powerless, unworthy victims, while parts and playing roles in this game of life, but in the bigger scheme of thing unconditionally worthy, intrinsically powerful creators.

The reason that these false beliefs cause us emotional pain is in order to alert us to the fact that we believe something that is inherently false. The emotional pain is your inner guidance system offering you powerful and accurate feedback that you are going the "wrong way" by believing a lie, but since no one ever taught us about this feedback system or how to use it, we falsely interpret emotional pain as proof that our most disempowering beliefs are true, further strengthening both the belief(s) and the pain.

If you fail at school, your lover leaves you or you lose status, you might feel like you are not good enough, and you might believe that you are not worthy, and, if this is the case, the belief of unworthiness triggers intense emotion, but emotions alone are not painful without the precipitating belief.

Nonetheless, we unconsciously interpret these emotions as proof that the belief is true, and the moment we believe a disempowering belief, we program it into the subconscious mind, thereby activating the corresponding program. *Never even realizing that the purpose of these painful emotions is to show us that we believe a falsehood, so we will let it go.*

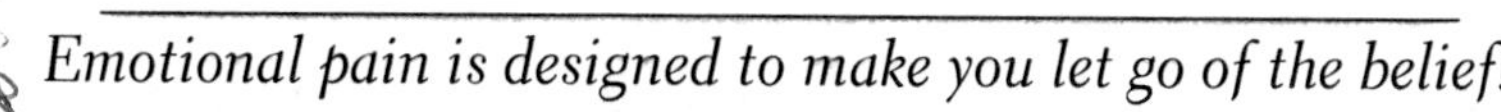

Emotional pain is designed to make you let go of the belief!

Unfortunately, that is not what usually happens. Instead of saying to ourselves, "*Wow, it feels really bad to believe that I am unworthy, so it must be untrue,*" we grasp onto the disempowering belief, and along with the emotional pain (shame, regret, guilt, etc...), we do whatever it takes to push the pain down so we can't feel it; favorite strategies include denial, distraction and dissociation.

An emotional wound results when a disempowering belief is entangled with repressed emotions and then stored in the body.

Free-will allows you to believe anything you choose (consciously or unconsciously), however, your True-Self would never believe that you are powerless, unworthy or a victim. Believing something that the True You would never believe indicates the EGO is in the driver's seat, and, because it also hinders your ability to embody your True-Self, disempowering beliefs must be released and emotional wounds must be healed.

Emotions Stored in Fat

The most common way for your body to store repressed emotions is in the production and maintenance of fat cells.

Since the body needs to store repressed emotional energy somewhere, a larger body is often required for storage - making it difficult to lose weight and keep it off; if you don't first release stored emotional energy (wounds), the body will hold onto extra storage space (fat cells) due to necessity.

Many people are emotional eaters due to the fact that they are repressing their emotions, and they need to make additional storage space as they need it, in real time. In response to repressing emotions, the mind/body computer says, "*More repressed emotions coming own - increase fat storage,"* and, at the same time, the mind/body-computer initiates cravings of fattening foods so it can quickly manufacture more space in the body to store newly repressed emotions.

Imagine that you are eating a slice of cake and really enjoying it, when suddenly you start thinking about a traumatic memory. Painful emotions surface, and because you don't want to feel them, you push them down. Now, the body has to store those repressed emotions, and, therefore, those calories that would have been easily metabolized are now made into fat to be used as storage space.

The bottom line is, emotions are either processed or stored.

Most of us don't like extra body fat, but it is a much better storage facility than vital organs that you need in order to survive. Chronic extra fat may impair your health on some level, but long-term storage of painful emotions in your vital organs could be deadly. Having said that, emotional wounds can be stored anywhere in the body, and, often are, especially ones that are long-term.

Fortunately, the mind/body-computer has an ingenious safeguard designed to initiate the release of stored emotional issues.

Emotional Triggers to the rescue!

Indeed, the EGO uses emotional reactions to generate energy, and also to put up a defensive front, yet, simultaneously, these same emotional reactions offer powerful opportunities for healing, but only if you are conscious during the process. By being conscious and proactive, you can override the EGO and you can activate the higher purpose of all emotional reactions - turning a trigger into a tool for healing.

Without emotional triggers we might not even know that we had emotional wounds. This also indicates that we need other people to trigger our issues or we wouldn't know they existed, or that we had to heal them. The underlying good news is that everyone who triggers your emotional issues is unknowingly serving you, and conspiring for your healing and awakening, just as you are for them.

> *Signpost on the path*
>
> *Emotional triggers can be used as tools for healing*

If there is no emotional wound, we simply do not get triggered.

We are only triggered if there is something

to trigger, and that is the point.

If the Powerlessness Program is operating, you might be triggered anytime you feel that someone is trying to control you, bully you or have power over you, or, if the Victimhood Program is operating, you might be triggered anytime someone seems to threaten your wellbeing or makes you feel like a victim, but, not surprisingly, most triggers are the result of the Worthiness Program - when this program is operating, we are triggered whenever we perceive that our worth is in question, or someone or something makes us feel unworthy.

Let's look at the ways in which this pivotal trigger shows up:

Judgment Trigger

Being judged by others is a huge trigger because the moment you experience judgment, the EGO hears it as proof of unworthiness, and, if we are deemed unworthy, for any reason, it triggers a fear of rejection or abandonment. If you recall from a previous chapter, rejection and abandonment are like death according to the EGO, and, therefore, judgment must be avoided at all costs.

All judgment that causes emotional pain or an emotional reaction is self-judgment. Another's judgment of you cannot harm you unless you take it on, own it, and use it to judge yourself. In actuality, if you look closely, you might see that when others judge you, it is almost always a reflection of your own self-judgment.

The worst part about judgment is that when we feel judged, we unconsciously react by withholding love from ourselves, thereby dissociating from the present moment and consequently misaligning our True-Selves.

Identity Trigger

Since our sense of worth is often intertwined with identity, anything that threatens our perceived identity is considered a risk to the EGO, and, therefore, when others question our identity, or we lose even a portion of our identity, the EGO is programmed to react defensively to protect our worth. If your worth is not dependent on an identity, there can be no trigger in this regard. Identity includes the roles we play in life, as well as aspects of character and personality.

Emotional Needs Trigger

The most common emotional trigger has to do with emotional needs. As previously discussed, when we forget that we are unconditionally worthy, the EGO develops a primary emotional need that signifies worthiness, such as respect, approval, acceptance, understanding, appreciation, etc… We unconsciously believe that when this emotional need is met by others, it proves we are worthy, but this also means that the well-meaning EGO is diligently on alert for evidence that this need is ***not*** being met, and, even the slightest indication could be a big trigger.

If your primary emotional need is to be seen, for example, and you go into a store where the clerk seems to ignore you, your EGO could be triggered. This is why we sometimes overreact to small things, and we don't know why. Certainly, being ignored by a store clerk isn't going to change your life significantly, yet, to the EGO, it signifies unworthiness, and, as a result, your worth must be defended.

When your Primary Emotional Need (P-E-N) is ignored, the EGO triggers an emotional reaction to defend your worth. An emotional reaction results when:

- Your P-E-N is approval and the EGO senses disapproval.
- Your P-E-N is respect and the EGO senses disrespect.
- Your P-E-N is acceptance and the EGO senses rejection.
- Your P-E-N is understanding and the EGO senses not being understood.
- Your P-E-N is being heard and the EGO senses not being heard.

- Your P-E-N is appreciation and the EGO senses being taken for granted.

Based on the Past

The EGO is programmed to calculate all current experiences and possible future events based on past experiences, and especially ones that resulted in disempowerment or trauma in some way. A past situation may seem minor on the surface, but to the EGO it is permanent cause to be on guard - the EGO is always prepared to keep you from repeating experiences that could decrease your worth or result in powerlessness.

Needless to say, this means that the EGO is on super-high alert for anything that might resemble an emotional wound. Therefore, it is vitally important to identify and heal all emotional wounds so that the EGO is not constantly triggered to defend you.

Underneath the Reaction

In order to understand emotional triggers, it is important to look beneath the surface of the emotional reaction. As you dig deep, many feelings may come up but keep inquiring until you uncover the disempowering belief at the core. Your inquiry should reveal three elements:

- Emotional Reaction (the emotion experienced as the reaction)
- Underlying Emotion
- Disempowering Belief

Emotional reactions are always in response to a deeper emotion and that underlying emotion is always invoked by a disempowering belief, for example:

- Anger may be in response to feeling hurt because we believe that someone has deemed us unworthy.
- Frustration may be in response to feeling overwhelmed because we believe we are powerless.
- Jealousy may be in response to feeling rejected because we believe we aren't good enough.

> ꧁Signpost on the path ꧂
> *Transcending the EGO requires the healing of all emotional wounds*

Emotional reactions perpetuate dysfunction

Sometimes the best way to handle a difficult situation is through an emotional reaction, as everything has its place and purpose, but, in the long term, chronic emotional reactions are terrible strategies for self-empowerment, and even worse for transcending the EGO.

Emotional reactions are often the way, in which, the EGO protects us, but this defensive strategy actually creates more issues than it solves. It's fairly obvious that chronic emotional reactions alienate others and adversely affect relationships, but chronic emotional reactions also perpetuate disempowerment, dysfunctional dynamics and unwanted negativity.

When we react to an emotional trigger, we reinforce the dynamics that are responsible for the trigger, thereby perpetuating unwanted situations and relationship challenges. For instance, if you react to feeling unappreciated, you give power and energy to being unappreciated, and, whatever you focus on, you increase with the power and energy of your focus - you won't receive appreciation by giving your attention to not being appreciated.

Every time you have an emotional reaction, your True-Self goes unconscious, and the EGO takes control, and this is precisely why unhealed emotional issues keep you from living as your True-Self.

Feelings Rising to be Released

The current presenting issue may seem insignificant on the surface, but, if the EGO relates it to a past unhealed emotional issue, the wound is activated and all the emotions stored within the wound come to the surface; suddenly, we are overwhelmed with intense emotion, even though the current situation may be minor.

Clearly, this explains why even a small trigger can affect us in a big way.

When we have a stored emotional issue, repressed emotions are "packaged" together in a compacted cluster of non-moving energy. Unless triggered by a current day issue, or reminder of the past, dormant emotional wounds stay closed. However, when triggered, stored emotional energy is activated and we experience "*feelings coming up*" - causing us to feel the same painful emotions that we originally experienced and pushed down. This is why we might say that an issue made our feelings come up – the stored emotional energy is, in fact, *rising up to be released.*

Until we are conscious and courageous, it is instinctual to "re-press" painful emotions, oftentimes, by means of denial, dissociation or distraction.

Repressing emotions might give us temporary relief, but it also increases the size and intensity of the wound. As we push the original emotional wound back down, we have also added the emotions associated with the current issue. Every time we do this, the wound gets bigger and denser, ultimately taking up more space in our bodies, inhibiting the flow of Life Force Energy and adversely affecting our lives in greater capacities.

As long as emotional wounds are stored in the body, we will attract one emotional trigger after another because:

1. The EGO uses emotional triggers to generate energy.
2. Your mind/body wants to release the stored emotional energy and heal.

Since emotions get stored in the body by way of repression, they have to come out the same way they got in. Repression locked those emotions in your body, and expression will free them. This means you need to feel your emotions when they come up, and you must allow the feelings to process through until they are released.

Emotional triggers cause stored emotions to come up in order to be released, and the process of releasing emotions is feeling them.

Healing is Feeling!

It's important to mention that you don't have to be triggered in order to heal an emotional wound. You can consciously choose to release any wound without being triggered, but, in order to do so, it is usually necessary to locate the wound in the body, activate it, and allow it to process through by feeling it until it is completely released. Emotional triggers are extremely helpful because they usually locate the wound and activate it, so you don't have to.

If emotions were repressed due to emotional overload, it is also important to release the story that caused the overload, as well as releasing the belief that originally triggered the overload. Without the disempowering belief, you should be able to feel and process stored emotional energy as it rises.

Stop Labeling Emotions

Before you can embrace, feel and process all your emotions, you need to remember that there is no such thing as good or bad emotions. All emotions are gifts and equally valuable. When we refer to negative emotions, it does not mean that the emotions are bad, but, rather, they are simply emotions we prefer not to experience. When we refer to positive emotions, it doesn't mean the emotions are good - they are simply emotions we prefer to experience.

If you can drop your judgments and preferences regarding emotions, feeling your emotions can be like masterfully surfing ocean waves; whether the tide is going in or out, you are balanced and in harmony with the motion of the ocean.

The Master Key to Emotional Healing

When you believe that you are unworthy, or your worth is conditional, it makes it all the more difficult to feel your emotions because certain emotions are interpreted by the EGO as proof that you are not worthy, and the EGO must protect you against unworthiness at all costs. For instance, according to the EGO, feelings of rejection or abandonment are evidence that you are not worthy of love or life, and, therefore, the EGO will try to block you from feeling these emotions by invoking intense emotional pain so you don't want to feel them.

Hence, when you know and own your worth, the EGO doesn't block you from feeling any emotion, because nothing triggers unworthiness. Therefore, you can feel emotions as they surface, making it safe to process emotional wounds until they are healed.

> ꧁Signpost on the path꧂
> *The secret to healing emotional wounds is knowing your unconditional worth - and power!*

When you own your intrinsic worth, it is safe to feel any and all emotions.

Most importantly, all emotional wounds are the result of forgetting your unconditional worth and intrinsic power, so it only makes sense that healing requires that you fully reclaim your worth and power.

Reclaim Your Power

When we experience emotional pain that results in trauma or woundedness, we perceive it as a loss of power - believing that someone or something has taken our power, and we cannot get it back.

Of course, no one can take or steal your power under any circumstances. Your power belongs to you, and you are the only one who has access to it, and, despite how it may seem, you are the creator of your life. You might ask, *"If I am creating my life, why would I create negativity?"* Until we are conscious and awake, we unconsciously create our lives based on our deepest beliefs.

Whether you realize it or not, life is always responding to your beliefs by manifesting the tangible equivalent, and, in fact, life can only mirror your beliefs.

Moreover, the purpose of life is to demonstrate your beliefs to you, so if your life is great, it means your beliefs are empowering, and if your life is mostly challenging, it means that your beliefs are disempowering. What about children? Sometimes, prior to birth, children choose to experience certain challenges for various reasons, but, children also take on their parent's beliefs and unknowingly manifest those beliefs, and, of course, manifested experiences reinforce precipitating beliefs - this is how we unconsciously base our lives on our parent's beliefs, but once we take on a parental belief, it's ours and we own it.

At anytime, we can claim our power, take responsibility for the manifestation of our beliefs and transform our lives. However, if you believe that your power has been stolen, or you make someone responsible for your experience, you unconsciously give your power away - making yourself powerless to change or heal. You lose power every time you make external conditions, be that family, religion, culture, birth-sign, lineage, government or unseen spiritual forces, responsible for your personal circumstances.

We may blame others and shift responsibility onto things outside our control in an attempt to reclaim our power, but you can never reclaim power by shifting blame and responsibility. In fact, the opposite is true; every time you blame someone for something, whether it is blaming your mother for your relationship issues or your partner for your loneliness, you disconnect from your power, making yourself a victim. Healing can never happen as long as you identify with being powerless or a victim.

Healing requires that you reclaim your power by taking responsibility for every experience in your life, even if you don't know how or why you created it. You cannot heal a wound that was created in a relationship when you continue to blame the other person. The only way to heal is to let go of blame, including the need for apology, acknowledgment or restitution.

You don't need anything from anyone in order to heal.

However, if you feel unworthy, it is nearly impossible to take responsibility for all the experiences in your life, due to the fact that taking responsibility for difficult life experiences can provoke deep feelings of shame, and shame is the same as feeling worthless, which is devastating to a fragile EGO, and can result in depression or emotional paralysis.

Therefore, the key to reclaiming your power is first remembering your intrinsic worth!

This is why your Worthiness Practice must be done every day until you absolutely know and own your unconditional worth, and, at that time, you will have the capability to feel, express and process any and all emotions.

The bottom line is that emotional healing requires the release of all disempowering beliefs, while at the same time, remembering the truth of your being.

The Formula for Healing Emotional Wounds

The formula for healing emotional wounds can be summarized:

1. Affirm your unconditional worth and intrinsic power
2. Take responsibility for the wound
3. Process emotions (See "Ride the Tide" Healing Process below)
4. Reaffirm your unconditional worth and intrinsic power
5. Repeat as needed

"Ride the Tide" to Healing - an emotional healing process

The following process can be done anytime you are emotionally triggered: be aware that this is not a substitute for professional help.

- Always begin and end this process by affirming your unconditional worth and intrinsic power.
- *I Am unconditionally worthy! I Am intrinsically powerful!*
- Find a private space where you feel safe and you can "get into your body."

There is no way to feel your emotions, if you are not in your body, so it is essential to get in your body and feel what it is like to be in your body. Many of us are so good at dissociating from the body that we don't even realize that we are doing it.

One way to ground yourself in the body is to place your awareness on one body part at a time, starting with your feet and slowly moving your awareness upward, all the while breathing deeply. It is important to do this process without self-judgment, as judgment is the quickest way to disconnect from the body.

> *Signpost on the path*
> *To be the True You, learn to Ride the Tide of Emotion*

Once grounded in your body, get to know what you are feeling, and really feel it. It is very helpful to name emotions in order to "make friends" with them (you might want to research a list of emotions and use it as a reference).

At first, you might only be feeling the emotional reaction that caused you to begin this process, *but what is under the emotional reaction?* Anger and frustration, for example, are surface emotions. Under each of these emotions is a more meaningful emotion(s), so allow yourself to go deeper and see what there is to feel without resistance. Whatever you feel is perfect so trust your senses.

Breathe deeply….

As you begin to experience deeper emotions, it is essential to surrender to these revealing sensations, allowing yourself to really feel without resistance, and also allowing your emotions to manifest anyway that is natural; you may cry, wail, laugh or scream - do what you need to do in order to express all your emotions.

Remember, if emotions come up but you push them down or avoid them, they will not get released - it is in the process of expression that emotional wounds are released. The key is to experience and express your emotions until you feel a release. Oftentimes, we stop the process and push our emotions back down when they become most intense, but this impedes healing because the release is often *just beyond the peak of emotional intensity.*

As it is darkest before dawn, it is most intense before the release.

It is possible that in feeling and expressing your emotions, you may be inspired to take action, such as speaking your truth to someone, cleaning up a mess, writing a letter or expressing yourself in some other way. When you receive these impulses, it usually supports healing, but try to express your emotions in ways that are empowering for all involved. Although it can be very positive to express your anger, it might not be a good idea to act out of anger, for various reasons.

As you allow yourself to feel emotions as they come up, there will likely be accompanying thoughts. The thoughts are manifestations of the core disempowering belief(s), and, therefore, reveal the belief. Active beliefs are ripe for release.

Belief Shifting Process

As you now know, belief is the one and only off switch for subconscious programs. Therefore, to assist you in turning off the Worthiness Program and Powerlessness Program, here is a powerful Belief Shifting Process.

Although most of our beliefs are unconsciously formed in response to life experiences, we each have the innate ability to consciously choose our beliefs. This means that we have the power to adopt or release any belief simply by choosing so - yet, this is the most challenging thing to do.

It is very difficult for the mind to grasp that you can drop a belief simply because you choose to, and you can adopt a new belief in the same manner. It's all about choice, and, therefore, any belief shifting process is only to convince your subconscious mind to let go of a belief and/or adopt a new one. Having said this, one of the most powerful belief shifting processes is healing and reprogramming your past-self; whether from childhood or adulthood, yesterday or yesteryear, this process can be done with any belief.

Healing Your Past-Self

When we trace our most limiting core beliefs back to their origin, we often end up at an early memory. It is possible to use this memory as a means to shift a belief; by healing the younger part of you, who adopted the belief you wish to release, you can change the past. Healing your past-self allows your present day self to heal simultaneously. Since the subconscious does not know the difference between real and imagined, or past and present, when you imagine a different past, your subconscious believes it is so; allowing healing to unfold.

Here's how to do it:

Step 1. Name the belief you desire to release. In identifying a belief you want to release, keep in mind that the disempowering core belief is virtually always regarding worthiness.

Step 2. Go into a state of relaxation/meditation.

Step 3. Ask your True-Self or Infinite Intelligence to show you where this belief originated. Trust what you see and experience, even if it doesn't make sense or you are seeing/experiencing something that you do not actually remember. If you don't recall a particular past event, but only a time period, try to find a memory that represents the belief you want to shift. Even if you have to fill in details with your imagination, do your best to "locate" a particular moment in time.

Step 4. As the Observer, witness the past event, and "notice what there is to notice" - particularly the moment your past-self chose the belief (you now desire to release).

Step 5. Access your current wisdom regarding this belief. If you desire to change a belief, it likely indicates that you have an awareness that the belief is untrue. Tap into this awareness by mentally focusing on it.

Step 6. Imagine that you can communicate with your past-self; sit or stand in front of him/her, and make sure you get his/her attention. Your past-self must be aware of your presence in order to proceed to the next step. Introduce yourself as the wiser/mature version of him/her.

Step 7. Imagine that your past-self can speak to you; allow him/her to tell you how he/she feels. Listen carefully without interrupting. Your past-self needs to know that you hear and understand him/her, so, when he/she is done talking, compassionately repeat or paraphrase what you heard, adding in statements of support and understanding. Never judge your past-self as judgment will shut down this process.

Step 8. Now, talk to him/her about the belief that was chosen, and show him/her why it is false. In other words, let's say, that your past-self adopted the belief that he/she is not important because your parents were distant and disinterested. Explain to your past-self that your parent's behavior have nothing to do with him/her. Maybe they had problems of their own, and although they weren't the best parents, they still loved him/her, for example. Keep explaining until it makes sense to your past-self. Allow him/her to ask questions and comment.

Step 9. Determine the primary emotional need that was not met in this past circumstance; acceptance, approval, understanding, appreciation, being heard, etc..., and meet this need in your past-self. Give him/her the exact emotional support he/she lacked in that moment. Keep doing it, until your past-self feels satisfied. In our example above, the need was to feel important - you would meet this need by speaking to your past-self, in such a way that he/she feels important. You know exactly what it means to him/her to feel important, appreciated, heard, understood or whatever your P-E-N might be. Treat your past-self in a way that you wanted to be treated.

Step 10. Install the belief of unconditional worthiness. It is very important to make sure that your past-self knows his/her unconditional and intrinsic worth. You cannot emphasize this enough. You install the belief by making your past-self ***feel*** his/her intrinsic worthiness. With sincere conviction, speak to him/her in such a way that he/she knows that you believe he/she is worthy. Then ask your past-self to affirm, "I Am Worthy" at least ten times. If there are any other beliefs you wish to install, do so now in the same way.

Step 11. Ask your past-self what he/she needs from you, and whatever it is, give it abundantly. It might be a sense of safety, a hug or some other expression of love. Your past-self might even want you to take him/her to the park or ice cream parlor; create that experience virtually by imagining that it is really happening now.

At some point in this process, you may feel an energy shift in your body; as your past-self releases the false belief that shift will ripple forward to the current moment. If you don't feel anything that's perfectly fine, and no indication of the process not working. Everyone is different – some feel it and some don't.

Step 12. Ask your past-self if he/she would like to reside in your heart. If the answer is yes, imagine taking a miniature him/her to the *warm* area of your heart.

Step 13. Check in with your past-self on a daily basis, and ***especially when you feel emotionally triggered.*** When you check in, talk to him/her, listen and give him/her what he/she needs just as you did in this process. Check in every day until you experience a permanent shift and the old belief is no longer playing out. Also, keep in mind that there is often a Lag Time - the amount of time needed for the reality of everyday life to catch up with the new belief. So, do your best not to react to current day experiences that represent the old belief.

If there are multiple memories regarding the belief, you can do this process for each one, beginning at the earliest.

This process is not limited to childhood memories; it works exactly the same way for adult memories and trauma you wish to heal, but it is helpful to deal with the earliest memory regarding the belief.

Optional Process (you can do this process after the one above)

Depending on the circumstance, you may want to teach your past-self how to be empowered. To do this process, imagine that you can go to the moment just ***before*** the emotional situation that triggered the false belief. Empower your past-self by teaching him/her how to set protective boundaries and communicate in effective ways. Once you empower him/her, imagine that he/she experiences the situation that created the belief, but this time from a state of empowerment. You should be able to imagine an improved outcome where your past-self is empowered and stays empowered – maybe even avoiding the event altogether.

For a free belief shifting quantum process go to www.Nanice.com/Believe

---

One more thing, if you want to heal a past relationship trauma, but you are in the midst of current relationship abuse, you may experience blocks in the healing process, because as far as your subconscious mind is concerned, you are still subjecting yourself to emotional abuse or trauma. Even though you have a different partner and a new relationship, if the dynamics are the same or similar, for all intents and purposes, nothing has changed.

Clearly, it is essential to release the past emotional wound, allowing your past-self to heal and become more empowered, but healing also requires certain boundaries that will prevent current and future emotional injury. If you are still experiencing abuse in a present-day relationship, it is extremely difficult to heal past abuse.

Yes, this means that you must teach others how to treat you, and even how to speak to you, and, it also means that you must be willing to disengage from relationships where others are not respecting your boundaries.

Let's Recap

- Emotions are your mind's interpretation of moving energy in your body, and, they are also the way your body informs cells of the current condition.
- It is not the events in our lives that cause emotional trauma or emotional pain, it is the beliefs that we adopt in order to explain experiences, with unworthiness virtually always being the core belief.
- Emotional pain is designed to alert you to, and make you let go of, false and disempowering beliefs.
- Suffering can be alleviated by releasing resistance and feeling emotions, and without resistance emotions are experienced and allowed to flow, resulting in increased Life Force Energy.
- Repressing emotions removes the motion from emotion, turning moving energy into non-moving energy, resulting in the formation of emotional wounds - and because they are stored where they are stuck, physical issues often manifest in those same areas.
- When you are emotionally triggered, stored energy gets stimulated and begins to move, bringing up past emotional pain, but, if you react by repressing this pain, the stored energy is pushed back down, along with the current emotions - increasing the size of the emotional wound.
- To fully heal, you must address the core cause of the problem which is virtually always an energy flow issue caused by repressed emotions.
- The secret to healing emotional wounds is affirming your unconditional worth and reclaiming your power by taking responsibility for the wound, even if you don't know how or why you created it, and, then fully processing stored emotions.

The word "healing" comes from the word whole, indicating the return to wholeness. The return to wholeness is the reunion with True-Self.

Chapter 33

PREVENT EGO HIJACKING

When your True-Self is embodied, you're going to want to sustain it as long as possible, therefore, you need to prevent EGO Hijacking as best you can.

When we are emotionally triggered, the EGO automatically takes control as a defensive general, and it is going to protect us by fight or flight. Keep in mind that the reaction of flight is not so much about literally running away, although that may be possible, but, it is more likely an emotional sort of flight, such as shutting down or dissociating; like a tortoise, we retreat within a protective shell. However, if our defensive mode is to fight, our weapon of choice is likely the "weapon of emotion" known as an emotional reaction.

EGO Hijacking occurs whenever you are emotionally triggered and "give in" to an emotional reaction; for example, your significant other forgets your birthday and you react with anger and jealousy because he always remembers his friend's birthdays, so you feel less important. During this emotional reaction, your anger and jealousy act as a defensive shield that is intended to protect you from further emotional injury.

As you now know, emotions are energy in motion, but emotional energy is not limited to the internal body. Emotions quite easily ripple out into the space around us, and this means that we each have the ability to affect the energy in the environment. If you have ever been in a room with a very angry person, you know exactly what I mean – anger permeates the space around the enraged person. Because emotional energy is tangible, it can be consciously used to repel or attract just about anything, but, instead of having emotional mastery, as we were intended, most of us are unconscious slaves to our emotions. This is mostly due to the fact that the EGO knows exactly how to use emotions to motor-vate us, as well as protect us.

In times of danger, instead of protecting ourselves with metal armor and a sharp sword, the EGO depends on the enormous power contained within an emotional reaction. Anger, frustration, jealousy and a host of other volatile emotions have the inherent ability to act as powerful forms of defense, for the purpose of protecting our power and worth. As reactive emotions ripple from within, the space we inhabit is engulfed with energetic information that warns everyone in proximity to beware! Without even saying a word, emotions like anger speak volumes.

Even when the EGO is dormant, it is still on alert – perpetually looking for any signs of possible risk to your worth or wellbeing, it is ready to jump into *reaction* in the blink of an eye. If the EGO perceives judgment or rejection, for instance, a defensive measure is triggered, and, if your True-Self does not quickly override this trigger, the EGO will activate an emotional line of defense – in the form of an emotional reaction, the EGO will send anger, frustration, impatience, rage, etc... to the defensive front-line.

When you are no longer emotionally triggered, the True You can remain conscious and embodied indefinitely, but, until then, understanding your triggers is key to sustaining embodiment.

It is helpful to make a list of all the situations, relationships and experiences that specifically trigger you. Once you make this list, you will likely see that most triggers have to do with disempowerment, which is always a result of subconscious programming. The only reason we are ever triggered by anyone or anything is because subconscious programs are running.

The True-Self Override

It is possible to override emotional reactions via your True-Self but this is not a short-cut for healing. It is essential to address emotional wounds and release them, but, keep in mind that emotional triggers may stay active even after a wound is healed, especially when the "motor" had a lot of momentum. If you have healed your emotional wounds, but you are still experiencing triggers, it is possible to override those triggers via your True-Self.

> *Signpost on the path*
>
> *Always discern when to process an emotional reaction and when to override it*

Once your True-Self is fully integrated, it is unlikely that you will get triggered very much, or at all, but until integration is complete, it pays to clearly identify any triggers, so you can consciously avoid them. This includes steering away from people, situations and conversations where you could be triggered, but, also having a plan in place, so if you are triggered, you can easily process it and quickly move through it.

Consciousness is Key!

If you are conscious of your triggers, your True-Self can override most emotional reactions, so, even if the EGO gets triggered by the possibility of judgment or rejection, for instance, it is neutralized and your True-Self remains embodied. This means that when you are triggered, you pause to remember your unconditional worth and intrinsic power, and you reassure the EGO that there is no risk to your worth and no threat to your power, and, therefore, you can choose to let go of the trigger because there is no reason for it.

Let's say you are experiencing True-Self embodiment and you are having a wonderful day of inspiration and flow, when out of the blue, you get a negative phone call from a parent, partner or friend; as you perceive his/her judgment, you sense that familiar tight or uncomfortable feeling indicating the EGO has been triggered. If you are not conscious, your True-Self is immediately hijacked, which results in an emotional reaction of some sort, and the day goes downhill from that point on, but, if you are conscious, you can override the trigger. The instant you sense that familiar feeling that precipitates an emotional reaction, Stop, Drop and Roll. You probably recognize this terminology from a fire prevention class, but, if you think of an emotional trigger as if it is the first spark of a fire, this terminology works great.

As soon as you recognize a potential trigger:

- **Stop** - take a deep breath and remember your unconditional worth.
- **Drop** – drop into your heart and reassure the EGO that there is no danger.
- **Roll** – allow the potential emotional reaction to roll off your back.

By avoiding EGO hijacking, your True-Self remains embodied, and every time your True-Self overrides an EGO reaction integration strengthens.

It's important to be aware that a trigger doesn't have to be external; a single negative thought can be a trigger, as well as a shameful memory or future fear.

The Truth about Rejection

Another type of emotional reaction occurs when we do to ourselves what we fear others doing to us.

Until we are awake and conscious, it is human nature to do to ourselves what others have done to us, or even what we fear they may do. If we fear judgment, we judge ourselves, if we fear abandonment, we abandon ourselves, if we fear rejection, we reject ourselves. I've heard people say, *"I'd rather do it to myself before someone can do it to me."* Yes, it might be a strategy to keep the illusion of power, but it is also insanity to self-inflict the very pain we are trying to avoid.

Let's say that your partner ends the relationship because he/she now loves another. At the first sign of rejection, you unconsciously react by rejecting yourself – how? By trying to understand why you have been rejected, you look at all your faults and you judge yourself without mercy. Maybe you alternate between blaming your partner and shaming yourself, but, nonetheless, once you feel bad enough, you unknowingly dissociate, or maybe you ingest something to feel numb. In this process, your True-Self is misaligned or even evicted, and for all intents and purposes, you have essentially rejected your real self, and this is why rejection feels so terrible.

It is not the rejection by another that is so devastating – it is the rejection of self that cuts to the bone.

Upon self-insight, it is fairly easy to see that the greatest pain of rejection or abandonment comes from ourselves. It's true that no one can hurt us more than we hurt ourselves, but it is also true that no one can even hurt us, if we don't first set the stage by judging, abandoning or rejecting ourselves.

But, don't fret – there's a simple solution. Instead of doing to yourself what you fear others doing to you, do to yourself what you really want them to do. What do you really want? You want love.

So, if you are on the receiving end of a break-up, or experiencing any kind of rejection, Stop, Drop and Roll. Don't react by shunning or shaming yourself. Instead, respond with enormous unconditional self-love and nurturing.

Instead of withholding self-love because you feel judged, abandoned or rejected by another, embrace yourself with open arms and a warm heart full of self-forgiveness, compassion and pink fuzzy love - love yourself abundantly, by being kind, nurturing and understanding – be the best friend to your best-self.

If rejection of your True-Self is the cause of so much pain and suffering, the solution is self-love.

Also, keep in mind, because the EGO is triggered whenever it senses rejection or abandonment, your True-Self is swiftly misaligned or evicted, and the EGO interprets this as being rejected ***by*** your True-Self. This is a convoluted game the EGO plays by telling you that you are not worthy because your True-Self has rejected you and doesn't want to be with you. This game can be transcended with consciousness.

When you realize that your True-Self has been displaced, say to yourself, *"My True-Self is not rejecting me nor could ever reject me. I am my True-Self and I love myself unconditionally."*

Avoiding Triggers via Forgiveness

Most of us have forgiveness backward; we want to forgive and forget so that we can stop feeling negative emotions, but in order to forgive or let go, we must first choose to disengage from the emotions.

No doubt, it can be difficult to forgive and let go if the EGO is holding on to a past situation and using it as a "motor" for energy. For example, if you still get energy from arguing with your brother about something that happened in the distant past, the EGO will hold onto it as a "motor." When you no longer get emotional energy from a past "wrongdoing," it will be a great deal easier to forgive and let go.

Believe it or not, most grievances are caused when emotional needs are ignored or stepped on. If your primary emotional need is respect and you experience disrespect, anger is often provoked as a defensive strategy in order to protect your sense of worth. As long as you feel disrespected by this person or she never apologizes for disrespecting you, the wounded part of you feels unworthy in her eyes, making it nearly impossible to forgive.

Does this also give you some insight into the reason why others may be angry with you? Did you ignore or step over a primary emotional need, making your friend or relation feel unworthy *in your eyes*?

If the person you are angry with, is also angry with you, chances are you are both ignoring each other's primary emotional needs. Many arguments go something like this; one partner says, *"You don't hear me"* and the other responds, *"You don't accept me."* If you listen carefully, most people will tell you their primary emotional need - then it's up to you to offer what they need, or not - but, if you do, make sure to do so without expecting that your need is met in return.

Indeed, sometimes it appears that someone has done something so terrible to us and it seems much greater than issues of non-acceptance, non-approval, disrespect, being taken for granted, etc..., but when you look deep, you can see that relationship issues almost always funnel back to primary emotional needs, because when that need is not met by those important to us, we feel unworthy. Underneath any presenting issue, you will find one or both people feeling unworthy, and projecting it onto each other, thereby believing that the other person deems them unworthy.

You might say that you are angry because your spouse cheated on you, or your best friend betrayed you, but you are really angry because it made you feel a *certain way* that you unconsciously connect to unworthiness. Ask yourself, "*How did this situation or experience make me feel?*" If it made you feel rejected, you likely associate acceptance with worthiness. If it made you feel judged, you likely associate approval with worthiness.

If you want to forgive someone, you must let them off the hook; let go of the need that this person meet your primary emotional need. This requires that you know and own your unconditional worth and it is not dependent on anyone or anything.

Let's Recap

- The EGO defends your power and worth with emotional reactions, such as anger.
- EGO Hijacking occurs whenever you are emotionally triggered and "give in" to an emotional reaction.
- If you are conscious of your triggers, you can override most emotional reactions by remembering your unconditional worth and intrinsic power.
- As soon as you recognize a potential trigger, Stop, Drop and Roll!
- It is an EGO reaction to do to ourselves what we fear others doing to us, so, if we fear judgment, we judge ourselves.
- No one can hurt you, if you don't first judge, abandon or reject yourself.
- Instead of withholding self-love because you feel judged or rejected, embrace yourself with love and compassion.
- Most grievances are caused when emotional needs are not met, and, therefore, forgiveness requires you to let others off the hook.

Chapter 34

Essential Element # 4 - Self-Love

There is a direct relationship between self-love and consciousness; the more we love ourselves, the more we can stay present and be conscious, and the more we can experience True-Self embodiment.

The vibration of our True-Selves is the high vibration of love, so when we withhold self-love, we inadvertently misalign, making ourselves energetically incompatible with who we really are.

There is no way around it, the path to True-Self integration requires self-love.

Who Says Self-love is Selfish?

I don't recall self-love being part of the grade school curriculum. Do you remember a parent, teacher or clergyman instructing you to love yourself? Probably not. In fact, many of us were indirectly taught that self-love is selfish, and you should always think of others first. As a result, we are afraid that if we love ourselves, we will be judged selfish or egotistical. It is difficult to learn to love oneself when this false idea is subconsciously ingrained, but learning to love yourself is exactly what you must do in order to be your True-Self.

> *Signpost on the path*
> *True-Self requires True-Love*

What is Self-love?

Before we can define self-love, we must consider the *biggest* picture. We must consider that the Universe (and everyone in it) is made of divine love. Divine love is the infinite energy of the Universe, and, because there is nothing else to make anything out of, everyone and everything is comprised of this loving energy. It's love or nothing. Since you and I are also made from this love, it should be no surprise that the Prime Creator of the Universe unconditionally loves each of us.

Divine love that makes up every "micro this" and "macro that" should not be confused with human love. The emotion that we associate with human love, even in its purest form, is no more than a cloudy reflection of Divine Love.

Divine love is unconditional and intrinsic in each one of us. There is nothing that we must become to gain this love. There is nothing that we must do to prove that we are worthy of this love. There is nothing that we must exchange, sacrifice or compromise in order to receive this love. Period.

This love is guaranteed and without conditions or exceptions. If you exist, you are loved by Source. Even if you forget that you are infinitely loved, you are no less loved. If this is the divine love of Source, what is self-love?

Self-love is the allowance of divine love to flow to you and through you, so that you radiate Life Force Energy.

When you withhold self-love by doubting or judging yourself, you not only disconnect from your True-Self, you also inhibit Life Force Energy.

Self-Love Translates into Life Force Energy

Life Force Energy is the energy of love, so if you do not feel worthy of love, you block energy.

How much Life Force Energy you receive at any given moment is directly related to self-love. Although you may falsely base your *worthiness of love* on external factors and the approval or disapproval of others, you are the only one who decides how much love you are worthy of, and, as a result, you allow or inhibit the flow of Life Force Energy.

When you truly know that you are loved unconditionally and there is no doubt of your worth, divine love flows to you continuously, and like an infinite waterfall, you are tapped into the Prime Source of energy.

The most important byproduct of True-Self embodiment is the flow of Life Force Energy, but it also works both ways. If your intention is to connect with Life Force Energy, the result will likely be True-Self embodiment.

The Life Force Energy Store

Imagine that there is a Life Force Energy store where you can purchase Life Force Energy, but, instead of needing money to make this purchase, you need unconditional self-love. The amount of Life Force Energy you can purchase is relative to the amount of self-love you experience and express. You cannot fool the "Energy Giver" - pretending to love yourself does not work. You can beg, plead and try to manipulate, but there is nothing you can do to get more Life Force Energy. It all depends on what you have to offer in the Universal Currency of self-love.

The "Energy Giver" compassionately offers you a free lesson on how to receive unlimited Life Force Energy.

The lesson is simple:

Self-love = Life Force Energy

Unconditional Self-love = Unlimited Life Force Energy

The Dynamics to Self-Love

There is nothing that you need to do to experience love, but there is plenty to undo. When you stop judging, doubting and denying your worth, self-love flows.

Self-love requires believing in yourself, trusting yourself and knowing that you are intrinsically and unconditionally worthy.

- Self-Belief – the absence of self-judgment; believing in yourself and your abilities.
- Self-Trust – the absence of self-doubt; listening to your body and inner guidance, and following this guidance.
- Self-Worth – to know and own your unconditional worth.

The formula for Self-Love is:

Self (belief + trust + worth) = Self-Love

In the eyes of Source, you can make no mistakes and you can do no wrong. Source sees you and knows *who you really are*, and no matter how far from the light you may wander, divine love remains with you, always and forever.

Self-love is to feel the love of Source – to welcome the love that is specifically flowing to you and for you.

The Demonstration of Self-love

Self-love is allowing the flow of divine love, but it must also be demonstrated in the ways we treat and feel about ourselves, including our bodies, lives and past-selves.

Love Your Body

Imagine that your consciousness has been placed within your body, so that your body is a sacred temple that houses your consciousness, in order for you to experience life in this physical reality.

The temple that is your body is specially created for you and is designed to provide everything you need in order to experience the life you intended to live. Unlike man-made temples, the temple of your body is also a vehicle that will take you where you want to go, allowing you to experience everything desired in this reality. It is extremely resilient, flexible, intelligent and intuitive, and it is even self-healing. Your interactive body allows you to feel great pleasure through all the senses; beautiful music, intoxicating scents, delicious tastes, breathtaking sights, and indescribable sensation, from the gentlest breeze against your cheek to the most wonderful delights.

> *Signpost on the path*
> *You are not only worthy of love, you are actually made of the very love that you seek.*

Your body gives you the ability to create great works of art, incredible innovation and mind-expanding possibilities on every level. It allows you to play, dance, sing, paint and procreate, as well as experience the full spectrum of emotion – from love to hate and everything in between.

No matter what you ask your body to do, it never judges you. Your body loves you unconditionally and will undergo extreme challenges for you. Even if you disregard or ignore your body's warnings, it does its best to compensate and be there for you, but, as much as your body is committed to supporting you, it needs something in return. That special something is love!

The more you love your body, the more it receives Life Force Energy, and the healthier it can be, so it can continue to perform in all the ways you choose.

Withholding love from your body is the same as withholding love from yourself.

When you negatively judge your body, it believes you without question. When you tell your body, it is not good enough or you criticize your body for being "too much this" or "not enough that," you are unknowingly withholding love, and, as a result, you are cutting off Life Force Energy. When you allow others to judge your body, and you believe those judgments, your body experiences betrayal and Life Force Energy is also inhibited.

Your body will do its best to function without adequate Life Force Energy, but, eventually, it will suffer and break down, and you might experience illness, injury or disease.

Healing the body requires loving the body exactly as it is right now. You cannot judge your body and love your body at the same time. When you love your body without conditions, your love becomes a conduit for Life Force Energy to flow in the direction of your love - Life Force Energy heals whatever needs to be healed.

Your body does not have to be in tip top shape in order to love it. You can love it right now, and, if you desire to improve it, your body will respond infinitely better to love than it ever did to judgment.

Everything you put in your body counts!

Ingesting low vibration products, such as processed foods, preservatives, chemicals, toxins and artificial anything can lower the vibration of your body. Everything you put in and on your body has a vibration and when your body interacts with food and other products, your body takes on energy.

Many awakening people are becoming vegan in order to avoid ingesting hormones and chemicals, as well "animal fear.

Your body is an entire eco-system with trillions of cells and even more healthy bacteria, and they all work for you and are programmed to serve you – you could even say that you are their god. Because each cell and bacteria have consciousness, and that consciousness can be instructed and programmed, you can tell your body what to do, but you must not be a condemning god who punishes and withholds love, but, instead, if you want your body to respond positively to your command, you must be a loving and kind god.

It is incredibly important to talk nice to your body - when you are negative about your body, you lower your body's vibration and when you speak well of your body, its vibration naturally rises. Not surprisingly, self-love is one of the best ways to increase your vibration.

Note, when you are conscious and awake, it is possible to override harmful effects of any substance, simply with the power of your intention.

Love Your Past-Self

When you think about your past-self (from yesterday or yesteryear) do you feel guilt, regret or shame? Many of us are in the habit of judging our past-selves for stupid mistakes or things we still regret. What we don't realize is that when we judge *who we used to be*, we withhold love from our former selves, while also inhibiting present day self-love. You cannot love your present day self any more than you love your past-self. If you withhold love from your past-self, due to guilt, regret or shame, it is the same as withholding present day self-love.

We all think we make mistakes and have lengthy lists of things we could have done different or better, but, the thing is, it is our past choices that have allowed us to grow and evolve into who we are now. Your past-self did the absolute best he/she could do at the time. Judging your past-self does not help you in anyway, and, in fact, it keeps you stuck at the exact moments in time where you hold judgment. Additionally, if your energy is stuck in the past, it inhibits the flow of present day Life Force Energy.

If you are going to practice self-love, it means that you must love all of you - your past, present and future self. You cannot love your twenty year old self, but hate your fifteen year old self.

There was not a single moment of your life in which Source judged you, and withheld love, so why do it to yourself? Maybe it is time to forgive your past-self and set him/her free, and maybe it is time to speak with your past-self, appreciate his/her challenges, and courage, and finally offer unconditional love.

As you shower your past-self with unconditional love, that love ripples forward and immediately reaches you in this moment.

Love Your Life

If you love yourself, why would you be living a life you hate? When you truly love yourself, your natural inclination is to create a life you also love. It is not possible to love yourself and hate your life or vice versa - the two go hand-in-hand.

Oftentimes, a sign of *self-love scarcity* is tolerating an unhappy job or unhealthy relationship, or maybe living in a way that compromises wellbeing.

When you love yourself, you do what it takes to create a life you love. You do not settle for limitation, mediocrity or living a life that doesn't support the real you. Through self-love, your life is a canvas, and you are the ultimate painter.

Do you see that there is a big difference between proving your worth by improving yourself versus improving the dream that is your life?

The content of the dream makes us no more or less worthy, as all experiences offer and hold the same value, but this doesn't mean we cannot create the best dream possible - why not? Isn't this a sign of self-love? Why would you want to suffer in a bad dream when you can have a wonderful dream?

Only you know the dream that is the best and brightest for you, but when you choose it and align with it, the Universe guarantees delivery - because your best dream is the Universe's dream for you!

If it is not possible to change current circumstances, for one reason or another, can you release resistance and love the life you have; fully knowing that even in its most challenging expression, it is still a divine gift?

Sometimes, we are afraid to love our current day lives because we think that if we love a less than ideal life, we cannot change it, or won't want to change it. So, to be on the safe side, we withhold love, so that we will make the necessary changes, but, sooner or later, we realize that the strategy of resistance never works.

What you resist, persists because you get energy from resisting and the EGO will not release sources of energy.

Self-Judgment

If you want to make changes in your body, mind or life, you must give up self-judgment, as self-judgment is the glue that holds your challenges and issues together. When you are no longer generating energy from self-judgment, the things you want to change or improve can be accomplished through inspiration, and the enlightened desire that comes through True-Self embodiment.

Enlightened desire is the desire to reach and experience your personal potential; how strong, flexible and beautiful can the body be, how ingenious the mind, how enlightened the spirit? The desire does not come as an attempt to prove worth, or push away unworthiness, but, rather, as the natural unfoldment of self-expression, curiosity and inspiration.

In order to reach the state of inspirational desire for *exploring your greatest potential,* not only must you drop self-judgment - you must embrace yourself wherever you are. Instead of judging and resisting a condition, you must allow it; approaching it from a space of compassion. You don't have to accept it, as implicit in acceptance is non-acceptance (*you will never say or think, "I accept something" if you are not first judging it*). When we allow, we release judgment and resistance, and energy flows - offering possibility and even transformation.

The process of allowing invites that which you allow to shift and evolve into a higher version that you call forth through your loving desire. If you want a better body, love the one you have right now. If you want more money, love the money you have right now. If you want a better home, love the one you have right now. *The more you love where you are, the more energy flows and the more power you have to manifest.*

Self-Love List

If self-love is an essential component to True-Self embodiment, it makes sense to do whatever it takes to develop an abundance of self-love. The following exercise asks you to think about all the things you like and love about yourself. Even if you have resistance at first, make sure you complete the exercise because it will make a huge difference in how you see and feel about yourself. On a full sheet of paper, brainstorm "What do I love/like about myself?"

To help you generate some ideas, please consider:

- What do you love/like about your body?
- What do you love/like about your mind?
- What do you love/like about your spirit?
- What do you love/like about how you live your life?
- What do you love/like about yourself that doesn't fit into any of these categories?

Mirror, Mirror on the Wall

For a minimum of five minutes each day, stare into a mirror, looking into your own eyes. Drop all judgments and resistance, and simply look at yourself in the mirror and say, "I love you." As you say "I love you" to yourself in the mirror, also notice that the self in the mirror is saying it back to you. Do this every day for at least one month. It's normal for this process to feel odd or uncomfortable at first, but do it anyway. There are enormous gifts to be discovered.

Divine Love is Found in the Now

Your greatest gift is received when you are present. This is the gift of divine love. It is gift wrapped and waiting for you in every moment, but you must be present in order to experience this *present of love*. If you are re-living the past or pre-living the future, you will miss the love that is here for you in this moment.

Being present requires that you drop resistance and embrace this moment with unbiased awareness. It is through your non-judgmental awareness that love can flow.

When you are present in this now, the loving energy of Source flows through you, bringing health, abundance, creativity, inspiration and love. If you are not present, you misalign with this love, and you misalign with your dreams and desires.

You are love, you are light and all is well.

TRUE LOVE IS SELF-FULL

Does taking time off or doing things for yourself make you feel guilty?

Part of you knows that it is necessary to take time for yourself, but another part feels incredibly guilty for even thinking of it. What's going on here?

Wanting to do something, but feeling guilty for doing it, is a symptom of Split Energy Syndrome.

Split energy results when the EGO's agenda clashes with the desire of your True-self.

The EGO's main agenda is generating energy by motor-vating you to prove your worth, and because this program never takes a break, the EGO requires you to be consistently productive – doing all the things you need to do so that others find you worthy; this includes fulfilling the roles you play, making money, living up to expectations and proving that you are needed - all so that you are deemed worthy of life and love, by those around you.

Any desire or inclination toward "useless behavior" is immediately thwarted by the EGO; useless behavior is any behavior that does not ensure current worthiness or potentially increase it. It is not that the EGO thinks you don't deserve some time to yourself or special care, it's just that the EGO is not programmed in that way. Self-care (beyond basic needs) is not on its agenda.

The EGO needs a way to persuade you away from behaviors that don't produce value according to the Worthiness Program – no big surprise, its secret weapon is guilt. The EGO gets you to stick to the agenda by motor-vating you with guilt – just the thought of putting off your "to do" list is enough to produce painful bouts of the stuff. In order to avoid this unforgiving emotion, you probably do whatever guilt tells you to do, or, if you do bypass it, shame may come knocking on your door.

Shame says, *"Who do you think you are that you can choose yourself over others?"*

Shame has a way of making us feel worthless. Or, maybe we hear the EGO whisper, "Selfish" and we believe that it is true. We are programmed to believe that it is wrong, and possibly even evil, to be selfish. Instead, we must aspire to selflessness in order to feel good about ourselves, but *selflessness is just another sneaky aspect of the Worthiness Program.*

Indeed, the crafty EGO may even motor-vate us to put everyone before us because we are supposed to be kind, giving and loving. Don't fall for this hoax – it's just another way to prove worth. Yes, that's right, the EGO motor-vates us to put others first (and ourselves last) to demonstrate we are good, nice or even spiritual so that others see us worthy and hopefully they will give us approval, acceptance, appreciation or whatever our primary emotional need might be.

If you are doing one thing in order to get another, it has "EGO" written all over it. When you are selfless, so that you can get credit or attention for your act of kindness, your selfless act has invisible strings attached and it is tainted with EGO-driven energy.

For many of us, being called "selfish" is worse than any four letter word, and, in fact, the fear of being labeled "selfish" often causes us to ignore our own important needs and deepest desires. When our entire lives are shaped around the foreboding dread of appearing selfish, not only do we suppress expression, we also disregard what would bring us the most joy in life. We might even stay trapped in jobs and long term relationships well past their expiration date, simply because we are afraid that our choices might be deemed self-serving to others.

On the spiritual path, or even the path of being a "good person," we are often told to think of others before ourselves. Maybe as children, we were taught that it is bad to be selfish or we were even punished for thinking of ourselves first. In theory, it might sound nice to put the needs of others before our own, but when we constantly put ourselves last without question, we stay asleep and disempowered. *How can you awaken, when you are ignoring your Self?*

I spent the first twenty three years of my life pleasing others. Whatever someone asked of me, I always said yes. That sounds like a beautiful way to live except for one big problem. Every time I said yes to the desires of others, I was unconsciously saying no to my own. It was, as if, the entire world was vastly more important than me, but I didn't know any better. It was the way I was raised and there was a big pay-off for always pleasing others. But the pay-off didn't make up for the huge emotional cost of my own well-being.

To be perfectly honest, I was terribly afraid of being called *selfish* so I bent over backward to avoid this debilitating label, but it didn't work because no matter how much I did for others, if I even thought of myself first, or I said no, I would be called *selfish*. Even though I would do back flips to prove them wrong, under the surface, I had growing resentment.

The first problem with always putting yourself last is that it perpetuates the Worthiness Program, because when you always put others first, it tells the subconscious mind that your needs and wants are not as important as the needs and wants of others, and, therefore, you are less worthy in comparison. It is a vicious cycle because when you don't know your worth, you degrade yourself and negate your own personal needs, thereby increasing your sense of unworthiness.

The second problem with always putting yourself last is that it perpetuates the EGO while displacing your True-Self; it is only the EGO that says you must not be selfish, and if you always listen to it, not only does it grow stronger, it also keeps you from embodying your True-Self.

Falsely believing that our needs are less important, or we are not worthy of self-care, lowers our vibration and perpetuates True-Self displacement. Additionally, if you are not accustomed to listening to your own needs and responding fully, how can you ever recognize the voice of your True-Self? If you are not following the inner guidance of your Wise and True Self, there is no way to be in proper resonance, and without vibrational resonance, your True-Self will remain somewhere between slightly misaligned and fully displaced.

When we keep putting ourselves last, eventually we become emotionally and maybe even physically depleted. This pain is our inner guidance system telling us that something is wrong, and we have to change in order to heal. If we continue to ignore our own needs and desires, our physical or emotional bodies may give out – forcing us to withdraw our attention from others and focusing our attention on healing ourselves. Maybe, then, we even use illness as an excuse to take care of ourselves. But, we don't need the excuse of illness or emotional distress in order to start putting our needs first.

Surely, it is time to question this idea of selfishness. Maybe we have been taught all wrong. After all, if selflessness was the way to go, wouldn't we all be so much happier?

After years of putting everyone first, I had a big wake-up call. Because I suffered horribly from chronic fatigue and I became consistently sick and depressed, I knew I couldn't live the way I was living anymore, so I courageously, and, for the first time, decided to say, "No." I said no to everything that I didn't want to do and anything that felt out of integrity for me.

Do you know what happened? Everyone called me *selfish*, but because I had chosen to take care of myself this time, it went right over my head. I think my mom and boyfriend even got together to discuss how selfish I had become. But, no matter how many times I was called selfish, I didn't budge, and it didn't affect me. I was clear and confident for the first time in my life, and I began to feel better. My energy returned and my outlook on life began to brighten. As I was taking care of myself, I was beginning to remember who I was - and it felt so good to be me again. "No" became my mantra, and my key to emotional freedom.

Embracing Sacred Selfishness

Sacred Selfishness is about honoring yourself. You are a sacred being in physical form, and *who you are* on all levels deserves love, respect and the utmost kindness. In order to embrace Sacred Selfishness, you must let go of all negative beliefs about being selfish. You must stop feeding yourself ideas that keep you from self-honoring, and you must stop worrying about what the world might say, or think.

Sacred Selfishness may mean speaking your truth, taking care of your emotional and physical needs or ending a relationship or a path that is not working for you. Sacred Selfishness might also mean following your heart, spending time alone, and only doing things when you want to do them. It might also involve letting go of "shoulds," "have to's" and emotional baggage like guilt, regret and obligation. As you begin to take better care of yourself, set boundaries and teach others how to be in relationship with you, you experience Sacred Selfishness and you become Self-Full.

Sacred Selfishness is about giving yourself permission to take care of you!

The truth is, **you were meant to be responsible for your own life.** You have been born into a sacred body and a beautiful life. Who do you think is supposed to care for it? Your first responsibility is to you. Remembering that you are the caretaker of your body, as well as your life - *how might you live better?*

Once you master self-responsibility, then, and only then, can you be of contribution to the world. You cannot give to anyone if you are empty inside. The giving must only come from a surplus of well-being. Well-being is the result of self-responsibility. When you are self-full, you naturally have an abundance to give without any cost to yourself.

Sacred Selfishness Means Choosing Yourself

Many of us go through life putting ourselves last because we have never chosen ourselves for the starring roles of our lives. We have carelessly given that role to everyone else - partners, parents, kids, friends, co-workers - anyone but us. The thing is, *if you don't choose you for the starring role of your life, no one else will.*

Life is asking you to choose yourself. Not to negate yourself, put yourself second or disregard yourself for any reason, at anytime, but to choose you - not just once and be done with it, but over and over again. Especially, not to wait for someone else to choose you because that can never work. If you don't choose you, first and foremost, how can anyone else choose you? But, when you do choose you, you become empowered and fulfilled and then it appears as if the entire world chooses you, and they do.

Once you have chosen yourself an inexhaustible number of times, there is a point where the choice becomes seamless and there is no longer a choice. It is, as if, something deep inside ignites and fullness births you, raising you up to be *who you really are*

Living as your True-Self, in all your magnificence, you are perpetually filled with inspiration, abundance and Life Force Energy.

From this space of self-full magistracy, the drama falls away and you are left with the purity of your own free spirit. Inspired by Source, a new paradigm of life is experienced through you, and by you.

> *Signpost on the path*
>
> *To become authentically Self-Less, you must master Sacred Selfishness*

Becoming Selfless

At some point, the most unexpected thing occurs. The self-full self that is now completely you disappears before your eyes, and what is left is *a self that is Self-Less.*

Because you are full and need nothing from anyone or anything, you effortlessly evolve into selflessness. This is the organic evolution from Self-full to Self-less. This is the state that the mystics tell us to attain, but what they fail to mention is that the path to selflessness is in choosing yourself and becoming so self-full that you need nothing.

We are taught that selflessness is a spiritual attribute and if we are on the spiritual path, we may adopt the idea of being selfless, but being selfless does not make us more spiritual. *Selflessness is a byproduct of spiritual awakening, but you do not wake up by being selfless.* In fact, artificial selflessness often keeps people asleep because putting yourself last, keeps you disconnected from your True-Self, and, if you are disconnected, you are asleep.

If we overlook our own needs and put ourselves last so that we can be selfless, we are putting the cart before the horse – limiting our ability to grow and evolve into a higher version of who we have known ourselves to be.

After many months of saying no, and meaning it, everyone stopped calling me selfish. Probably because it no longer made me sway to their wishes. But, then something very unexpected began to happen. Because I was taking really good care of myself, I had a great deal more energy and good feelings. That energy and good-will naturally overflowed from me and I had the desire to say yes - to help where help was needed and to be of service in whatever way was called for. At some point, I realized that I was doing the same things for the people in my life, as I had done in my "pre-selfish" era, but now it was coming from an entirely different place inside me. I was at choice. I wasn't saying yes because I couldn't say no. I was saying yes because I was inspired to say yes, and I had the natural energy to support that choice.

Instead of obligation and guilt being the fire in my heart, love became the guiding force. It turns out, love is infinitely more self-sustaining than EGO-driven guilt or obligation.

Ultimately, Sacred Selfishness allows you to experience a sense of wholeness, where love for yourself overflows naturally. From Absolute Fullness, you naturally desire to serve and it is done with unconditional love because that is *who you really are*, and, as a result, you experience unlimited Life Force Energy and enthusiasm.

When you finally need nothing - you have everything to give.

If you want to be the best you that you can be, you must honor yourself in every way. As you accept your own value and worth, you will naturally care for your divine body and sacred life, and, as you do, you will remember *who you really are*, and you will naturally awaken as your True-Self.

This is the sacred journey to awakening as your True-Self.

Let's Recap

- True-Self Integration requires unconditional self-love, which means believing in yourself, trusting yourself and knowing that you are intrinsically and unconditionally worthy.
- When you are present in this now, the loving energy of Source flows through you, bringing health, abundance, creativity, inspiration and love.
- Always putting yourself last perpetuates the Worthiness Program, by telling the subconscious mind that you are less worthy.
- When you withhold love from your body, past-self or current life, you withhold love from yourself, and withholding self-love displaces your True-Self.
- Self-judgment blocks self-love.
- Love of self is demonstrated by creating a life you love.
- Being present is an act of self-love because this is where love flows.
- Sacred Selfishness is about honoring yourself and giving yourself permission to take care of you!

In the following chapters, we will explore:

- The Open Door to True-Self!
- Over 20 EGO Pitfalls and how to avoid them
- Reprogramming the EGO
- Tips for Channeling Life Force Energy
- How Not to be a Negative Energy Sponge
- The Art of True-Self Living!

Chapter 35

The Open Door to True-Self

Indeed, there are four elements to True-Self integration, self-love, unconditional worth, intrinsic power and healing emotional wounds, but let's not overlook the open door to instant embodiment.

Presence is the key to instantly being the True You!

You don't need to heal, change or fix anything in order to embody your True-Self. You only need to be present - here and now. True-Self embodiment can happen anytime you become fully present.

Presence is the result of being conscious in the present moment, but what does it mean to be conscious?

The word conscious comes from the word Consciousness.

Consciousness is the eternal back-drop for life. It is the space from which everything springs forth and ultimately returns. What happens in the space of Consciousness may have a beginning and an end, but Consciousness, itself, has no beginning and has no end. What happens in the space of Consciousness may be finite and definable, but Consciousness, itself, is infinite and indefinable. Consciousness is the absolute source of all creation, and the bottomless well from where Life Force Energy flows. Consciousness is, in fact, the sum of all existence, and because everyone and everything is made from Consciousness, we can conclude that everyone and everything possesses Consciousness. Indeed, the rock experiences consciousness vastly different than the sea, and the sea experiences consciousness vastly different than you and me, yet, despite expression and manifestation, it is all the same One Consciousness.

Consciousness is creative, which is why we call it Creative Consciousness. There is really no definitive point or purpose to the creation of anything in the Universe, so there is nothing to prove, attain or accomplish. Consciousness just does what Consciousness does – it creates and it experiences its creations, and that's it. It is so simple, that if we are searching for the meaning of life, we might miss it entirely.

With infinite Universal Energy anything is possible and nothing is out of reach.

Desiring to create and experience every facet of every possibility, Consciousness perfectly fractured into quad-zillions of conscious pieces – like a holograph, each containing the whole, but seemingly separate. Along with the birth of every being in all of creation, you are an individual aspect of Consciousness, and, as such, you are on an extraordinary mission, sent by Consciousness.

You were given life in order to experience a specific version of reality that can only be seen through your eyes and experienced through your life. Your gifts, challenges and individual perspective collectively influence your participation and perception of life, making no other being exactly like you, thereby offering surprising variety that comes from free-will.

Providing Consciousness with rare experiences that only you can offer, by being you, your purpose is to live this unique version of life, and, moment to moment, relate your observations back to Consciousness, but, in order to do so, ***you must consciously experience your life***, otherwise, there really is no point. This means that in order for Consciousness to experientially grow from your life experiences, *the True You must be conscious.*

When you are conscious as your True-Self, the channel is open and you allow Consciousness to experience life as you, and through you, but, when you are not conscious, the channel is closed and you block Consciousness. If you can imagine, when you are unconscious, your eyes are shut and Consciousness cannot see, and, when you are conscious, your eyes are open and Consciousness can see.

You serve Consciousness and fulfill your purpose whenever the True You is awake and conscious.

What's in it for you? Aside from divine fulfillment, as a channel for Consciousness, you are plugged into Life Force Energy and this energy flows through you, naturally resulting in peace, joy or bliss (your mind's interpretation of Life Force Energy flowing through your body in abundance).

If you are sleep walking through life, and the EGO is in control, your unconsciousness serves no one and nothing - which is fine, but you miss the point of being here. If you are not consciously experiencing your life, Consciousness does not grow or expand, and your personal result is likely feelings of non-fulfillment, varying degrees of anxiety and bouts of depression.

Here is a secret that can set you free...

It really doesn't matter what you do, or how you do it, as long as you are conscious as you do it. There is no failure or success, no good or bad, no positive or negative - because to Consciousness all experiences are equally valuable.

Through your eyes, ears, mouth, nose and kinesthetic sense, you have the ability to witness and experience something that can never be duplicated in all of creation. This includes every moment of your life, and, if you are not present in the moment, it is lost forever, because it can never be repeated. Possibly, there will be other ones like it, but this one-of-a-kind moment will never come again, so, if you are not conscious, this precious moment is gone for eternity.

Your life is vibrant living art, and when you release all inhibitions and find the courage to be who you really are, the Divine shines through the exquisite expression that is you.

It is true that most of humanity goes through life in an unconscious state of living. Sleep walking through relationships and fearfully hiding through uncomfortable situations, the EGO obliging works over-time, and, in fact, you could say that the EGO runs the world, but this is all about to change. Humanity is on the precipice of global awakening - chaos and havoc are signs that this is happening, due to the fact that the collective EGO is giving one last hooray, but the "motors" of humanity are seizing and it is time to awaken.

Awakening is synonymous with our True-Selves becoming conscious, and, if you are now reading these words, *you can be sure that the True You is in the process of awakening.*

Awakening is inevitable and you couldn't stop it, even if you wanted to, but there are many things that you can do to ease the journey. The information and guidance in this book are intended to support you in this sacred process. Knowing that awakening unfolds as your True-Self becomes fully conscious, the more you practice over-riding the EGO and being conscious in the present moment, the quicker the True You will awaken.

Being Present

Being Conscious is Being Present.

Being present can be described as mindful awareness - being aware of "what is" in this moment without resistance, story or trying to change it in anyway. You are the witness to life as it is, but this is not a stagnant process. Indeed, you are a participant in life as much as you are the conscious witness. Living in the moment, allows you to respond authentically, as your True-Self, manifesting in spontaneous living, as well as the manifestation of desire.

When the EGO is dormant, subconscious programs no longer control your life, and, therefore, the True You responds to the moment as it is – this one aspect of True-Self Living transforms your entire life, and combined with the abundant flow of Life Force Energy, you have the capability to live your greatest dreams and explore your most fascinating adventures.

Mindfully living in presence allows you to have and attain goals, but the process is not EGO-driven. When your dreams and goals are the ones that Source has for you, simply by following inner guidance and living moment to moment, you are on the path, and even though it is not necessary for joy or fulfillment, success in eminent.

There are so many ways to be present in any given moment, and the choice is up to you.

You might be conscious of your heart beating in your chest, the taste of cold water on a hot day, the smell of cookies baking in the oven, the sound of trees blowing in the wind, the feel of electricity in the air on a stormy night, or you might even be conscious of the entire Universe pulsating through you, and around you. Your full awareness on any aspect of creation aligns you with Life Force Energy, and the flow of energy fills you up from the inside out.

Meditation, doing what you love to do, having fun, etc.., can all set the stage for Presence, but, as soon as you get distracted, start worrying or you are triggered in some way, your True-Self goes unconscious, and the EGO automatically re-engages. You cannot fool the EGO, pretending to be present when you're not, which means that even a little distraction prevents you from being present. It's all or nothing.

No doubt, it is very difficult to stay present when subconscious programs are running and you are frequently triggered - indicating the need to turn them off and the importance of doing so.

However, you don't have to worry about staying consciously present for the rest of your life – that huge goal just keeps you from being conscious in this moment. In fact, don't worry about the future at all, because it is only now that counts. The only moment you ever need to be present is now.

Every moment that you are conscious in the now accumulates, and, as you spend more and more time in the present moment, those moments turn into hours, days, weeks, months and years, and, sooner or later, you will be consciously living in the present moment full time.

In the process of becoming conscious on a permanent basis, the EGO is transcended and your triggers, fears and insecurities are permanently nullified.

Being conscious is another way of saying that your True-Self is embodied because the "you" who is conscious is the True You.

The more you invoke your True-Self, through consciously being present, the more attuned you will be to embodiment, and the quicker you will notice when the EGO takes charge. This awareness allows you to make the necessary adjustments or fine tuning to override the EGO, while the True You stays in the driver's seat.

If you only remember one thing...

Remember that the EGO is programmed to turn on whenever you are not fully conscious and present in this moment. *Going unconscious is the On Switch for the EGO.*

This also means that because the EGO is not programmed to operate in the present moment, consciously dropping into presence **deactivates** the EGO, but only for as long as you are present.

Presence is the Off Switch for the EGO.

Mindful Curiosity

When you recognize that the EGO is in charge, please understand that you cannot "get out of EGO" by resisting it because resistance only feeds it, and since fighting against the EGO is not an act of consciousness, it is not a fight you can ever win, or a good strategy to transcend the EGO.

As long as you are unconscious the EGO is in charge.

When you recognize the EGO, instead of resisting or judging, notice what you notice and simply be mindfully curious. Maybe ask yourself, "What is this space of EGO that I'm in?" Look around and see what you can learn from it. The more you understand the EGO and its hidden workings, the greater your power to transcend subconscious programming.

In the judgment of being unconscious, the EGO continues to operate.

In the allowance of being unconscious, the True You becomes conscious.

The practice of allowance is the practice of letting go, and the more you let go, the higher your consciousness will rise.

Letting Go

True-Self embodiment is much more about undoing than doing.

There is nothing that you must learn or become in order to live as your True-Self. Instead, there are many things that you commonly do and think that cause the True You to go unconscious, and simply by releasing these disempowering practices, you will create a welcome home for your True Being.

It is the disempowering practice of holding on (to anything) that makes us go unconscious and lose presence, and, therefore, one of the best True-Self Practices is letting go!

During moments of letting go, the True You automatically becomes conscious in the present moment, consequently, aligning with the flow of Life Force Energy, and resulting in the experience of blissful wellness.

Letting go sounds so simple, but, for most of us, letting go is the hardest thing to do. The reason for this is due to the fact that the EGO is holding on because it is programmed to protect you, and, therefore, it is not going to let go, unless it is assured that it is safe to let go. This means that the EGO needs to know what it is letting go to - if you do not know what you are letting go "to," letting go can trigger fear.

This is where your own spiritual beliefs come in.

When you let go, you are not letting go to just anything - you are letting go to something infinitely greater and wiser than the human you - be that an all-loving Creator, Source, Universe, Divine, Big G.... or whatever it is to you.

Yes, this requires trust, but that is the point. Letting go requires that you trust whatever it is that you truly believe in, but you must find out for yourself. Do not take the word of religion, parents, society or anything else. You must make this discovery yourself – on your own terms.

You also need to know exactly what you are letting go of...

If you look closely, you will see that the only thing that we can ever really release is our thoughts – we cannot let go of tangible people, places and things because we never really have them anyway. The only thing we ever possess is our thoughts about anything, but thoughts can be powerful prisons.

Since we believe our thoughts are always true, we unconsciously attach identity to all of them, and this false attachment imprisons us, eventually causing pain and suffering.

But, of course, the divine purpose of pain and suffering is to make us let go of disempowering beliefs and limiting thoughts.

However, we don't need to wait until we are in pain – we can just let go of painful thoughts and beliefs. More on letting go of thoughts shortly, but the practice of letting go that I have found to be most powerful and effective is letting go to this moment.

You don't have to let go of everything at once for the rest of your life - the EGO would definitely revolt, and it would not work. The real trick to letting go is simply letting go in this present moment only, but this includes a full letting go: letting go of your roles, masks, relationships, possessions, desires, attachments, obligations, stresses, worries, expectations and all else. Remember, you can only let go of your thoughts and beliefs about these things because there is nothing else to release.

You can reclaim any, or all, of it later, but for the current moment, there is absolutely nothing that you have to hold onto. In ***this moment***, you can fully free yourself, and take a deep breath.

Experiencing this space of freedom requires conscious practice, but the more you practice *just being,* the more you will reprogram the EGO, and the easier it will become to let go in all circumstances. You will likely discover this space feels so good that you will want to experience it all the time, and, as a result, when the EGO takes over, it will feel so uncomfortable that you will want to make the shift back to your true inner being immediately.

As you let go in the moment...

Place your focus on your breath as you release all your mental attachments, thoughts and beliefs to this moment. Breathe into the space that letting go opens up for you. Repeat several times a day, or discover your own best way to let go. Letting go is as easy as exhaling.

Letting go to this moment brings you immediately into presence – where your True-Self resides and all your power dwells.

In the process of True-Self integration, it is important to recognize that there will be days when your True-Self is fully embodied, and days when your True-Self is misaligned or even watching from a distance - being kind and patient with yourself will smooth out the bumps in the road and allow for even more embodiment.

Let's Recap

- Your gifts, challenges and individual perspective collectively influence your participation and perception of life, allowing you to experience a specific version of reality that can only be experienced as you.
- Your purpose is to live this unique version of life, and relate your observations to Consciousness, but, in order to do so, *the True You must be conscious.*
- There is not a single thing that you came here to do or fulfill, and, in fact, it really doesn't matter what you do, or how you do it, as long as you are conscious as you do it.
- There is no failure or success, no good or bad, no positive or negative – because to Consciousness all experiences are equally valuable.
- Awakening is synonymous with your True-Self becoming conscious.
- Living in the moment allows you to respond authentically, as your True-Self, manifesting in spontaneous living.
- *Going unconscious is the On Switch for the EGO.*
- *Presence is the Off Switch for the EGO.*
- It is the disempowering practice of holding on (to anything) that makes us go unconscious and lose presence.
- During moments of letting go, the True You becomes conscious in the present moment, consequently, aligning with the flow of Life Force Energy, and resulting in the experience of blissful wellness.

Chapter 36

Avoiding EGO Pitfalls

The EGO is so pervasive that we don't even recognize it most of the time. Oftentimes, we only identify it when it is blatantly out of control, or, more accurately, *blatantly controlling.*

It can be a little overwhelming to realize just how much the EGO runs our lives, but, nonetheless, if we are to become conscious and live our lives as our True-Selves, we must be completely self-honest, and we must pinpoint all the ways in which the EGO *calls the shots* so that we can consciously make choices that are in integrity with our True-Selves.

An important aspect of transcending the EGO is understanding all the ways in which it operates, and motor-vates your behavior. Once you fathom the dynamics of the EGO, and you ascertain its tools and tricks, you have the power to override unconscious programming. By identifying patterns, the unconscious becomes conscious, and, as a result, the Space of Choice naturally unfolds.

When you are unconscious, there is no space between your external environment and your internal reactions, but once you are conscious, a huge space opens up where you can choose to make choices that support your True-Self. So, instead of falling into the same pit over and over, you will have the awareness to notice the pit, and because you will know how to avoid it, you will be able to break disempowering patterns, thereby overriding the EGO's programmed reactions.

> *Signpost on the path*
>
> *The journey of True-Self is a journey from unconscious to conscious - from asleep to awake*
>
> ---
>
> If we are to transcend unconscious behavior, we must first become conscious in order to understand the hidden dynamics that cause that behavior. In this sacred process we embrace the power to wake-up as our True-Selves.

By exploring common EGO Pitfalls, the following section will help you put some more pieces of the puzzle together, while also offering guidance and guidelines that will help you create a practice that supports True-Self integration.

Once again, if you want tangible shifts in your life, just reading the words is not enough - you must take the necessary actions on a consistent basis, for as long as it takes to experience results.

At the end of each EGO Pitfall below, you will find a suggested True-Self Practice; intended to help you avoid that particular pitfall and/or help you climb out if you've fallen in. Since the following twenty plus EGO Pitfalls are not in any particular order, you can begin your True-Self Practice anywhere that resonates for you, but it is usually best to start with one True-Self Practice at a time, and add on once you navigate the pitfall successfully, but always do what feels best to you – above all else, *trust yourself.*

By creating your own True-Self Practice, you have the power and know-how to override EGO programming, while aligning with *who you really are*.

Keeping a journal also supports the journey, so you can track the process.

EGO Pitfall #1 - Resistance

The EGO automatically resists everything that it discerns as a threat; anything that might reduce your sense of worth, lower your status, disempower you, overlook your primary emotional need or deflate the EGO in anyway, but it also resists the unknown because the unknown represents similar danger.

Because resistance motor-vates you to move away from the undesirable, it generates energy, and, therefore, the EGO favors resistance.

> ***Signpost on the path***
>
> *When in resistance, beware of EGO*
>
> *Because resistance is often the EGO's response to an emotional trigger, resistance generally indicates that the EGO has taken charge.*

The problem is, resistance cuts us off Life Force Energy, which means that when we are in resistance, we lack the natural energy to create what we really want - making it much harder to move away from that which we resist and much harder to move toward that which we prefer. Without the flow of Life Force Energy, if we are to make any changes in our lives, the EGO must generate energy, but EGO generated energy can cause more problems than it solves - giving us even more to resist.

If you desire "smooth sailing" to any dream, desire or goal, never take action while in resistance, because if you try to struggle through resistance, everything will be twice as hard and take twice as long.

The moment we resist anything, we disconnect from the present moment, we go unconscious and the EGO takes control. In comparison to the possible pain associated with an unwanted experience, being cut off from our True-Selves makes us feel a million times worse.

We all know that when we like something, we automatically hold on to it, and when we don't like something, we tend to resist, but the only reason we ever resist anything is because we don't like how it makes us feel, or how it might make us feel, yet, resistance often shows up as fear, anger, frustration, hate, impatience or judgment - in other words, by resisting one "bad feeling" we may end up feeling even worse.

Resistance is the result of believing that something (or someone) should be different than it is, but it is never the object or subject of our resistance that causes us emotional pain - *it is the resistance itself.*

The opposite of resistance is not acceptance, as non-acceptance is implicit in the word acceptance. We only try to accept something as a result of not accepting it. If we are really in the space of acceptance, we generally don't think about it in terms of acceptance, but, if acceptance is tainted by the subtle essence of resistance, what is the opposite of resistance?

The opposite of resistance is allowance

By allowing "what is" we don't push against the unwanted, we don't give energy to it and we don't call it to us. The state of allowance is non-judgmental and non-controlling. When we allow the outside world to be as it is, we have no desire to interfere or improve, and there is no opinion that we know what is better or best. We trust life and we trust the Source of life.

In this gentle state, there is no need to change a thing - and because we are not trying to "change or control," life can easily, and often quickly, shift and evolve on its own. When we react, we resist, and when we resist, we feed energy to that which we are resisting, unconsciously perpetuating the undesirable.

It is undoubtedly true that "*what you love, loves you,*" but, equally as true, "*what you resist, loves you too.*"

Your energy acts like an invisible magnet drawing the focus of your energy to you, so, whatever you put energy on through love or resistance is fueled by your energy, and is drawn to you, according to the law of attraction.

Indeed, it can be scary to allow things to be as they are, especially when they appear to contradict what you really want, but, here's the thing; the Universe knows who you are and also knows what you want, because this is also what the Universe wants for you. The Universe actually communicates to you through your dreams and desires because your dreams and desires are the dreams and desires of the Universe for you! If you trust this, and you also trust that the Universe is conspiring on your behalf, even when it seems otherwise, there is no reason to resist anything because you confidently know that things always turn out well for you, and somehow even the worst experiences inevitably turn out to be incredible gifts in disguise - all supporting your unique journey and the manifestation of your dreams.

In the space of allowance, you give the Universe plenty of room to create on your behalf, even when things aren't looking favorable. You don't have to know how things will turn around - just trust in the divine plan, knowing fully that the Universe has a whole bunch of miracles in its bag of tricks - even when everything seems to be moving in the wrong direction, it can all shift in the blink of an eye.

As the EGO looks for "what is wrong" in order to defend us, we find exactly that, all the while missing the Abracadabra of the Universe that can only be seen and experienced through our True-Selves.

The key to allowance is trusting the Universe.

The more you trust the Universe, the more trustworthy it becomes.

It is not that the Universe is ever untrustworthy, but when you don't really trust the Universe, chances are you are focusing more on what you do not want, and so the Universe brings to you more of what you do not want because that is simply how the Universe works.

Where energy goes the Universe flows.....

This means that wherever you put your energy, via your mental focus, you are actually telling the Universe that this is what you desire, and it responds accordingly. When we get what we do not want, it seems as if we cannot trust the Universe, but this is only because we do not understand the laws of manifestation.

When we truly trust the Universe, we tend not to focus on the undesirable, but rather we focus on what we really desire, knowing and trusting that the Universe responds accordingly in divine time and in the perfect manner. As we trust the Universe in this way, it delivers, and we experience a more trustworthy Universe.

If you don't trust the Universe, it is nearly impossible to allow life to be as it is, but when you do trust, it is quite effortless to allow life to unfold before you. Your part in the process is listening to your inner guidance (which comes from the Universe) and taking only inspired action. If you are making things happen or trying to control outcomes, you can be sure that it is the EGO pushing toward its own pre-programmed agenda – manifesting as stress, overwhelm and frustration, and leading to challenges that could have easily been avoided, if you were following inner guidance and acting according to inspiration.

The True You does not resist anything because there is no reason to resist.

Allowing "*what is*" to be exactly as it is invokes the highest expression of love. It is neither holding on nor letting go. It is graciously witnessing the divine dance that can transform a "denser version" of anything into its fully enlightened expression.

When you allow life to be as it, you suddenly have access to beauty unseen by most.

Without resistance, life is so much sweeter and you can feel so wonderful in the flow of Life Force Energy that it really does not matter what exists before you. Without resistance Source radiates through you, and this divine radiance transforms the world around you.

Allowance is the true secret to being present, living as your True-Self - and always being in the flow.

The Shift

The Art of Dropping Resistance and Dropping into Allowance

In the spirit of avoiding an EGO Pitfall, it is especially helpful to be super conscious of resistance. The quicker you notice it, the easier it is to turn resistance into allowance. Gently notice what you are resisting, and why you are resisting it. You might mentally "play out" your resistance – what might happen as a result of resistance? Does resistance in this circumstance support or hinder your highest intentions? Does it help or hurt the situation? Once you see the bigger picture, resistance may just loosen on its own without any further technique.

If resistance does not loosen through the process of noticing and/or playing it out, try this:

Step 1 – Breathe

Take ten deep breaths, focusing on the inhale and the exhale; slowly inhale to a slow count of five, hold your breath for a slow count of five, slowly exhale to a slow count of five, hold the exhale to a slow count of five – repeat ten times. By the end of ten breaths, the resistance should loosen.

Step 2 – Imagine Giving it Up

The next step is to imagine giving your resistance, and the focus of your resistance, up to a higher power. You can imagine it floating up, or a big hand coming down and swooping it up, or maybe it just evaporates and disappears. Whatever method you use, you should feel a noticeable relief.

You might also affirm "trust and allowance," such an affirmation might be, *"I trust that my current experience is divinely orchestrated, and because the Universe is conspiring on my behalf, I now allow my life to be exactly as it."* A shortened version, *"In trusting the Universe, I allow my life to be exactly as it is."*

Whatever you do, don't resist the resistance!

When you experience resistance, the last thing you want to do is resist it; judging resistance or trying to push it away, only adds more resistance. *Resisting resistance only creates more resistance*. You cannot overcome resistance with more resistance.

But, you can overcome resistance with allowance.

Here's the trick, if you cannot easily practice allowance with the initial focus of your resistance, try allowing your resistance, and, if you cannot allow your resistance, try allowing the resistance of your resistance. **The point is to find some level of allowance.**

In aligning with the energy of allowance on any level, you resonate with allowance, so even if your initial resistance remains unchanged, you are vibrating with allowance. Your moment to moment vibration affects every component of your life in the present moment; it does not matter what you are allowing - as long as you are resonating with allowance.

True-Self Practice

- Allow life to be as it is.
- Stay in the present moment.
- Trust the Universe.
- Find some level of allowance in all circumstances.

EGO Pitfall # 2 - Self-Importance

Self-importance is a sneaky pitfall because it can show up in so many different ways. In the shift from EGO to True-Self, it is extremely helpful to notice all the ways in which self-importance infiltrates your life, so that you can make more conscious choices.

To pinpoint self-importance, notice all the "shoulds" you apply to others. For instance, if you find yourself feeling annoyed at your friend or partner for not being on time or forgetting your birthday, ask yourself, "What must I believe in order to feel annoyed?" If you believe that others *should* act certain ways, it is only due to self-importance. Whenever the word "should" shows up in this way, you can be certain that it is the EGO demonstrating self-importance. Without self-importance you wouldn't take anything personally, you wouldn't have to defend yourself, and you would be free of annoyance.

Consider the True-Self Practice of not making anything about you and not taking anything personally. This process will help to loosen self-importance, allowing you to experience reality without the filters of the EGO. Seeing the world through transpersonal eyes changes the way you see the world – *and the world changes.*

The EGO always wants to be on top so it constantly sorts for opportunities to be better at something. Notice when you have this inclination and make a different choice. Rather than having to be better or best, refrain from one-upmanship, and allow others to be on top; you might be surprised how this one shift improves certain relationships.

The EGO also demonstrates self-importance by *topping a story,* so, even if you think your story about the topic at hand is more informative or interesting, let it go - relinquish the spotlight. This was quite big for me; evidentially I used stories to get attention and I always had one for any occasion. It was difficult to break this EGO-habit at first, but, after a while, it actually became quite enjoyable to be the attentive listener. Without competing for the limelight or trying to make everything about me, I began to hear things I never heard before.

It is also an excellent idea to create a practice where you do not take credit for everything. This could translate into not competing for credit, as well as allowing others to take the credit, even if you participated. It could also translate into *random acts of anonymous kindness*. When you are no longer doing things for credit (or to get your primary emotional need met), it cleans up a tremendous amount of convoluted energy.

Self-importance is also responsible for labeling, keeping score and other forms of judgment.

Once we become aware, we might be astounded at the amount of labeling we do. Nonetheless, each time you notice that you have categorized, stereotyped or pigeon-holed a person in anyway, imagine releasing the labels, even if they are positive - all labels keep us from seeing the real person behind the shadow. It might feel unnatural at first, but do your best to *really see* all the people in your life; beyond the masks they present to the world, look into their eyes and listen attentively without judgment or interference.

As soon as you notice that you are keeping score, measuring worthiness or judging in some other way, simply drop it, and approach the situation or relationship from a higher perspective where value and worth are intrinsic. The EGO is programmed to see separation so that it can calculate worth in order to protect survival but our True-Selves always recognize Oneness. The more you consciously focus on this universal fact, the more you will experience the magic and wonder that comes from this divine truth. The word, "Namaste" means the Divine in me honors the Divine in you; receiving the world in this way changes your world.

True-Self Practice

- Do not take anything personally.
- Do not make anything about you.
- Refrain from one-upmanship.

- Let others take the credit.
- Drop labels.
- See everyone beyond their masks.
- Release judgment, measuring and keeping score.

EGO Pitfall # 3 - Shifting Responsibility

Despite the best intentions of the EGO, there are bound to be times when you "appear to be unworthy" - this includes any behavior that others might judge, from making a simple mistake to less than perfect results, or it might be what we consider less than desirable circumstances, regarding a partner, home, job or finances.

Depending on our particular programming, the EGO associates mishaps, accidents and negative experiences and circumstances with unworthiness, and, in fact, worth may be adversely impacted when anything goes wrong or is not up to current standards, according to society, culture, family, religion, etc.... This may mean that you feel unworthy, and you project it onto others by believing that they see you unworthy, which may or may not be true.

Some people blame themselves for everything that goes wrong, and that in itself can be a "motor" for the EGO, but, generally speaking, the EGO prevents self-blame because it can quickly morph into shame, which is the same as saying that our lives are of no value, and we are not deserving to live. Since even minor everyday mishaps can trigger shame, the EGO defends your worth by shifting responsibility.

Blame

The EGO is programmed to believe that if a mistake, mishap or negative situation is your fault, it makes you unworthy, but, if you shift blame onto someone else, you can prove it is not your fault, and you remain worthy.

For most people, shifting blame is quite instinctual; if we stub our toe on a box in the middle of the room, we immediately blame the person who left it there, or if we are late for an appointment, we blame anyone who got in our way.

If you could hear the energetic field of communication underneath blame, you would hear one EGO say to another, "It's not my fault, it's yours - I'm not worthless, you are!" This is why we automatically react defensively when someone blames us for something - especially if we didn't do it.

Of course, this means playing the blame game all day long with family, friends and those with whom we live and work - no wonder little issues turn into big distractions and ongoing disharmony.

Most people throw blame around like a hot potato - doing all they can, not to be the one to get burned, but what happens when there is no one to blame? Excuses to the rescue!

Is it possible that you rely on excuses all day long without even realizing it?

When there is no one to blame, or we are not in the habit of blame, the EGO compels us to make excuses that will justify, rationalize or show a reason for our behavior or negative circumstance; each successful excuse allows us to remain blameless and our worth is protected.

We might justify a behavior or circumstance when we know that it might not be "right" but, based on our interpretation of the facts, we try to provide a good reason that it was called for. We might rationalize a behavior or circumstance when we try to prove that it is logical or rational, or that it makes sense according to our story.

Excuses are like "made up" *free cards* that we haphazardly throw around to explain "bad behavior" or life situations that others might judge inferior. Secretly hoping these *free cards* get us off the hook so that we are not responsible for our own "less than ideal" circumstance, so we can remain worthy in the eyes of others. .

Whenever we make an excuse, we are covertly saying, "I have no control over myself or my life"- thereby perpetuating the Powerlessness Program.

Excuses may include limiting physical, emotional or mental conditions, as well as temporary or chronic disabilities, but the most common excuses are time and money, with other common excuses including fatigue, stress, PMS, various disorders or being too young or too old. We might also use excuses related to specific life challenges, childhood issues or being a victim in some manner. Excuses may even stretch beyond the planet, such as the effects of a full moon, mercury retrograde or other astrological influences. Whether it is too much *this* or not enough *that,* nothing is too big or too small when it comes to excuses.

Many might argue that certain conditions and factors really do play a part in our lives, and, indeed, they can, but this is simply not the point. Personal and global history demonstrates that virtually every challenge can be transcended, and, in fact, many people have turned their "limitations" into powerful strengths.

The point is, the EGO relies on excuses to keep unconscious programs running, and, if you want to reprogram the EGO, you must override its functions.

Therefore, it is pivotal that you understand that the EGO compels you to use excuses in order to protect your worth, but, at the same time, every single excuse perpetuates the Worthiness Program.

If that's not enough to convince you to release excuses, every time you use a limitation as an excuse, you reinforce the limitation in your subconscious, plus, the more you use a condition as an excuse, the more it grows, perpetuating the condition and possibly other dysfunctional dynamics.

Chronic excuses may also keep you from looking at the cause of your challenges, but, equally relevant, if an issue provides an excuse, the EGO will prevent you from overcoming it because it is an effective worth-protecting strategy.

If you frequently rely on excuses, you will need continuous excuses in order to rely upon – trapping you into an unwanted cycle of dysfunction.

Losing Power

Mishaps, mistakes or less than ideal behavior or circumstances all imply unworthiness to the EGO, but these dynamics also cause us to feel out of control and powerless. As a way to regain power, the EGO manipulates us to shift responsibility onto another person or blame an excuse.

However, when we shift responsibility, we actually disempower ourselves.

Believing that someone or something has power over us, or even power to affect our reality, disconnects us from our own intrinsic power, and as long as we believe that something is out of our control, we are, in fact, powerless. Therefore, shifting responsibility, whether through blame or excuse, perpetuates the Powerlessness Program.

The Real Shift

Reprogramming the EGO requires that you stop shifting responsibility in all areas of your life.

The first step is to non-judgmentally observe when and where you shift responsibility. It helps to keep a journal and write down your observations to review later, discerning blame from excuses.

The second step is to make a conscious choice to give up excuses and refrain from blame. When something goes wrong or you are afraid of being judged, instead of projecting your feelings of unworthiness onto others, own your feelings, but also *tell the EGO that you are worthy* and it does not have to protect your worth by shifting responsibility.

The third step is to empower yourself. Whether you are consciously, or unconsciously, creating your life, you are no less responsible. Real intrinsic power comes from taking full responsibility for every single experience, because you are the creator of your life - the more responsibility you take for all aspects of your life, the more empowered you become.

In moments of mishap, will the EGO rush in with blame or excuses,
or will the True You override the EGO by choosing empowerment?

Refrain from Blame

If your automatic "go to" reaction is blame, replace it every time by taking responsibility and empowering yourself. Ultimately, this means that you are not verbally blaming others, and it also means that you give up all thoughts of blame so that blame is no longer a part of your consciousness.

Say Sorry

Give yourself permission to take verbal responsibility when appropriate; acknowledge your part in an issue or mishap and apologize with sincerity. Do not say you are sorry if you aren't because lying and misdirection only feeds the EGO, and no one will believe you anyway. You don't always have to verbalize responsibility, but your willingness to do so helps to reprogram the EGO.

Give Up Excuses

The secret to eliminating the need for excuses is letting go of what others think, and, in fact, *it is none of your business what other people think about you.* As long as you try to control the thoughts of others, you will need excuses to defend your value in their eyes, but it never works. If someone is judging you, an excuse isn't going to change a thing, so let them think as they wish, and make it none of your business. *This is true liberation!*

True-Self Practice

- Refrain from blame.
- Give up excuses.
- Take responsibility.

EGO Pitfall # 4 - EGO Defense

The EGO is always on guard, ready and willing, to protect your esteem, but every time it does, you stumble into a pitfall.

EGO says, *"Defend Yourself!"*

In the event that someone judges you or criticizes something in which you are identified, such as a person, place or thing, the EGO has a slew of strategies designed to defend your worth, such as:

Denial - denial can be such an automatic defense that we don't even realize when we are "in denial." If you are judged for doing something wrong, the EGO might react by denying that you had anything to do with it or maybe even down-right lying.

Offense - another ploy of the EGO is to take an offensive stand, so, if criticism is directed at you, the EGO might manipulate you to divert the criticism back on the accuser by making his/her faults or mistakes seem larger in comparison; to do so, you must either top the criticism or find a whole new topic to criticize. If your spouse criticizes you for leaving the top off the toothpaste, you might come back by saying that he/she leaves the top off more often than you, or pointing out some other faults that make you seem *better by comparison.*

Emotional Reaction - a very common method of defense is anger or a similar emotional reaction. An emotional reaction creates an energetic shield to protect you from offense, while, at the same time, an emotional reaction can be fierce, acting like an aggressive weapon, intended to take down your opponent.

Dissociation - another defensive strategy is to close down or dissociate. You may see the other person's lips moving but you have no idea what she is saying - turning off or going unconscious removes the possibility of further emotional harm.

Avoidance - the EGO's defense may be by means of changing the subject, pretending you didn't hear the remark or avoiding the issue in some other way, possibly by putting pressure on someone else.

Deflection – another strategy of defense is pointing out all the reasons why you don't deserve judgment, demonstrating that the positive outweighs the negative, and, therefore, you are no less worthy.

Most of us can agree that taking the defense creates problems in relationships, and the fact that it doesn't feel good tells us there is a better way.

The Shift

As long as you defend yourself in anyway, you reinforce the Worthiness Program and, oftentimes, the Powerlessness Program, as well. Many defensive strategies also boost the EGO, generate energy and fuel the EGO for future lines of defense. Breaking these dynamics requires the transcendence of defense.

True-Self says, *"Know Thyself!"*

Here are several alternative True-Self responses that can replace EGO defense:

Do Not Take Anything Personally – if it is not about you (and it never really is) there is no need for defense. With practice, criticism can easily roll off your back without causing emotional injury to you.

Refrain from Reacting – instead of reaching for anger or another emotional reaction, take a deep breath, and consciously choose your response.

Stay Conscious - there is no reason to go unconscious or dissociate when you remember your worth and you consciously own your power. Use this opportunity to embrace your worth and power.

Communicate - oftentimes, it is appropriate to share your feelings; let the other person know how their judgment made you feel, for instance, and possibly teach him how to offer you feedback so that you can benefit from his viewpoint.

Set Boundaries - you might also set a boundary that supports you, by letting others know that any form of judgment is out of bounds. Yes, you do have a right to set boundaries and refuse judgment.

Don't Believe – don't believe everything you hear; just because someone judges you, it doesn't mean that it is true or right, so be discerning and don't take on another's beliefs about you.

Agree – a radical response is to agree with any forthcoming criticism. Instead of resisting, just go with it. Without being concerned whether it is true or not, you can simply allow others their opinions.

Pay Attention – you might want to pay attention; see if there is any truth to the criticism, and, if there is, consider using it to make positive changes in your life. *When the EGO is not defensive, there is a great deal more room for possibility.*

Respond with Love – we often withhold love when we feel judged or criticized, but this doesn't feel good to anyone. Instead, keep your heart open and your mind clear; choose to see the other person beyond judgment, and allow your love to flow to both of you. ***When in doubt, choose love!***

Take Notice – if your first inclination is a defensive strategy, pause and take a deep breath. This may be an opportunity for self-insight and higher consciousness. Notice how the judgment makes you feel and notice the power you give to the one judging. You can wisely use this information by noticing where you doubt your worth or how you give your power away. To support this process, carefully review the chapter on emotional triggers.

Always remember, the more you know your worth, the less you will care what others think or say about you.

True-Self Practice

- Track your defensive strategies.
- Notice how each one makes you feel.
- Take full responsibility for your own response.
- Develop empowering True-Self responses (using the list above).

EGO Pitfall #5 - Self-Consciousness

Being self-conscious is a major symptom that we are tracking our worth in the eyes of others – needing the world to deem us worthy or maybe even see us as "better than." Self-consciousness makes us want to control the way people see us, and, as a result, we change our worldly presentation accordingly, or we do our best to avoid being seen.

> ☙Signpost on the path❧
> *What others think about you is none of your business!*

If you need others to see you a certain way, and, if you care what others think about you, there is no way to avoid this pitfall, but there is a permanent cure to self-consciousness that will allow you to avoid this pitfall altogether.

The cure to self-consciousness is owning your worth!

When you own your worth, there is no longer a need to be self-conscious because it doesn't matter what anyone says or thinks, and when you no longer fear being judged, there is no need to hide. Imagine, as you let go of the need to be liked or loved by others, you fulfill this need yourself, and because you like and love yourself, there is no need for others to provide reassurance in anyway.

Whenever you are aware of being externally focused, needing something from the outside world, shift your focus inward and find what you are seeking within. It will also help if you can resist seeking feedback, and even allowing both compliments and criticism to slide. Especially be aware when you are changing your behavior because you fear judgment, and, instead, offer yourself approval and reassurance.

Imagine, as you give to yourself what you emotionally desire from others, you fill up with love and support from the inside out, and as you stop projecting self-judgment onto others, you are free to be yourself, without fear of shame or rejection.

When people judge you, remember that it is only their EGOs that are judging. Maybe say to yourself, *"I don't care what my own EGO says, so I certainly don't care what other EGOs say about me."*

On the path to True-Self Confidence, ask Source to show you how you are seen from these unconditionally loving eyes, and practice seeing yourself the same way. When you see yourself through the eyes of Source, your entire world awakens.

It is true that when you fully own your worth, you simply don't care what others think, believe or feel about you, but, please don't confuse this with "not caring about others." You can care about someone without needing to control their thoughts, beliefs or feelings about you.

You might also think that if you fulfill your own emotional needs, you don't need relationships, and this simply isn't true. It is true that you won't need relationships in the same old way, and, as a result, your relationships will evolve and become more harmonious and satisfying.

True-Self Practice

- Replace self-consciousness with consciousness.
- Let go of the need to be liked or loved.
- Give to yourself what you emotionally desire from others.
- Stop projecting your own self-judgment onto others.
- See yourself through the eyes of Source.

EGO Pitfall #6 - Crowd Pleasers

Many of us have no idea what we like, or don't like, without the opinions of others. To play it safe, and not risk our worthiness quotient, we rely on those with greater worth and power to dictate our likes and dislikes. We allow family, friends, co-workers, specific organizations or pop-culture to decide the value of things before we even consider them; the value of clothes before we wear them, the value of neighborhoods before we live in them, the value of people before we befriend them, the value of apps before we install them and the value of consumer products before we buy them. Certainly, it can be helpful to read reviews before going to a movie or consulting references before hiring a professional, but what happens when you need others to decide the worth of art before you can like it, or the value of a song before you can listen to it?

EGO says, *"Follow the crowd!"*

The EGO is programmed to follow the crowd because the worth of a person, place or thing is pre-determined by the majority rule, and by agreeing with the majority, we automatically improve our worth, or at least we don't compromise it.

Our modern day tribes dictate our preferences and pre-ordain our choices, allowing us to avoid judgment for liking something different, but the cost of EGO satisfaction is self-suppression, and this only perpetuates all EGO programming, and, as a result, it is a huge EGO Pitfall.

Your Power of Choice!

True-Self says, *"Be your own unique being."*

Overriding unconscious programming requires a very different way of living, such as:

Make your own choices – ignore the majority rule, and decide for yourself in all areas of your life. Your tastes, preferences and opinions are a unique expression of *who you really are*, and when you express yourself, you align with the True You.

Be Adventurous – the only way you will discover your unique style and expression is to walk the pathless path. There is no greater adventure than the one that calls forth your True-Self.

Practice Discernment - an important aspect of expression is discerning your preferences, but this requires the willingness to try things that are often off *the main street of reality.*

Think for Yourself - be an independent thinker, but don't just rely on logic; remember to listen to your inner guidance because this is how your True-Self communicates.

Create Experience - experience everything for yourself and don't take anyone's word for anything. Only through direct experience can you know what you like.

True-Self Practice

- Don't blindly follow the crowd.
- Make your own choices.
- Try new things.
- Assert your preferences even when you are the minority!

EGO Pitfall #7 - Trying to Change Others

As you go through the process of discerning the EGO from *who you really are,* it is common to notice everyone's EGO with heightened awareness. You may feel the inclination to point it out or try to change others in order to help them, and you may want others to change so that it is easier for you to stay on track and not get your EGO triggered. Unfortunately, that is not the way it works, and, if you try to change another, you will find yourself in a frustrating EGO Pitfall.

> *℘Signpost on the path☙*
> *Avoid detour - do not try to change another soul!*

You can only change yourself, so it is important to always remember that the process of awakening as your True-Self is about you and not about anyone else. If you concern yourself with others, you will inevitably misalign with your True-Self, and, if you do, you are no help to anyone. Instead, play the observer and allow others to be exactly as they are.

Having said this, the more you live as your True-Self, the more you will naturally call forth the True-Selves of those around you, and once you master living as the True You, the world will want to know your secret; so, when they come knocking on your door, you can effortlessly teach by example.

- When you are present, it invites others to be present.
- When you allow others to be who they are, they tend to drop judgment, as well.
- When you open up, it creates the space for others to do the same.

True-Self Practice

- Don't try to change anyone.
- Refrain from judging others.
- Allow everyone to be who they are.

EGO Pitfall #8 - Money

Who would have thought that money would be an EGO Pitfall? But, it should really be no surprise - after all, money is entangled with worth and power, and, in fact, we are brainwashed to believe that the more money we have, the more worthy and powerful we are - with the reverse also being true. Additionally, money is tied to survival and anything that has to do with survival is dominated by the EGO.

Just the thought of money, or not having money, can trigger the EGO, and, if you are not conscious enough to avoid the trigger, you will likely find yourself in the EGO's Money Pitfall. Indeed, when people fight over money, you can be sure that it is their EGOs that are in battle.

The best way to avoid this pitfall is by fully understanding that money is a manifestation of Life Force Energy.

> *Signpost on the path*
>
> *The lack of money symbolizes the lack of Life Force Energy*

Since there is only one energy in the entire Universe and everything is made from this one energy, you must have adequate access to it if you are to manifest anything - including money. Manifestation requires the core substance of Life Force Energy as the baseline, and, therefore, if you have a scarcity of energy, experienced as anything from mild fatigue to major depression, there is a likelihood that it will also show up in your finances.

Have you ever noticed the relationship between exhaustion and scarcity? The more exhausted a person tends to be, the less money they generally have. When physical energy is in deficit and you don't even have enough energy to live your life, there is a good chance that finances are equally deficient.

Living mostly on EGO generated energy ultimately results in a scarcity of energy in all areas of one's life.

EGO-Driven Money

It is true that many people make a great deal of money when the EGO is running the show, so, what's that about?

On occasion, an EGO is so big and inflated that it generates an enormous amount of energy, and from this artificially-generated energy, certain EGO-driven people can materialize artificially generated energy into money. In other words, if they are driven to accumulate wealth, the energy generated by the inflated EGO is used to manifest wealth. This may not sound so bad, but it is not without great cost. Oftentimes, these same EGO-driven people suffer from chronic and severe health issues and their relationships generally suffer just as much. They may have wealth and the illusion of power, but they are miles away from peace, joy and fulfillment.

The secret to financial abundance is channeling an abundance of Life Force Energy as your True-Self, and materializing it into wealth through the conscious intention of your quantum mind.

Prosperity consciousness is the result of being in the abundant flow of Life Force Energy and using the power and focus of your mind to alchemize that energy into financial prosperity. This means consciously utilizing the power of thought to focus on the successful manifestation of your desires - focusing fully on what you want, even if you are currently experiencing the opposite.

Life Force Energy + Focused Intent = Manifestation

You can substitute wealth with virtually anything because everything is made from the same one substance.

True-Self Practice

- Take your primary focus off money.
- Focus on channeling an abundance of Life Force Energy (an upcoming chapter will show you how to increase the flow).
- Use the power of your mind to attract wealth.

EGO Pitfall #9 - The Guilt and Obligation Trap

EGO says, *"Work hard and be all things to all people, and only when you are done, can you have some fun."*

According to EGO programming, when we are doing what we love to do or having fun, we are not proving our worth, so it is a waste of time; if it was up to the EGO, we would be working all the time.

The EGO commonly motor-vates us with the trickery of the word "should" but this is just another hidden pitfall - even if you can avoid obligation, you might still find yourself in the EGO pitfall called guilt.

Whenever you hear yourself saying or thinking that you should do something, you can be almost certain that it is the voice of the EGO. Many of us live our lives rotating between fulfilling our "shoulds" and experiencing guilt when we have the courage to override EGO-driven obligation.

Indeed, when we choose fun over duty, we are overridden with guilt, but from a grander perspective, this is completely illogical and counter-productive because having fun and following your own inspiring guidance opens the door to your True-Self.

Consider the moments in your life when you embody your True-Self. Can you see that there is a direct connection between doing what you love to do and True-Self embodiment?

The World's Best Reason for Having Fun

Next time you question your desire to take time off, or you feel guilty for wanting to have some fun, remember that having fun and doing what you love to do "drops" you in the present moment where your True-Self can be found, and, in fact, this is one of the easiest ways to experience embodiment.

If doing what you love to do and having more fun in your life allows your True-Self to be experienced, doesn't it make sense to spend more time having fun and enjoying yourself?

The key is to participate in activities you love to do, but without the guilt. If you experience guilt, you miss the point, and you misalign with your True-Self.

Knowing that joyful living is a direct path to True-Self emb
how can you consciously create more joyful moments on a dai

True-Self Practice

- Drop your "shoulds."
- Do more of what you love to do on a regular basis!
- Release guilt and obligation.
- When there are things that you absolutely have to do, find a new way to do them - without resistance.
- Be "at choice" for all you do!

EGO Pitfall #10 - Multi-tasking

With so much to do in our busy lives, it is almost impossible not to multi-task. On the surface, it appears that doing two or more things at once saves time, but appearances can be deceiving. First of all, when we try to do more than one thing at once, we are tossed out of the present moment, which, of course, means that the EGO takes control (if it's not already). Additionally, to make sure we get it all done, while we live up to standards, the EGO's goal-oriented programming causes needless stress and self-judgment.

The Shift

Why have the EGO do any task, when the True You could do it better?

With your full attention on one task at a time, your True-Self is called forth, and consequently, an abundance of Life Force Energy to get the job done. Presence has the magical ability to make the ordinary quite extraordinary. When the Divine shines through, doing the dishes or laundry become sacred tasks not to be missed, and the natural byproduct is joy and peace.

True-Self Practice

- One task at a time.
- Full attention on each task.
- Be Present!

EGO Pitfall #11 - Self-Sabotage

Have you ever felt inspired, but later lacked the energy to follow through?

Moments of inspiration occur when your True-Self is embodied and fully aligned; at these times, a great idea feels wonderful and seems quite doable! You are psyched for a new experience of life or materializing a cool idea, but, for some reason, you lose confidence, energy or vision, and inspiration fizzles-out before you even begin. Sometimes we refer to this as procrastination, laziness or lack of motivation, but those things are just symptoms of a deeper dynamic that turns inspiration into procrastination.

[illegible]on and great ideas are always a result of True-Self embodiment, but, if your [illegible]e-Self gets displaced, the EGO is left to deal with these inspiring ideas, except they are not so inspiring to the EGO, whose job it is to protect you from unknown dangers.

If you wonder why you have so many starts but few finishes, it might be because your True-Self inspires you but doesn't stay around long enough to see anything through to completion.

Embarking on a new idea requires going out of your safe comfort zone which means risking judgment and possible rejection. Since the EGO is programmed to protect you from taking risks, it will do whatever it needs to do in order to shoot down inspiring new ideas; it's secret weapons include fear, procrastination, fatigue and inhibiting motivation, but, let's not forget about the EGO's most formidable weapon - self-doubt.

Since the EGO has no way to navigate unknown territory, anytime you wish to venture into the unknown, or try something you never tried before, the EGO attempts to stop you by flooding your mind with self-doubt – like a powerful energetic barrier, self-doubt pushes you back down into your comfort zone.

EGO says, *"You can't do it, you'll fail, people will laugh, you're not good enough to succeed, why even try, you'll be disappointed, and on and on…. "* until all your dreams and desires are deflated.

The EGO is not trying to be mean or insensitive – it is only doing what it is programmed to do, and in this case, it is programmed to keep you in the familiar and mundane. By undermining your ability, you remain small, but safe – the EGO has done its job.

When the EGO is in control, your inspired dreams are out of reach.

Desiring something you have no way of attaining is painful, so maybe you forget about it, or maybe you try to force yourself to take action, but EGO-driven *brute force determination* can't overcome procrastination, laziness, self-doubt or lack of motivation, because the EGO created these road-blocks in the first place. However, if a goal or outcome supports the EGO's agenda, increasing worth or control, it will likely provide appropriate motor-vation for you to succeed.

The Shift

The True You knows *who you really are* and also knows that there is no risk or danger in the eternal scheme of things, so it is safe to try anything and explore all possibilities, but, if your True-Self doesn't fully inhabit your body on a permanent basis, the EGO will squash these dreams.

The EGO is not out to hurt you or harm you in anyway, nor does it wish to sabotage your success. It may look and feel like self-sabotage, but it's not – it's more like having **two managers** on different shifts with opposing missions. Even EGO-driven behaviors that seem to be most harmful and self-sabotaging are actually the result of programming that is intended to protect you, and your worth.

Don't be mistaken, it is not a battle between the EGO and True-Self; when your True-Self is sitting in the commander's seat, the EGO is dormant. It is only when the commander's seat is vacant that the EGO takes control.

If you have a choice between taking action as your True-Self versus the EGO, choose the former. Your dreams and desires are meant to be lived and experience the EGO is not equipped for the necessary journey to get there. If you want to manifest your inspired dreams and compelling desires, you must do so as your True-Self.

Indeed, it can be difficult to overcome the EGO's fearful voice, but overriding self-doubt tells the EGO that you believe in yourself, and when you consistently "shush" the doubt-laden EGO, and you confidently move past fear and self-doubt, sooner or later, there will be no reason for the EGO to shut you down.

True-Self Practice

- Don't take important actions when the EGO is in charge.
- Don't make important choices when the EGO is in charge.
- Use procrastination, doubt and fear as EGO indicators.
- Do not fight or argue with the EGO (you won't win).
- Using a consciousness practice align with your True-Self.
- As the True You, listen to inner-guidance, following tangible instructions.
- Take inspired actions.
- Repeat as needed.

EGO Pitfall #12 - The EGO's Distorted Filter

It is no secret that the EGO filters everything through the past, using past problems as guiding factors to make safer choices, and, as such, the EGO is constantly calculating and using those calculations to trigger programmed responses - resulting in a reaction of some nature (a reaction is repeating a past action).

The EGO is smart, but it is only a program and *a program can only do what a program is programmed to do* ..... Therefore, you can be smarter than the EGO!

The EGO sees and experiences life one-dimensionally, through the lens of survival and protection, and, therefore, it is likely that you will miss the exquisite magnificence of life – limiting your perspective to the dirty lens of gray colored glasses.

The key to out-smarting the EGO is being conscious and present, so that you can recognize the EGO's patterns and consciously interrupt those patterns by making new empowering choices that the EGO would never consider.

When you find yourself triggered or experiencing a common reaction, take a deep breath, and question yourself, *"Is this really true? How do I know it is true? What if it wasn't true?*

Consider that without the EGO's programmed reactions, there is a whole new, and possibly enlightened, response to all situations, experiences and relationships. Every time you question your reactions, you take a little bit more of your power back, and, if you are successful in interrupting a pattern, you just might avoid EGO Hijacking.

Life as your True-Self allows you to see and experience the whole world, and everyone in it, through the rose-colored glasses of Source, except they're not really rose colored and Source doesn't actually wear glasses, but you get the point.

True-Self Practice

- Stop, Drop and Roll
- Question reality: Is this really true? How do I know it is true?
- Respond from your True-Self in the present moment.

EGO Pitfall #13 - The EGO Takes Credit

Imagine that you start painting as a hobby, and, absolutely, loving it, you embody your True-Self, and you discover that you have a real gift. Your paintings are fun and provocative, and, before long, you begin to get publicly recognized as a painter. The EGO discerns that your art-work increases your worth, and, automatically makes it a "motor" - because increased worth amounts to more energy. Now seeking recognition and praise for your creativity, your True-Self is booted from the job and the EGO is now in the role of painter, but, with the EGO depending on the results for a sense of worth, the free-flowing nature of your painting dramatically changes, with stress and rigidity taking its place.

This is an EGO Pitfall that trips up many creative and innovative people.

When we first begin to explore a gift or desire, there is no emotional investment or pressure to succeed, and this keeps the EGO out of the creative process. Because our creativity is flowing through our True-Selves, we are the receptive vehicle for Source, and the results are exquisitely unique and divinely compelling. As long as we are still beginners, the EGO doesn't see our amateur creativity as an opportunity for worth, and our True-Selves continue to be inspired. This can all change once we experience a sense of accomplishment from the work we produce - as the EGO grasps onto a new "motor" for worth. From that point on, inspiration is clouded by motor-vation.

Maybe this is when we experience writer's block, artist's block or the equivalent for our particular form of creativity, or, if we don't experience a block, quite possibly, the essence of our art has lost its sparkle, and we don't why. Even if we are able to maintain similar results, the ease and exhilaration experienced by our True-Selves are now beyond reach, and, the pure fun of creating is lost in a cloud of stress and expectation.

With conscious awareness, this can all be avoided by keeping the EGO out of the creative process. It is important that, no wonder how amazing your creative results, you don't attach your identity or sense of worth to any of it. Remember, only by the grace of the Divine are we able to express creativity. Being in gratitude to the Source of our inspiration helps to keep us humble and receptive.

Hence, even when your True-Self has a *victory*, don't allow the EGO to claim the rewards.

True-Self Practice

- Create as your True-Self.
- Intercept the EGO's tendency to take credit.
- Recognize the Source of your creativity and express gratitude.
- Practice humility.

EGO Pitfall #14 - Hiding in the Shadows

The EGO says, *"Look at me!"* but the EGO also says, *"Don't look at me."*

We often identify the need for attention with the EGO, and, although this is true, it is also true that the EGO often compels us to hide so that we are not seen. Hiding in the shadows or refusing to take the spotlight is an EGO strategy designed to protect our worth. So, instead of trying to prove worth by getting recognition, appreciation or attention, the EGO has us on the defense - hiding in the shadows. After all, when we are seen, we are vulnerable to negative judgment, so, rather than failing, looking like a fool or allowing others to laugh at our inadequacies, it is safer to retreat and avoid emotional risk.

There is nothing wrong with being a private person, but, if a greater part of you desires expression and you suppress yourself, you will inevitably disconnect from your True-Self, which can result in unhappiness and lack of fulfillment. If the True You desires creative expression, the best you can do is get out of the way. As you discover your intrinsic worth, and you release the need for external feedback, you actually won't care what the world says or doesn't say, and you will be free to be *who you really are.*

True-Self Practice

- Consciously choose to express yourself.
- Anchor your internal sense of worth.
- Don't look for feedback.

EGO Pitfall #15 - EGO Dependence

Many things can cause a True-Self visitation; falling in love, having fun, expressing gifts, laughter, compassion, contribution, etc... If you are not conscious of your True-Self, it is natural to think that an experience, event or another person made you feel incredible or joyful, but as soon as you credit an external source for your experience, you give your power to this "false source."

The person, place or thing may have helped to align you with a True-Self experience, but, if you believe that you need the person, place or thing in order to feel this way, you will make yourself dependent on something external, thereby falling into a pitfall and misaligning with your True-Self.

Notice, when you enjoy yourself, you let go and become present, effortlessly coming into resonance with your True-Self.

The thing to remember is that you don't need any conditions to let go or to become present - you can do it anytime, any place, under any condition. Instead of crediting things outside your control, when you experience what might be your True-Self, own it.

True-Self Practice

- Own your True-Self experience.
- Don't depend on externals for embodying your True-Self.

EGO Pitfall #16 - Perfectionism

Perfectionism is sneaky – on the surface it sounds like it could be a good thing. After all, what's wrong with perfection?

It is true that perfectionism is a strategy for success, but when you measure success, by your ability to be consistently perfect, success is perpetually out of reach. Like all strategies, the strategy of perfectionism, sooner or later, does the opposite of what it was intended to do - turning this strategy into an EGO Pitfall.

If you look closely, like a wolf in sheep's clothes, you will see that perfectionism is just another name for self-judgment. In the name of perfection, we give ourselves permission to be self-critical and undermining every time we fall short. Never quite meeting our own standards of perfection, *because good is not good enough*, we become our own worst enemies.

If there is such a thing as perfect, and we believe that we must live up to this unrealistic ideal in order to succeed, we set ourselves up for perpetual disappointment, failure and maybe even depression.

A Matter of Worth

If you look even closer, you will see that there is a huge connection between perfectionism and self-worth. Perfectionism is a strategy to gain a sense of worthiness, but the conditions are usually so high and difficult to meet that the attainment of self-worth never comes. When your sense of worth is entangled with being perfect and/or producing perfect results, you must meet your self-imposed conditions in order to feel worthy. Even if you are able to meet your own standards of perfection, the sense of worth doesn't last long, and you will need another perfect accomplishment in order to sustain or regain feelings of worth.

Don't let perfectionism be an excuse to beat yourself up!

When we are driven by perfection, we often miss the point of why we are doing what we are doing. Perfection drives us in such a way that the goal or results become more important than the process, and when we bypass the process, we miss the whole point of life.

The Shift

The cure for perfectionism is waking up, and remembering that you are unconditionally worthy, and no matter what you do, or how you do it, you are no less worthy. You are off the hook – you don't need to prove anything to anyone (not even yourself) in order to have worth.

As long as you seek perfection, you will miss it by a mile, but without the need for perfection, so much more is possible. When we are ***driven by love***, everything that we do transforms. It is no longer about perfect results – it is about the desire to express love in whatever we are doing. When we are driven by love, there is no room for fear of failure, or needing to be the best in order to be worthy. Love of self, love of others and love of the task at hand produces excellence. Needless to say, this is the perfect environment for the True You, and just by substituting ***love*** for perfectionism, you will experience your True-Self a great deal more often.

From now on, you can drop the conditions of perfectionism that you have made-up, and you can also drop any facades that keep you hiding. As you free yourself from self-imposed restraints, you can dance in the sun or sing in the rain.

Your only job is to be you!

True-Self Practice

- Recognize the judgment in perfectionism.
- Drop perfectionism – let yourself off the hook.
- Get present with whatever you are doing.
- Allow love to be the driving force.

EGO Pitfall #17 - The Waiting Pit

One of the most common EGO Pitfalls is waiting - waiting on hold, waiting in traffic, waiting for a friend, waiting, waiting, waiting... If we anticipate a wait, maybe it's not so bad, but when we believe that we shouldn't have to wait, these circumstances make us feel surprisingly powerless - usually because we feel that someone or something is controlling us or stealing our time. Regardless, the moment we get impatient or frustrated, the EGO is triggered and it is downhill from then on.

If there are no accidents in life and everything is perfectly orchestrated specifically for you and me, this must also mean that even when we are forced to wait, there is a higher reason for it. Maybe we are being lined up for some future opportunity, maybe we are stressed-out and this is an invitation to rest or maybe our belief system simply attracts these sort of things. Nonetheless, if we allow the EGO to be triggered, it only makes matters worse - feeling bad, possibly waiting longer and we could miss that synchronistic opportunity because we are misaligned with our True-Selves.

Instead of reacting to situations that make you feel powerless, what if you could use "waiting" as a doorway to your True-Self? With the conscious use of mindfulness, waiting can be a portal to presence.

Here's how

When waiting in traffic, waiting on hold, waiting in line or waiting for a friend, identify the trigger of powerlessness, and, instead of falling into the pitfall, use this time and space to practice letting go. Breathing deeply, allow yourself to let go of the current story (about the wait) and drop into presence; notice what there is to notice in the present moment - wake-up and be alert here and now. You might experience colors becoming brighter, sounds intensifying or an intoxicating scent. Being Present is much like a natural drug - without any negative side-effects.

Rather than suffering through resistance, surrender through mindfulness.

True-Self Practice

- Identify how powerlessness triggers impatience, frustration, etc....
- Use waiting as an opportunity for mindful presence.

EGO Pitfall #18 – Control

It's fairly obvious that the EGO motor-vates us to control people, places and things in order to protect us and keep things predictable, and because it seems natural to control, most of us fall into this EGO Pitfall over and over again, but there is a way to avoid it altogether.

Yes, we control because we have been programmed to be controlling, but the core reason that we continue to control is because we do not trust life to take care of us, and we believe that if we don't try to control things, life will fail us and those we love. Even if our controlling ways are somewhat successful, if we do not trust life, we are likely anxious, depressed and overwhelmed. When we are disconnected from life, we are also unplugged from the source of feeling good.

Peace and joy flow from a deep connection to life that can only be accessed through trust and letting go.

But, how can I trust life?

Look around and observe life - life flows effortlessly. The sun rises and sets each day on precise cue. The tides roll in and out in flawless harmony. The planets rotate like a well-choreographed dance through the Universe. Everything is perfectly orchestrated without your control. Even the organs of your own body perform with the greatest of precision. Your heart does not wait for you to say, "Beat." Your breath does not wait for you say, "Breathe." It all goes on without you – yet it is ALL for you! What is the source of all these miracles that go on moment after moment without interruption? It is the *Source of all this*, and infinitely more, that you can trust...

> *Signpost on the path*
> *Go directly to Source*
> *- do not pass go*

The Universe possesses infinite knowledge down to the smallest detail. Nothing is overlooked. This same omnipotent consciousness is applied to everything in the Universe from the tiny cells in your body to the largest galaxy in all of creation. The full attention of the Universe is equally upon each second of your existence. At the core of this awareness is unconditional love. This is what you can trust. This is what you can let go to.

Despite how it sometimes seems, the Source of life knows what it is doing at all times. When you try to control things, you misalign with life and then everything is more challenging because you are disconnected from this Source. When you let go and trust the power of the Universe, this power has the innate ability to serve you in all ways.

Letting go is the key to invoking the Power of the Universe.

But, what happens after you let go?

Do you just go with the flow and allow life to unfold around you? Well, this is certainly one option, but there is another. We are here to co-create and dance with life, so that your unique dance through the Universe is like no other.

Your ability to co-create lies in the power of your mind.

Life originates and unfolds in a *Mental Universe* of information which we call reality, therefore the only thing that can be influenced is the mental aspects of the Universe, and when this is mastered, the Universe unconditionally conforms.

Your innate ability to co-create and influence the flow of life lies in the power of your mind, and, therefore, the way to influence anything in the Universe is through thought; not by controlling circumstances but by controlling thoughts; this includes intention, visualization and imagination.

Be the Master of Your Own Mind.

At first it may be nearly impossible to stop or control your thoughts, but you do have the power to let go of thoughts that do not support you simply by turning your attention away from them time after time, for as many times as it takes, until those thoughts stop appearing. You might have to turn your attention away from a single negative thought a thousand times before it loses power and disappears, but it is worth it. How long would you cut through chains in order to free yourself? As long as it takes because the alternative is staying imprisoned.

True-Self Practice

- Consciously choose to release control on a daily basis.
- Let go and learn to trust the Universe.
- Practice releasing thoughts and focusing your mind.

EGO Pitfall #19 - Not setting boundaries

In the EGO's attempt at proving worth, we often end up trying to please everyone so that we will be liked and loved. Consequently, this results in weak or non-existent boundaries, and without proper boundaries, we are magnets to hidden pitfalls.

Because the EGO is triggered when others cross our non-existent boundaries, it is easy to see that setting and enforcing boundaries supports True-Self embodiment. For instance, if you are triggered when your partner yells at you, it indicates the need for a boundary that states, "People are not allowed to yell at me."

As we previously explored, triggers are an indication of emotional wounds and it is essential to release the wound, but healing also requires certain boundaries that will prevent future emotional injury. If you are still experiencing abuse in a current relationship, it is extremely difficult to heal past abuse (even from a different relationship).

Yes, indeed, this means that you must teach others how to treat you, and even how to speak to you, and it also means that you must be willing to disengage from relationships where people are not respecting your boundaries.

Also, remember some of the most important boundaries are the ones in which you set for yourself, such as saying no when you don't want to do something and speaking your truth when need be.

Boundaries have the inherent ability to nurture the True You, while allowing you to express and explore more of *who you really are*, but setting boundaries also helps to deactivate the Worthiness Program and Powerlessness Program; this is due to the fact that every time you set and enforce a boundary, you show your subconscious mind that you believe that are worthy and empowered.

At some point, all boundaries fall away because people will automatically know how to treat you, but, at the same time, it won't matter how other people act - your True-Self will stay embodied regardless of anyone's behavior. Until then, respect your True-Self with strong, clear and empowering boundaries!

What boundaries do you need to set in order to be the True You?

The key to discerning this answer is noticing when and how you are triggered, and considering the possible boundaries that will allow you to stay trigger-free.

True-Self Practice

- Specifically identify how your triggers represent the need for boundaries.
- Set and enforce appropriate boundaries.
- Communicate your boundaries and be willing to disengage from challenging relationships.

EGO Pitfall #20 - Boredom

It is never your True-Self that gets bored. It is always the EGO.

Boredom occurs when the EGO is not totally dominant yet your True-Self is not fully embodied. This makes boredom the "in between space" where you are teetering between the EGO and True-Self.

The EGO makes us afraid to be bored, as if not having something to do every moment of the day might kill us, but, actually, this is exactly how the EGO perceives boredom. When you are bored, no "motors" are running and no energy is generated, and since you need energy to live, the EGO concludes that boredom is a threat to survival. Of course, the EGO is ready to take control, so it tries to motor-vate you by making you feel restless or unsatisfied so that you will do something to generate energy and fill this "pointless void" known as boredom - but this is just another sneaky pitfall.

Boredom was once my worst enemy, until I made a conscious decision to embrace it. So, instead of resisting boredom, I dove right in - hoping to learn everything about this uninteresting "non-experience" as I could.

I noticed that when I was bored, my mind was not really attached to anything, as it usually was. I also noticed that there was time and space to do or try something new or different. Since time and space were rare commodities for me, I decided to indulge. With time and energy, and a clear mind, I realized that this "boredom thing" could be a very valuable resource.

The curious thing about embracing boredom from this perspective is that as soon as you become interested in it as a resource for creativity, boredom is obliterated - what starts out as plain boring transforms into intriguing possibility.

So, I made boredom my best friend and together we created ...

One day, my five year old grandson, Alta, came to me with an exasperated sigh, he announced, *"I'm bored!"* Expecting me to mirror his low energy, he was shocked when I excitedly declared, *"That's awesome!"* Confused yet curious, he responded, *"Awesome?"*

Now, with his full attention on my words, I replied, "*Yes, Awesome! It's great to be bored, because when you are bored, you can do, be and create anything that you desire.*" His soulful eyes began to sparkle with new ideas.

Boredom is the ultimate blank canvas for creativity, because when you are bored, you are not pulled in different directions - your energy is not split - your mind is not racing. Every possibility is at your fingertips.

What you do with boredom defines your power as a conscious creator.

If you resist boredom or complain about it, you will get sucked into "boring land," where nothing seems interesting or worth your time, but, if you notice the blank canvas where you can create anything that you desire, that canvas becomes an exciting playground of endless potential.

But there is even more…

Boredom is a portal to True-Self embodiment.

It can be challenging to transcend an over-active EGO that keeps us running in all directions, and especially one that is never satisfied, however, when you experience boredom, the EGO is not very active, so you don't need to overcome it in the usual ways.

Boredom is an indication that our "motors" are not running, which means that we don't need to turn them off in order to transcend the EGO and embody our True-Selves.

You might say that boredom opens a portal that is not usually available most days. Because the EGO is not running "motors" and is not fixated on anything or anyone, you can use this rare opportunity to simply jump through the portal, greeting your True-Self on the other side (so to speak). Entrance into the portal, however, does require that you surrender to the spacious unknown.

Instead of allowing the EGO to fill the empty space of boredom, what would happen if you consciously chose to embrace the emptiness?

The first step is letting go of the need to alleviate boredom - this means that you must stop looking for something to do and you must stop seeking distractions. The second step is to become present in the now with your full non-judgmental awareness. As you consciously breathe, drop resistance, let go of the story and stop trying to change anything - simply notice how you feel. Do this for several moments and then extend your awareness out to the field around you.

Again, with unbiased commentary, notice what there is to notice; what do you hear, smell, see and sense? After several moments, shift your awareness within and continue the process moving back and forth between the inner and outer worlds. If you do this process with conscious intention and focused attention, you will transform boredom into deep meditation. In this delicious spaciousness your True-Self awaits – inviting you to slide into resonance … with the vast power and energy of the entire Universe. Now, as the True You, inspiration can flow, creativity can bubble up and you have direct access to unlimited resources.

True-Self Practice

- Embrace boredom.

- Consciously use boredom for creative expression and/or a portal to access your True-Self.

EGO Pitfall #21 - Feeding the EGO

> *Signpost on the path*
> *Warning, Do Not Feed the EGO*

You know your EGO better than anyone so you also know all the ways in which you feed it, but, if you need some clues, keep in mind that the ways in which we feed the EGO are often signified by our "motors," so if you can identify one, you can identify the other.

True-Self Practice

- Make a list of all the ways in which you feed the EGO.
- Taking one item at a time, decide to eliminate this "feeding."

Every time you override EGO programming or avoid an EGO Pitfall, you actively reprogram the EGO, but reprogramming often takes consistent new behavior over a period of time so be patient. Every empowering choice brings you that much closer to transcending the EGO and living as the True You.

Chapter 37

The 22nd EGO Pitfall - EGO Thinking

Since EGO Thinking is the most pervasive and all-consuming pitfall, it deserves its own chapter.

Your thoughts flit and fracture from moment to moment because the EGO is perpetually sorting for opportunities or reasons to prove, improve or protect your worth, as well as ways to gain control, and let's not forget - generate energy. This complex pattern most often manifests as what we call negative thinking.

Negative thinking is so pervasive that most of us don't even realize the frequency or intensity of our own negativity, so it might be very helpful to clarify the definition of negative thinking.

What is negative thinking?

Negative thinking is simply thinking about what you do not want, while positive thinking is thinking about what you do want.

Ask yourself, "Do I focus more on what I do want or what I don't want?"

For the majority of the world, the answer is the latter. Most people are unconsciously addicted to negative thinking and they don't even know it. Negative thinking includes the words you say and think, as well as negative self-talk, but there are several aspects of negative thinking that often pass by our radar.

> ℘Signpost on the path☙
>
> *Negative Thinking is Complete EGO!*
>
> *We often think of egotistical thoughts as those that say, "I'm better than… or look at me," but all negative thinking is just as much EGO-based.*

Negative thinking includes:

- Unhappy or negative visualization (past or future)
- Judgment of anything
- Self-doubt
- Self-judgment
- Perfectionism
- Mentally replaying unhappy memories
- Feeling sorry for someone – judging a person's experience is negative thinking
- Realism – realists are people who rationalize negative thinking
- Use of negative metaphors, such as, "I'm stuck between a rock and a hard place."
- Worry - you are imagining what you don't want

- Negative questions - if you ask, "What's going to go wrong?" your mind will sort for all the terrible things that could happen
- Complaining – even if it is really happening, it is still negative thinking!

Most of us don't even realize when we are thinking negatively because it seems to us that we are just reacting to the events in our lives, but negative thinking actually creates those events, first and foremost. There is no question of the chicken or the egg – first negative thinking, then negative events.

At this point, you might realize just how much of your thinking is actually negative, but, instead of being overwhelmed, this can be a moment of personal power - it is your awareness that opens the door to profound change.

Negative thinking is the direct manifestation of disempowering programs, so when the Worthiness Program and/or Powerlessness Program are running, you can expect corresponding negative thoughts. For instance, the Worthiness Program often provokes thoughts of judgment, comparison and not being enough, while the Powerlessness Program often provokes thoughts of control, disempowerment and victimhood.

The EGO is programmed to prove worth, gain control and generate energy, and, therefore, it continuously scans for known sources of worth, power and energy, and when it determines a good source of motor-vation, based on this criteria, it generates energy to motor-vate you, and, at the same time, it often uses your thoughts to communicate with you.

EGO says, "*You better win or look your best, don't look like a fool, everyone will laugh, don't be stupid or lazy etc…* "

At one time, thoughts like these may have motor-vated us to take action in order to prove our worth, but, eventually, they do the exact opposite. Listening to the EGO's negative monolog manifests as negative emotional energy, such as fear. So, instead of being motor-vated, we are paralyzed from taking action, but, nonetheless, the EGO keeps repeating the same negative thoughts because they were subconsciously programmed when we were very young, and the EGO cannot reprogram itself (this is a job for the True You).

Negative thinking alone is enough to cause anxiety,
but combined with negative emotional energy, anxiety is a sure bet.

The EGO generates energy to motor-vate us, but, when we ignore motor-vation, that energy has no outlet, so the EGO tries other means of motor-vation. Relentlessly flitting from one thing to the next, trying to get our interest, and, consequently, causing our thoughts to be scattered or fragmented - and, because there is no channel for the EGO's generated energy, the body doesn't know what to do with it.

Additionally, if we consider doing anything risky to our worth, the EGO might try to control our choices and behavior with fear or its close cousin self-doubt.

EGO says, "*You're not good enough, you'll fail, you've failed before, why try?*"

Fear and self-doubt shut us down and keep us from risky behavior, but, as a result, the energy that would have been used for expression is suppressed in the body as negative energy, along with fear, and, if the EGO is overwhelmed with this non-focused energy, the brain interprets this overload as anxiety.

Anxiety is the result of negative thinking and suppressed energy.

Not surprisingly, too much negative energy in the body at one time is debilitating and, if anxiety continues to build, the body could have an emotional breakdown - so something has to interrupt this cycle. Therefore, one of two things must result; either energy must be released or the system must shut down and reset.

Releasing energy could translate to frustration, anger, lashing out, blowing off steam or even abusing others. The release of energy is temporary and in all likelihood the cycle of anxiety and release continues – anxiety will build up again until it reaches the threshold where it must be released again.

If there is no release, depression may ensue.

Depression

Depression is the body's survival strategy
when overloaded with negative energy.

Depression works by cutting off external stimuli and relationships so that the EGO is no longer scanning for sources of worth, power or energy, and, if it is not scanning, energy will not be generated or accumulated within the body. Depression, partially or fully, disables your "motors" so that you have little or no external motor-vation, and, therefore, you disengage from the outside world, thereby protecting your mind and body from energetic overload.

Even though depression suppresses our senses and our "motors" mostly shut down, unless we are experiencing a full scale depression, where we are completely detached and despondent, fear and worry can still build-up inside depression, manifesting as more anxiety.

This means that even though depression makes us feel lethargic, we may still be accumulating anxious energy, and, if this trapped energy doesn't have an exit point, such as lashing out, the unconscious exit strategy could be a panic attack, and this is why depressed people sometimes have panic attacks.

Panic Attacks

A panic attack relieves internal pressure by releasing energy outward; you might even describe a panic attack as being attacked from the inside out.

We associate panic attacks with certain situations, such as closed spaces, heights, etc..., but it is not usually specific situations that cause us to panic. Indeed, panic attacks are often situational but the specific situation is simply the last straw, and, in fact, these situations are the trigger event, but they are usually not the prime cause as we have been led to believe.

Indeed, some people truly do have isolated fears about certain situations that result in panic attacks, but most people who experience panic attacks suddenly develop them overnight.

Most people experience at least a slight amount of stress on bridges or in confined spaces, but, if you don't already have anxiety, this increased energy probably won't make a difference. However, if you are already anxious, going over a bridge or in an elevator could be the energetic tipping point.

For the purpose of fight or flight, fearful situations always increase energy in the body, but usually an isolated situation does not produce the amount of energy required for a panic attack.

Panic attacks could be your body's way of releasing negative energy before there is an energetic overload.

Generally speaking, we are likely to experience anxiety prior to a panic attack, and, then, when we experience the trigger event, our negative reaction compiles on top of pre-existing anxiety, and, in order to avoid an energetic overload, massive energy is released - and our brains interpret it as a panic attack.

Much like a volcano, panic attacks don't just erupt out of nowhere - slowly over time, energy builds until an energetic threshold has been met and exceeded.

Just to clarify, the situational trigger is not actually the *breaking point,* but, rather, it is our thoughts and beliefs about the trigger that builds up negative emotional energy to the point of bursting.

Panic attacks worsen over time because there is more and more fear associated with it each time, increasing negative energy with every successive attack, and, therefore, resulting in a lower threshold where panic sets in more quickly.

The best way to avoid panic attacks is to dissipate anxiety before experiencing the trigger.

Since anxiety is an overload of emotional energy, it makes sense to express emotions because when we express our emotions, we release emotional energy. There are many ways to express ourselves, such as talking to a friend, therapist, coach or other professional. We might also express our emotions through creative arts, such as writing, dancing, singing, painting, etc...

Developing a physical outlet for your emotional energy is very helpful, such as exercise, hiking, biking, yoga, martial arts, etc... or, you might go to the mountains, desert or beach where you can be alone – to yell and scream as loud as you can!

It's also important to express any True-Self inspiration – so, when you feel inspired, don't allow the EGO to bring you down or drown you in doubt. Just make sure that when you take action, you are doing so as the True You!

Anxiety does not exist when you are present in the moment, so developing a daily meditation and/or mindfulness practice is an excellent idea. .

The best way to avoid anxiety, altogether, is to transcend negative thinking by Reprogramming the EGO and Mastering Your Mind.

Negative thinking doesn't seem like a big deal until you look at the bigger picture. Every time we listen to our negative thoughts, we reinforce disempowering beliefs and perpetuate unconscious programming, entangling us in a complex web that could lead to overwhelming fear, anxiety and even panic attacks. Although the dynamics and details could be different than described above, and this is just one example, every time we choose negativity, we unconsciously choose the EGO.

Since anxiety and panic attacks are both signs that our "motors" are burning out and the EGO is malfunctioning, they each represent a perfect opportunity for transformation, and True-Self embodiment.

Let's Recap

- Subconscious programs have their basis in disempowering beliefs, such as unworthiness and powerlessness and manifest as negative thoughts.
- All negative thinking is complete EGO, often manifesting as fear-based emotions.
- If the EGO generates energy to motor-vate us, but it is not working because we are paralyzed with fear, the energy has no outlet, and the body could become overloaded with negative energy.
- Large amounts of negative energy in the body is interpreted as anxiety, and, if it is not released or adequately alleviated, it could lead to depression.
- In an attempt to reduce anxiety, depression numbs the senses and turns off "motors."
- Anxiety may continue to build in depression, and, if it reaches a dangerous level, a panic attack could result, in order to release built up energy.
- To avoid panic attacks it is important to dissipate anxiety before experiencing the trigger event.
- To avoid anxiety you must transcend negative thinking by Reprogramming the EGO and Mastering Your Mind.

Chapter 38

Reprogramming the EGO

The ultimate goal is True-Self integration, *where you live fully as your True-Self*, but it might take a little time before this happens, so it is a very good idea to have a higher functioning EGO in the event your True-Self is displaced from time to time. In other words, if and when, your True-Self is in the corner playing the observer and the EGO is running the show, your higher functioning EGO doesn't sabotage the dreams and intentions of your True-Self. But, before we go any further, there is something you should know about the EGO.

In its highest expression, the EGO is meant to be your avatar so that you can experience the full spectrum of life in this realm.

The True-Self desires to experience all things but because the high vibration of the True-Self doesn't allow for a direct experience of certain "low vibration adventures," such as war, fighting, separation and competition, etc… we need an avatar so that we can play and experiment in this vast dimension of duality. The EGO allows us to experience life in a way that our True-Selves could never know, which sounds awesome, except for the fact that we have become removed from this intent, and, as a result, the EGO has taken over, causing us to believe that we are the EGO.

Because the higher-intent for the EGO has been forgotten, most of our lives are focused primarily around survival and generating energy, and, as a result, we are often engulfed in a complex dynamics that keeps us from the joy, peace and exhilaration that we were born to experience.

The good news is, it's never too late
to take command of your life and reprogram the EGO.

You might discover that there are many ways of reprogramming, but when we speak of EGO reprogramming, we are usually speaking about reprogramming the beliefs that run subconscious programs, such unworthiness and powerlessness.

It is no mystery that beliefs manifest as thoughts, and, therefore, by paying close attention to our regular thoughts, we can we identify underlying beliefs, and since thoughts represent beliefs, if we consciously change our thoughts, we will ultimately change our beliefs, thereby reprogramming the EGO. This requires Mastering Your Mind!

Master Your Mind

> *Signpost on the path*
> *Be careful what you think because your thoughts dictate the path!*

Mastering your mind requires mastering your thoughts, but the biggest problem is that we think that we are our thoughts.

When you refer to yourself, it is likely that you use your thoughts to define you. Thought, however, is more closely akin to the five senses, and, in fact, thought is simply another sense like seeing, hearing and smelling. Thought is intended to serve us, but somewhere along the way, the EGO took control, and now we must reclaim control and reprogram the EGO to serve!

To your subconscious every thought is a command.

There are many types of reprogramming processes, but the ability to focus is of central importance. Since you automatically give power and energy to the focus of your attention, consciously choosing the source of your focus on a moment to moment, day to day, basis can transform your life forever.

No matter how it seems, you can, and must, train your mind to focus. The EGO uses your brain to sort for negativity (threats to your worth), so you must override this survival dynamic and focus on the positive.

- EGO says, *"Be on guard!"*
- True-Self says, *"Master a positive focus!"*

Without a doubt, this absolutely means that you must stop listening to subconscious programs that have their basis in disempowering beliefs and manifest as negative thoughts in your head. Every time you pay attention to a negative thought, argue with it or try to negotiate a deal, you are indirectly saying that you believe it, and, if you believe it, it will run, and it will run your life. When you no longer believe a thought or belief, you won't argue, negotiate or pay attention. You might have to ignore or say no to the same negative thought a thousand times before it stops repeating in your head, but, when you finally stop believing, and you withdraw your power and energy, it will naturally deactivate the correlating subconscious program, and the negative thoughts associated with that program will stop re-playing.

Inner Guidance Network

It's quite common to be unclear about the negative connotation to a thought. Some negative thoughts are incredibly clear to discern, while others are a bit hazier. Fortunately, with the help of your inner guidance network (aka emotions), there is no mystery to whether your thoughts are positive or negative. *You can accurately use your emotions to discern negative and positive thoughts.*

When you think positive thoughts like, "Today is going to be a great day or I love my life" you feel upbeat. When you think negative thoughts like, "Today is dreadful, or I hate my life," you feel down or blue. Since you cannot think negative thoughts and feel good at the same time, it's safe to say that your inner emotional guidance accurately discerns all thinking patterns, *and, remember, all negative thinking is complete EGO!*

Just to clarify, when we refer to negative and positive thinking, we are not assessing right and wrong thoughts, but, rather, positive thinking means that you are focusing on what you want, while negative thinking means that you are focusing on what you ***do not*** want.

Release Negative Thoughts

The following guide will help you overcome or release negative thinking.

Take Responsibility

If you want to embody your True-Self, it is essential that you take responsibility for all your thoughts, but also notice that you are not your thoughts. This is the high level of conscious responsibility. If you can separate *who you really are* from your thoughts, your thoughts will begin to lose their power.

Positive or negative, you are not your thoughts – so, ponder this; if you suddenly stopped thinking, would you cease to exist, or would you discover yourself to be the awareness beyond the thinking....?

Focus on Solutions

If you are faced with a problem, focusing on the problem is a negative mental state, while focusing on the solution or focusing on finding the solution is a positive mental state.

Turn it Around

If you find yourself focusing on what you do not want, flip it around. If you know what you don't want, you also know what you do want. Flip it around as many times a day as necessary. Eventually, it will stick.

Add a "Yet"

When you say, "I can't do something," it tells your subconscious mind not to allow you to do it. However, if you add a "yet," it changes everything. By saying "I can't do it, *yet*," you are commanding your subconscious mind to prepare for doing whatever it is that you want to do.

Drop Your "Buts"

If you say or think something positive and you add a "but," you negate the positive. By saying, I really like this day, but I wish I didn't have to ...," you made the whole thought negative. Just focus on the positive and drop your "buts."

No excuses

Don't give yourself excuses, such as, "Everyone thinks negatively" – that will just keep you trapped in old thinking.

Detox Your Life

Until you gain control of your mind, do your best to be around positive people. If you can't detox your life of certain people, set an intention to stay centered as your True-Self, and don't take anything personally.

Set Boundaries

When I first detoxed my life of negativity, I would literally tell any negative-speaking people, "I'm sorry, you probably didn't know this, but I don't allow anyone to talk negatively about me or around me." I would say it very nicely and I would sincerely smile. Often people would respond with an apology or they would just change the subject. Either way, it always worked.

rate Your Mind

rate your mind with positive videos, books and music – anything that makes feel good and moves you in the direction of focusing on the positive. On my website at ***www.Nanice.com***, I have inspiring classes, videos, and meditations, designed to empower positive thinking.

Practice Imagining

Practice imagining your perfect life as if it has already happened. Imagination will unlock the positivity that already exists inside you. It is also a great idea to pre-pave your day by imagining how you desire your day to unfold.

Be Kind to Yourself

If you have been practicing negative thinking your whole life, it might take some time to shift it around. Be determined to do so, but, also be kind, patient and loving with yourself. Judging yourself for negative thinking is just more negativity on top of negativity. Being kind and loving is positive thinking and it will help overcome negative thoughts.

For Others

Instead of feeling sorry for someone or worrying about others, imagine those who have challenges rising above those challenges – see them strong, happy and successful. The most that we can ever do for another is to imagine them at their very best.

Practice Letting Go

There are many ways to let go of thoughts; here are some ideas to consider:

1. When you automatically believe your thoughts, it invites other similar thoughts to manifest in your mind, and, before you know it, you have a full blown story and the emotions that go along with it. The shift is simple. When that first thought pops into your head, don't believe it. Just let it be without inviting other thoughts to join. Just observe without believing or disbelieving, and see what happens.

2. Imagine that the negative voice in your head is the voice of Mickey Mouse or Donald Duck - hearing a negative thought in a cartoon's voice can disempower any thought.

3. Another interesting option is putting a negative thought in a bubble and popping it. It doesn't matter how you do it, as long as you drop the thought.

4. On those occasions when you forget a thought mid-sentence and you really want to remember what you were saying or thinking, do something radical - let it go. Don't try to remember the thought, unless, of course, it's life or death. Every time you drop a thought, in this way, you retrain your brain, making it much easier to release other thoughts at will. It's only the EGO that is so attached to all your thoughts – most thoughts don't really matter in the big scheme of things, so you don't need to be a prisoner to your thinking.

When you stop listening to your thoughts, your thoughts turn off, and you are present and aware as the True You, but as soon as you start listening to your thoughts again, you are vulnerable to EGO control. Understanding this Stop and Start Switch gives you immense power to call forth your True-Self.

Clearly, it takes intentional practice but the rewards of Mastering Your Mind are exponentially greater than the time and effort required. The more you Master Your Mind, the more conscious you will become, increasing your ability to choose thoughts that serve and empower the True You.

All negative thoughts are self-sabotaging

Unfortunately, we have been led to believe that we must be hard on ourselves in order to make changes in our lives, but negative thinking is not inspiring. Negative thinking is self-sabotaging - if you want to make changes in your life, but you are mentally beating yourself up, you are sabotaging potential results, because you cannot make positive changes while focusing on the negative.

The best way to make changes or improve your life is to focus on what you do want and create empowering thoughts that will support you in realizing your desires. If you can become your own best friend and cheerleader, you will discover that anything is possible.

Reprogramming the EGO requires that disempowering thoughts and beliefs be replaced with the truth of your being.

Remembering Your Worth through True-Self Embodiment

No matter how many years, or lifetimes, you have been practicing unworthiness or powerlessness, there is an all-knowing part of you, known as your True-Self, who knows your unconditional worth and remembers your intrinsic power. Who better to reprogram the EGO than the True You?

During states of True-Self embodiment, you have the ability to access the feeling of unconditional worth, as well as intrinsic power, and by intentionally focusing on your worth and power, your subconscious will begin to align with higher consciousness, and, over time, old disempowering programs will be replaced with the wisdom and knowing of your True-Self.

Remember, you cannot turn off a program, or do any type of reprogramming, while operating from inside the program, because the EGO is self-preserving and it will not allow you. Therefore, if you are to turn off unconscious programming or reprogram the EGO, you must embody your True-Self.

The Process:

Access your True-Self by dropping into a relaxed state of consciousness, using meditation or your favorite process of letting go. A True-Self Embodiment Process is also located at the end of this chapter.

Once relaxed as the True You, it is time to speak directly to the EGO.

Clear and concise affirmations work best - the most effective manner in which to reprogram the EGO is through "I Am" statements. Whatever you say after "I Am" is received by your subconscious mind and recorded, but, the catch is, *you must <u>believe</u> your command.*

For your subconscious to accept anything as truth, you must believe it. If you don't believe, your subconscious will reject it. This is why this process must be done when you embody your True-Self. Many times, people do positive affirmations when their EGO's are in charge, and the affirmations don't work because the EGO doesn't believe them. This is where your True-Self makes all the difference! When you speak to your subconscious mind, as your True-Self, you speak as someone who knows that you are unconditionally worthy and intrinsically powerful, and, therefore, your subconscious will believe it too.

In addition to affirming your worth, you can add other commands, regarding your power, abundance, health, love or whatever is most appropriate for you.

The following are some suggestions:

- I am unconditionally worthy.
- I am unconditionally worthy of love.
- I am unconditionally worthy of abundance.
- I am unconditionally worthy of health and well-being.
- I am intrinsically powerful.
- I am a powerful creator.
- I have the power to do, be, have or experience all I desire.
- I am abundant.
- I am unconditionally worthy of freedom.

Repeat the affirmations of your choice every day and preferably several times each day. At some point in the process, you will feel the positive resonance of the words in your body. It is important to remember that reprogramming is often a gradual process, and requires a consistent practice. How long, you ask? As long as it takes!

Florence Scovel Shinn is the master of affirmative commands - you can find a list at - http://www.florence-scovel-shinn.com/

Quick and Easy Embodiment

While in a meditative or relaxed state, let go of everything for a moment and imagine the energy of love filling your body. Once you feel a sense of lightness, peace or presence, do one of the following two processes:

1. Locate your Observer; this is the part of you who is non-judgmentally watching and this is also your True-Self. Once your True-Self has been located, consciously invite your True-Self into your heart area; your intention may be enough for your True-Self to move into your heart or you may have to imagine it happening. Either way is fine. Once you sense your True-Self moving into your heart, imagine it settling into your entire body. It may happen instantly

or it may take several minutes. If it takes longer than you think it should, be patient and allow the process.

2. The second way to quickly embody your True-Self is to imagine the life size silhouette of your True-Self standing before you and simply step in. Your True-Self can be facing you or you can both be facing the same way; try stepping in from the front and then from the back to see which works best for you.

These are just two ways of intentionally embodying your True-Self but you might discover a way that works better for you. Having fun and doing what you love to do almost always guarantee True-Self embodiment. Above all, always trust yourself.

For a guided meditation, designed to support your journey to True-Self embodiment - go to www.Nanice.com/trueself

---

During the process of True-Self integration, it is common to feel as if the EGO is dying, but this death is an illusion. When the caterpillar enters the cocoon, does he know that he is becoming the butterfly, or does he believe that he is dying? If he is identified with being the caterpillar, indeed, there is a death involved, but not of the caterpillar, but, rather, the death of identity. In holding onto identity, resistance keeps the caterpillar from becoming his true butterfly-self.

The EGO is not you!

Nothing is dying.

Who You Really Are is Awakening …

Chapter 39

The Key to Problem Solving!

Have you ever noticed that you have the ability to see the world with two entirely different perspectives?

The EGO sees the world in terms of worth, possible danger and what could go wrong. Although its perspective defines a very limited reality, if we don't know anything else, it seems perfectly normal, but without the distorted filter cast on by the EGO, your True-Self sees the world in terms of possibility and creativity - a limitless reality blossoming with potentiality.

Whereas the EGO is not trained to see solutions beyond its scope of programming, your True-Self has the power to see solutions that turn difficult challenges into great opportunities. There is not an issue in your life that cannot be solved or transcended by your True-Self. If you desire access to mind expanding solutions, your True-Self just happens to be the world's best problem solver!

This means that before you contemplate the solution to any challenge in your life, first take the time to embody your True-Self.

Split Energy Syndrome

We previously discussed Split Energy Syndrome in terms of self-care, but it's actually much more pervasive. Whenever we are confused about a course of action and cannot make a choice, we experience what is known as split energy; part of us wants one thing and another part wants something completely different.

Most times, split energy manifests when the EGO and the True-Self are in disagreement. Split energy probably happens quite regularly, but we may not notice it unless there is a decision to make. It can be an interesting tell-tale experiment to pay close attention to split energy and notice who gets the deciding vote - will it be the EGO or True-Self?

There is no way to make this important discernment unless you can clearly identify the "voice" of your True-Self and the "voice" of the EGO. They may, or may not, *sound* different to you, but there is likely a sharp distinction between the two when you know how to listen.

Just like emotions produce different sensations in the body, so does the EGO and True-Self. Maybe you never noticed it before, and that's okay, but once you master this discernment, you'll probably wonder how you never realized the difference.

The key to discernment is the quality of the *voice* and the sensation it produces in your body. The EGO includes attributes, such as judgment, rigidity, repetition, focusing on "what's wrong," compulsivity, closed-ness, and it manifests as feelings of worry, anxiety, stress, overwhelm, uncertainty, etc... Your True-Self includes attributes, such as openness, invitation, creativity, possibility, certainty, free spiritedness, trust, and it manifests as joy, peace, love, enthusiasm and a calm sense of knowing.

Determining the "voice quality" is a rather logical process, while noticing bodily sensations is quite organic and kinesthetic.

Your body is an intuitive quantum computer, constantly making assessments of your inner and outer worlds, producing accurate conclusions and offering continuous feedback, all occurring in the blink of an eye. This all goes on without our normal awareness, but only because we haven't been trained to pay attention to our body's innate wisdom. Only in extreme situations do we notice fear warning us to stay away or exhilaration tempting us to take a chance, but, nonetheless, the body produces clear signals all the time.

The more you become in touch with your body, and learn how to listen, the easier it will be, but you can begin right where you are.

Place your awareness on your inner dialogue and notice how you feel; pay close attention to the sensations in your body. Do you feel open or closed, loving or fearful, rigid or relaxed, stressed or calm?

As you pay attention to your thoughts and listen to your body, discerning the EGO from your True-Self should become second nature.

Decision Making Process

Do you have an important decision to make but you are lost in the "valley of split energy"? Instead of making the traditional pros and cons list, it can be a very empowering to *discern the source* of conflicting ideas, beliefs and desires.

This is how you do it:

1. Take a blank piece of paper and cut it into several smaller sized papers - 2 inches by 2 inches is a good size.
2. On each piece of paper, write down one thought, idea, belief or desire regarding the decision.
3. Once you have completed step 2, divide the papers into two piles - discerning which thoughts, beliefs, desires and ideas come from the EGO and which ones come from your True-Self. You might also have a third pile of "unknown origin." As you reflect on the items in the first two piles, you may get clarity on the items of "unknown origin." If you are still not sure, say each item out-loud and notice how it makes you feel. A good general rule is anything that makes you feel constrained or judgmental comes from the EGO and anything that makes you feel expansive and open comes from the True-Self.
4. Once you complete this process, the opinions of the EGO and those of your True-Self should be quite clear, but what you do with the results is up to you.

The more you identify the voice in your head, and the more you understand the dynamics of the EGO, and how it operates according to subconscious programming, the more clarity you will inevitably bring to all the decisions in your life. It is also very helpful to use a journal to track the results of listening to the EGO versus listening to your True-Self, and let the results speak for themselves.

Yes, it usually requires much more faith to listen to your True-Self, opposed to the EGO. After all, the EGO is programmed to guide you according to the "safe choice" -

keeping you protected within your comfort zone. Additionally, guidance that comes from the EGO is always limited according to our specific programming.

Your True-Self, on the other hand, does not limit you within any comfort zones, and unlike the EGO, its guidance is not necessarily logical and predictable. However, your True-Self has direct access to the wisdom of the all-knowing Universe, and, with that comes the inherent ability to foresee the unfoldment of every possibility and, as such, you are guided accordingly.

Indeed, listening to the guidance of your True-Self may put you out of your comfort zone, and may require a leap of faith at times, but there is no better guide.

Experiencing clarity one day and doubt the next is a symptom of shifting from True-Self to EGO. To regain clarity, recognize that doubt comes from the EGO, and, therefore, take the time to call forth your True and Wise Self.

Clarity and intuition are beautiful byproducts of True-Self embodiment.

Are you surprised just how much the EGO runs your life?

Upon identifying the EGO's inner dialogue, most people are surprised to discover that the EGO is frequently in the driver's seat, but this is no reason for discouragement. This is cause for increased consciousness. The more you consciously invoke the voice of your True-Self, the more you will embody your True-Self.

With consistent practice you will be able to call forth your True-Self on the spot, but, until then, it is essential to develop a mindfulness or meditation practice focused on your True-Self. It is also a great idea to consistently discern the origin of all your thoughts, and, if you can, write them down.

Chapter 40

A Day in the Life of Your True-Self

No doubt, it would be incredible to wake-up as our True-Selves and live happily ever after from that point on, but, since most of us have spent the majority of our lives living in the EGO's shadow, that's probably not very realistic. However, it is realistic to begin a journey that will transcend the EGO, while awakening our Real-Selves.

> *Signpost on the path*
>
> *Living as the EGO inevitably means living a lie*
>
> *If you want to live your truth, you must live as the True You!*

This Sacred Journey is a journey that you will take each day, but only one day at a time. *Why just one day?* If you imagine a life-long journey or a journey that could take months or years, it can seem overwhelming because the destination is out of reach, but taking a journey for just one day is doable. No matter what unfolds on that day, simply living the day makes it a success, and once the day is done, the journey is over, with a brand new journey beginning on the next day, but, if you miss a day, it's no big deal because you can begin again.

So, why not intentionally live as your True-Self for just one day?

You have nothing to lose and literally everything to gain!

Initially, you might want to embark on your first few journeys on days that you are not working, because there may be fewer restrictions and work-related triggers. As you begin to get the feel of what it's like to live as the True You, every day can be a True-Self day. After all, the point is to ultimately live as your True-Self all the time.

The following will guide you through a full day as the True You, but, if a full day is out of reach, consider living as your True-Self for a specific period of time, such as an hour or two, or intend to live as your True-Self for the duration of an event or interaction. Even one hour each day can make a profound difference. The more time you spend as your True-Self, the more you will naturally align.

Let's begin the first day of the journey!

Good Day True-Self!

Each day is a brand new start, so why not wake up on the True-Self side of the bed?

Getting up on the EGO side of the bed generally means rushing through a mindless morning plan while mentally confronting life's problems with resistance and even fear. If you allow the EGO to begin the day, chances are the EGO will also end the day, because once the determined EGO is in the driver's seat, it wants to stay there. Yes, of course, you can override the EGO and align with your True-Self at anytime during the day, but it's probably a great deal easier to avoid the EGO first thing in the morning, than to overcome it during daily busyness or even chaos.

So, how do you wake up on the True-Self side of the bed?

Get a good night's sleep

If you are tired and cranky, your mind and body are ripe for EGO inhabitation, but, if you wake up rested, you will have greater mental mastery, and a better ability to recognize and override the EGO, so that you can live as the True You.

Morning plan

If at all possible, wake-up early so that you have time for self-nurturing. For example, I begin every morning with a hot bubble bath, a cup of coffee or tea and I listen to inspiring music, while bathing and getting ready.

Don't begin the day by ...

Just as important as what you do in the morning is what you don't do; don't begin the day by checking emails or voice-mails or thinking about problems or grievances.

Many people begin their days by watching the news or reading the newspaper, but, let's face it, most of what you read or hear is very negative, and guess what this does? Every time you believe something hurtful or harmful, even if it is unrelated to you, your subconscious mind takes it personally, as if you are experiencing a threat, and the EGO is triggered to protect you.

You might argue that you need to know what's going on in the world, but, keep in mind that traditional news media intentionally focuses on negativity, and rarely, if ever, publicizes the whole story, or even the true story. Personally, I stopped reading, watching and listening to the news in the 1980s because I recognized how much that negativity influenced my energy and affected my day. I may be somewhat less educated on current world events, but it is a small price to pay for vastly improving my overall wellbeing.

Meditate

A morning meditation or mindfulness practice can set the stage for a True-Self day. Simple deep breathing exercises increase Life Force Energy and aligns you with being present. Do some research and find the best morning practice for you.

Pre-pave the day

At the end of your meditation or mindfulness practice, take a few moments to pre-pave the day. Start by saying to yourself, ***"Today, I live as my True-Self"*** and, then imagine going through the upcoming day as your True-Self – imagining positive outcomes and opportunities in all aspects of your life. By using your imagination to focus on your desires for a fulfilling day, you are essentially showing the Universe how to serve you. Remember, you serve the Universe by consciously experiencing your unique version of life, but you are not here on your own – the Universe serves you by hearing your dreams, desires and preferences and manifesting them on your behalf, but you must properly ask so the Universe can hear you, and you must also embody your True-Self in order to be aligned with receiving when the Universe delivers.

Surrender

Once you pre-pave the day, let it go. You've shown the Universe your desires, and, if you want the Universe to deliver your requests, you must let go so it can do its job. If you hold on and try to control, you stand in the way of ease, flow and synchronicity.

Make a choice

Consciously choice to stay present throughout the day. You know your triggers and common pitfalls, and you also know where you get stressed-out and go unconscious, so, just for today, consciously choose to stay present, even in challenging situations. If you can see yourself staying present throughout the day, it will pre-pave presence.

Don't rush

Make a decision not to rush. Rushing is another "motor" and in the end, it just makes us late anyway. So, give up the rush. On the way to work, school or wherever your day calls you, take it slow and be aware of the journey. Don't just try to get to the destination. There is no destination – the destination is just an illusion. So, if you miss the journey, you miss the point of life. As you intentionally go through the day, see what there is to see, feel what there is to feel, hear what there is to hear and notice what there is to notice. Smile at people, wish them well, bless their days and be conscious with each smile, wish and blessing, and it will come back to you like you won the lottery! If you find yourself waiting in line, on the phone or for someone you know, do your best to refrain from impatience and frustration, and, instead, use the time to drop into mindfulness – allowing life to be exactly as it is at this moment.

Reframe Mishaps

Perhaps, you experience a mishap during the day. Instead of reacting negatively, take it as a sign that you are not present. The only reason you ever stub your big toe or knock something over is because you are not conscious in the present moment. When we are conscious, we are able to sense our present environment to such an extent that we intuitively know how to avoid injury and mishap. Physical pain, or anything that goes wrong, wakes us up by calling us back to the present moment.

Mishaps and mistakes are powerful opportunities to get back in our bodies, and become conscious here and now. For instance, as you pick up dropped papers or broken glass, be conscious as you do it. In that same regard, instead of resisting a painful stubbed toe, sit down, breathe and really feel it.

Believe it or not, the willingness to feel pain can bring instant relief to suffering.

Practice Presence

Imagine that this is your first and last day on earth – how do you live your one and only day? You don't have to do a single thing differently because that is not the point. The point is *to be different as you do it!* Imagine, everything you do is for the first and last time, everything you see is for the first and last time and everyone you encounter is for the first and last time. With this concept as your guiding force, there is no chance of taking anything or anyone for granted, and, therefore, little chance of going unconscious.

Bringing your full consciousness to each moment of the day, and being present in all interactions will certainly transform your day.

Don't worry about living the rest of your life like this because that's too big to consider. Today is your only concern, and, in fact, this moment is the only moment to be present. That's it! Moment to moment - day to day.

Discern Your Thoughts

Throughout the day, consciously discern your thoughts and lovingly ignore those of the EGO, while following the direction of your True-Self. At first, this discernment could be confusing, but the more you actively pay attention to your thoughts and how they make you feel, the clearer this distinction will become.

Depending on your particular circumstances, you may discover that if you don't listen to the EGO, you won't do many of the things you normally do. Should you discover that the better part of your day is EGO-driven, instead of making drastic changes, simply be the Observer. As you go through the day, non-judgmentally notice what there is to notice. By dropping into the Observer, you automatically access your True-Self and can see your life through these very wise and allowing eyes.

Choose Love

As you flow through the day, doing your best to spot, and avoid, EGO Pitfalls, there might be times when you feel uncertain about your actions, choices or behavior. That's completely fine, but it might help to remember that your True-Self often says, *Choose love!*

Although this is not a rule, in many instances the True You would choose love, but this can mean many things to many people in many different situations. Choosing love could mean choosing self-love, which might translate into enforcing a boundary or simply saying no. Choosing love could also mean forgiving someone who *stepped on your toes* in some way. There is not a right answer here, but, if you always put others before you, then choosing self-love is probably the path most aligned with your True-Self, as least right now. However, if you have a history of pushing people away or holding grievances, choosing love might mean choosing forgiveness. Choosing love could translate into a multitude of other things, as well, so keep your heart and mind open for signs of inner guidance - only you can discern the best path for you, and you don't need to show up perfect. This is not a contest, competition or race. In times of uncertainty, you can ask yourself, *"What would the True Me do?"*

Also, consider that choosing self-love doesn't mean that we must close down to those around us, and, in fact, as we master self-love, and our boundaries are established, we never have to close down to anyone.

Integrity

As you move through the day, you might also experience some confusion around personal integrity, and you might stumble upon the two faces of integrity.

Believe it or not, EGO Integrity and True-Self Integrity could be in direct conflict.

Integrity to the EGO might encompass anything that increases worth, operates a "motor" or results in success, and this could possibly even include some version of lying, cheating or stealing.

Integrity to your True-Self might mean listening to your inner guidance, while at the same time, being open, honest and present, even if it means possible failure.

At first, EGO Integrity might be quite compelling, but only due to the fact that the EGO's version of integrity appears to "get what you want" and also because unconscious programs have been running your life, and without consciously overriding them, they will continue to run. However, with conscious awareness, you have the ability to override internal programming, and, sooner or later, you might come to find that True-Self Integrity aligns you with your dreams and desires. Plus, just to add icing to the cake, you might also find that True-Self Integrity aligns you with a new paradigm of relationships - potentially elevating every relationship to a higher consciousness.

Don't Get on the Worry Train

As your day unfolds, it is quite possible that a feeling of worry surfaces from time to time. In the past, this insidious form of fear may have taken hold of your senses or even taken you down to your knees. Fortunately, with your heightened consciousness, this type of debilitation is a thing of the past. So, instead of giving in to the EGO's compulsive, over-sensitive, warning system, you can recognize its voice and choose to listen to your True-Self.

EGO says, "You are in danger!"

True-Self says, "You are safe."

When the EGO's alarm sounds, don't react by jumping on the worry train, but, instead, get super present, and, if everything is fine in the present moment, there is really nothing to worry about.

If, however, you do get on the worry train, don't be surprised if it intensifies, and before long, it morphs into stress. Stress is symptomatic of a highly alert EGO that is super-sensitive to any threat that might decrease worth, and, therefore, implicit in stress is the pressure to succeed and the fear of failure.

EGO says, *"If you don't get the job done right and on time, you're unworthy."*

Stress is a good sign that we are unconsciously living in the future as the EGO, so, if you should experience any sign of stress, Stop, Drop and Roll before it becomes overwhelming.

Immediately ascertain that stress is an indication that the EGO is rearing its worrisome little head, and, consciously choose to take the high road, which is the only road you will ever find the True You. So, instead of giving into stress, remind yourself, *"I am unconditionally worthy, and my worth does not depend on any person, place or thing."* Then, come back to the present moment with your full consciousness.

I'll be the first to admit that, on the surface, reality is worrisome and stressful, but, fortunately, unlike the EGO, your True-Self doesn't live on the surface of reality. Your True-Self is directly connected to the wisdom and magic of an All-Loving Abundant Universe that has your back every step of the way, *but you must get out of the way,* or rather, you must get the EGO out of the way – especially if you want to be blessed with the wisdom, guidance and magic of the Universe.

Your only real job is to consciously live as your True-Self in each and every moment, and by being present in the now, you align with everything good and fine today, and tomorrow takes care of itself. Maybe you are thinking, *"If I'm living moment to moment, how do things get done?"* This is where it gets really interesting. I wouldn't have believed it if I didn't experience it myself.

Live in the Moment

By consciously living in the moment, everything gets done that must get done, deadlines are met, kids are fed, bills are paid and any prevailing messes are cleaned up, but if that's not enough of an incentive for living in the present, there's even more.

Living in the future causes stress and stress compresses present day time so you actually have less time to get things done. Conversely, living in the present moment, and really being conscious here and now, actually expands time so you have more time for everything. Scientists agree that gravity drastically affects time, and, just as true, consciousness affects time – indeed, time does contract and expand according to your current level of consciousness. The more stress, the less time. The less present, the less time. The more future-oriented, the less time. Imagine, you have the ability to expand time, simply by being present - the more often you are present, the more time you will experience.

Just as presence directly corresponds to time,
presence directly corresponds to your intrinsic power.

Okay, it's no big secret that living in the future provokes needless worry and stress, but that's not the worst part – living in the fearful future takes you out of the present moment where all your power dwells. Hence, if you are not conscious here and now, not only do you misalign with your True-Self, you misalign with your intrinsic power, and, furthermore, the limitless power of the Universe.

Claim Your Power

What can you do with this power?

Anything you desire, when you know how. Power is Universal Energy and from Universal Energy you can manifest your grandest dreams, as well as your most ideal solutions to all challenges. Your intrinsic power has the innate ability to alchemize Life Force Energy into anything you can possibly imagine, and it materializes as creativity, collaboration and innovation, which inevitably results in love, prosperity, wellbeing and fulfillment. So, if you live in the future through worry, fear or stress, you cut yourself off from Universal Currency that can be used to manifest your best possible destiny. Why spend your time worrying about the future, when you can consciously create your most ideal future?

Let's make an important distinction here – there is a tremendous difference between unconsciously thinking about the future and consciously creating the future. If you unconsciously think about the future, the EGO is triggered because you are not present, and once the EGO takes control, it will sort for any threats to your worth and power.

Therefore, if you are unconsciously thinking about the future, it will spotlight threats in relation to your future focus.

Consciously creating your future requires you to be conscious as you do it. Unquestionably, this means that the only time you should ever think about the future or imagine the future is as your True-Self.

Instead of randomly, and absentmindedly, thinking about the future, intentionally isolate pivotal times in your life to consciously imagine the future of your dreams; begin your day, week, month, year or decade by consciously imagining your most desirable day, week, month, year, decade, etc... At other times, if your mind drifts into the future, stop drifting and come back to the present moment, where all your power is accessed and expressed. There is just no point in allowing the EGO to think about the future because it can only preview the future in terms of past programming, often resulting in some variation of fear.

Navigate the Bumps

A day in the life of your True-Self has the potential for magic and miracles, but, navigating past the EGO can also make it a little bumpy at times, so, it's normal to experience ups and downs, bouncing back and forth between the EGO and the True You. It is very likely that you will easily align with your True-Self in some circumstances but in others the EGO will dominate.

If, and when, you do get hijacked by the EGO, don't panic or resist, as that will keep the EGO active. The best thing to do is take time out. The simple, yet powerful, process of *letting go* (that we have discussed previously) can allow you to regain consciousness in the present moment, consequently, realigning with your True-Self. Or, simply, wait for the next *True-Self Window* to open up, where you have the wherewithal to be present once again, thereby deactivating the EGO.

No matter how often the EGO is triggered, or how often you fail to avoid EGO Hijacking, there is no need for concern – it's all part of the process, and, as long as your intention remains on living as the True You, success is imminent.

Relaxation Practice

An enormous support to True-Self Living is a daily period of relaxation. It is extremely helpful to make time during the day where you can re-center yourself; even ten or fifteen minutes of deep conscious breathing or mindfully taking a short walk can do wonders for letting go and realigning with your True-Self.

Additionally, toward the end of the day, it is imperative to partake in some sort of Relaxation Practice. You absolutely need time and space to let go completely. Even the very best days need a comedown where you can surrender it all, *and be still.* Don't think of a daily Relaxation Practice as a temporary practice, because it is a permanent and integral component to living as the True You.

Your Relaxation Practice is the perfect time to perform a Day Review.

Day Review

In your mind's eye, review the day by non-judgmentally observing the flow of the day, and then pinpoint any "sticky spots" where the EGO was triggered or even took control. Do your best to identify the trigger(s), and, if needed, go through an emotional healing process, as described in a previous chapter, to release the underlying emotional issue(s), which ultimately means releasing the causal disempowering belief(s). Once you complete the process, mentally re-enact the triggering situation(s), but, this time, imagine making different internal choices and overriding the trigger(s). Now, with the True You remaining in command, continue to play out the remainder of the day.

Also, during your day review, notice if there were any moments when you could have been more conscious or when you could have dropped judgment or resistance. Once you identify any such times, mentally replay the situation(s), seeing yourself with higher consciousness and a sense of love and allowance - continue to mentally replay the day from there on. Since the subconscious mind cannot discern the past, present or future, every time you imagine a higher version of a previous experience, your subconscious believes it is true, which means that when you replay your day from a higher state of consciousness, your consciousness is heightened.

Listen to Inner Guidance

During your practice of relaxation, it is also essential to intentionally tune into your inner guidance; just make sure to ascertain the voice of your True-Self, so you don't mistakenly listen to unconscious programming. See what your inner guidance has to say about the day. Maybe it will show you an experience from a different perspective, or maybe you'll receive an intuitive hit that upgrades a goal or plan. You might also have specific questions to present to your wise inner self.

Rejuvenate

Your Relaxation Practice should also provide a sense of rejuvenation, where you feel re-energized and inspired for the day ahead. This might include yoga, exercise, martial arts or some other form of empowering movement. Too exhausted to even think about moving? End of day exhaustion indicates that you are over-extending yourself, and your inner guidance is suggesting that you re-orchestrate your days in such a way that you can easily avoid exhaustion on a regular basis.

The details of your True-Self Day will be unique for you, but it might include time with your loving family and/or friends, doing what you love to do and maybe even some type of contribution.

Let's also remember that your True-Self Body requires nutritious foods, clean water and fresh air, while your True-Self Mind requires inspiring thoughts and empowering beliefs.

Any day can be lived as your True-Self, but, here's the thing; if you have been untrue to yourself, staying in a job or relationship past its expiration date, for instance, every time you embody your True-Self, you are going to be confronted with the lie you are living, and, if you continually ignore the guidance of your True-Self, you set the stage for the EGO to take control. Your True-Self knows what is in your highest good, and the more you follow true inner-guidance, the more you will joyfully live as the True You.

Let's Recap:

- Ideally, every day will be lived as the True You, but, until then, it is essential to intentionally create one True-Self day at a time. The more you live as your True-Self, the easier it will be.
- Get up on the True-Self side of the bed, and begin your day consciously by meditating, pre-paving your day and surrendering to the Universe.
- Throughout the day, practice presence, discern your thoughts, listen to your True-Self and choose love over fear.
- Practice True-Self Integrity - live in the moment and claim your power.
- Navigate the bumps.
- End the day with a practice of relaxation and rejuvenation
- Review the day.

Chapter 41

Channeling Life Force Energy

Honestly, it may take time to fully integrate your True-Self, and there may be hours, days or weeks where your True-Self is misaligned or completely displaced.

When this is the case, you can keep the EGO from generating energy by consciously channeling Life Force Energy. It is true that when you align with the flow of Life Force Energy, it is likely that your body comes into resonance with your True-Self, so the one goal of channeling Life Force Energy can result in two positive outcomes; experiencing the flow of Life Force Energy and True-Self embodiment.

The top ways to channel Life Force Energy

Create a Need for Energy

One of the best ways to naturally generate Life Force Energy is by having a need for energy. If you just sit home watching TV, you don't need much energy, and, if you don't need energy, there is no reason for your mind/body to receive Life Force Energy. This means that if you choose to use your mind and body for fun, exercise or some type of creativity, there is a need for energy, and, as such, energy will be channeled from Source Energy.

The Universe works on an "as needed basis" so, if you don't need it, you don't get it, but, if you do need it, you can get as much as you need.

Most people wait for energy in order to do what they enjoy, but, in order to get that energy, you must begin taking action. We are not talking about your "to do" list or fulfilling obligations. We are talking about doing what you love.

When you are "in joy," you are connected to Source, and Life Force Energy flows.

You might create a greater need for energy by:

Dance, Sing or Paint

It doesn't matter how you express yourself as long as it makes you feel good - the more you do, the more energy you will access.

Move Your Body

Yoga, exercise, hiking, biking, weight training etc… all create a natural need for energy that overflows into our days, allowing us to have more natural energy overall.

Conscious Sex

Sex is often used by the EGO to artificially generate energy, but when both people approach sex with high consciousness, through a practice, such as tantric sex, or simply staying present, sex can easily generate Life Force Energy, and, in fact, second to procreation, this is the purpose of sex.

Laughter

The more you can genuinely laugh, the more natural energy you will experience. Laughter requires that you let go of control and approach life, or at least an aspect of life, with humor and lightheartedness. The more light-hearted you are, the more you align with the flow of Life Force Energy.

Experience Love

The more you feel and express love for another, or even for something you love to do or experience, the more energy you will access. In addition, anything that invokes a feeling of love will allow you to tap into the Source of love and channel Life Force Energy.

Breathe in Energy

Life Force Energy is in the air around us, so anytime we breathe deeply and intentionally, we call forth this natural and abundant energy. Deep and conscious breathing tells your subconscious mind that you are choosing life, and, therefore, you need Life Force Energy in order to live. It also tells your subconscious that you are safe and well, and it's okay to let go and relax.

Breath-work, such as pranayama, and the practice of yoga, allow you to consciously channel Life Force Energy, ultimately connecting with your True-Self in the practice of breathing.

Normal mindless breathing keeps you alive, but does not provide adequate Life Force Energy because ***you must be in your body and conscious*** in order to channel this pure Source of Energy.

When we speak about "being in the body," we are really speaking about True-Self embodiment, and, therefore, the feeling of "not being in your body" is a symptom of True-Self displacement.

The same goes for "being grounded" – when we speak about "being grounded," we are referring to the True-Self being grounded in the body – aligned and fully embodied.

Breath-work quickly and easily grounds you in your body, so there is no good excuse to avoid breath-work; it doesn't cost anything, you don't have to go anywhere and it's always available and infinitely abundant. Simply by consciously breathing, you have direct access to one hundred percent of the energy you will ever need or want.

Breathing Exercise

Take ten deep breaths, focusing on the inhale and the exhale; slowly inhale to a slow count of five, hold your breath to a slow count of five, slowly exhale to a slow count of five, hold the exhale to a slow count of five – repeat ten times.

Be Present

The state of presence aligns you with the prime source of unlimited energy.

If you are seeking the bottomless well of Life Force Energy, the location is Now! Your ability to connect with your natural energy source lies in this moment. The Source is here now - because only this moment exists. This means if you are living in the past or future, your natural energy is compromised, relative to your lack of presence.

Whatever you do, even if you don't like what you are doing, drop resistance and be present.

When we are distracted, thinking about something we would rather do, or something we should be doing, we dump energy needlessly. Bringing presence to each and every moment, even if you are engaged in an undesirable experience, allows energy to flow to you and through you, and then, you have an abundance of energy to complete the task at hand - likely making it much more enjoyable. When you become present in the moment, love naturally flows, and where love flows, Life Force Energy flows.

Here are some ideas:

Music

Music is like medicine - it has the power to transform you in an instant, so choose your music wisely. If you are aware, you can easily tell if your music choices raise your vibe and tap you into Life Force Energy or bring you down and trigger the EGO. You just need to listen to your body in order to understand the powerful effects of music. Why not choose music that brings you up and energizes you?

Art

The higher purpose of art is to invoke an experience. Like music, art can elevate you or bring you down. Choosing art that enlightens your heart and enriches your spirit raises your vibration and aligns you with Life Force Energy.

Nature

Everything in nature is in a constant state of presence. It is only humans who have the ability to dissociate from the present moment. Being in nature invites you to remember presence; as you let go and relax, the rhythm of nature can balance your body, mind and spirit, allowing you to connect to Life Force Energy.

Meditation

There are many types and purposes of meditation. When you partake in meditation that allows you to let go, the natural result is becoming present and connecting with the flow of Life Force Energy.

Senses

Life Force Energy can also be derived through the five senses - taste, touch, sound, sight and smell - but only when you are present and allow the experience of sensation. The more you love what you sense, the more energy it produces. If you judge what you are sensing, you immediately become unplugged, cutting off your connection to Life Force Energy.

Follow Your Dreams

Your dreams have the capacity to energize your life, but only if you follow them.

There is a symbiotic relationship in nature - just like you can see it in the flowers and the bees, it also exists between you and your life. Life will *feed you* with as much energy as you need, but you must need it for purposes of inspiration, contribution, enjoyment and the fulfillment of your dreams. If you have a dream, and you follow it, you will most certainly access an abundance of Life Force Energy in order to fulfill that dream.

Our dreams are the *dreams of Source* for us, and, in fact, the way in which Source communicates to us is through our dreams and desires, but, it doesn't end there. Source also equips us with everything we need; Source provides the dream, the inspiration for the dream and the necessary gifts we will need to fulfill the dream, and when we say "yes" to the dream, Source supplies us with all the Life Force Energy required to turn the dream into reality.

Inspiration is the creative force that guides you on your path, and directs you toward your grand dream. When you follow your inspiration, you experience an abundance of natural energy to take you where inspiration calls. Additionally, when you express your natural gifts, Life Force Energy flows to fuel the expression of those gifts. The more open and expressive you are, the more energy you need to express, and the more energy you will receive.

Our dreams may take us in the direction of contribution, and, of course, being of service to others through love and compassion channels Life Force Energy, but be careful of the EGO. If you are helping others out of guilt, obligation or because you feel sorry for someone, the EGO is likely generating energy, which will leave you feeling tired and drained in the end. So, when you follow your dream, take the time to discern inspiration from EGO-driven motor-vation.

If you stop dreaming because you think you are too old to experience the manifestation of your dreams, you will consequently age faster because you are telling the Universe that you are no longer a viable vessel for creation, and, therefore, you have no need for life-creating energy.

Your dreams fuel you with Life Force Energy and that rejuvenating energy keeps you young, so, if you want to stay young, you must allow inspiration to flow and you must follow your dreams wherever they take you.

It is never too late to dream, and you are never too old to make your dreams come true!

Let's Recap:

- Creating a need for energy increases Life Force Energy
- Life Force Energy can be channeled via self-expression, movement, connecting with others, laughter, etc...
- Breath-work is one of the quickest and most effective ways to increase Life Force Energy.
- Music, art, nature, meditation and using your senses all have the ability to increase Life Force Energy.
- If you are living in the past or future, your natural energy is compromised, relative to your lack of presence.
- When you become present in the moment, Life Force Energy flows.
- Life will *feed you* with as much energy as you need, but you must need it for purposes of inspiration, contribution, enjoyment and the fulfillment of your dreams.

Chapter 42

True-Self Time and Space

We tend to think of time as something tangible, but it's actually not real. Time is elusive and not all time is the same. Have you ever noticed that when you are stressed, there is never enough time but when you are relaxed and going with the flow, there is more than enough time?

Time is relative to whether you are living life through the EGO or True-Self.

When we are living through the EGO, stress, pressure and rushing condense time, and, as a result, we experience not enough time.

When we are living as our True-Selves, time has a way of expanding to accommodate our needs. As we trust the flow of the Universe, and give up fear-based stress and rushing, time expands, and there might even be an experience of timelessness. We may refer to this as being in the zone, where anything is possible, and sometimes we may even exceed logic and expectation, because this is also the space of magic and miracles.

It is impossible to access the state of flow and ease from EGO, due to the fact that the controlling EGO misaligns you with spiritual expansion. To access this exhilarating space of timeless possibility, where more is possible in less time, your True-Self holds the key. There is no doubt that you can actually experience and create a great deal more as your True-Self, and enjoy it all the more, as you do.

The EGO has its own "speed" and way of moving through life, and, if we move according to "EGO speed," we misalign with our True-Selves, so, we must slowdown, and when we do, we access more time and space to do all the things we were rushing to do as the EGO.

Life has its own divine speed that is one hundred percent in alignment with our True-Selves, so when we are able to listen to life and dance with the flow of life, we naturally sync up with our True-Selves. Becoming in sync with the flow of life is just another way of aligning with who we really are. So, what exactly is the speed of life and how do we sync with it?

Trusting the Flow

If you want to channel Life Force Energy, you need to be in the flow with Life Force Energy. If you are going faster than the speed of life, you are out of sync and misaligned with life's energy.

There is a natural rhythm to the Universe and when we are in sync with this rhythm, life unfolds seamlessly, but when we try to rush toward a destination or goal, we may actually *move faster than the speed of life*. Getting out of sync with life often results in a myriad of challenges and issues.

If your life is chaotic or you are stressed out, tired, fragmented, anxious, confused or things are breaking all around, chances are, you are moving *faster than the speed of life,* and the EGO is in charge.

> *Signpost on the path*
> *The more you trust life, the more energy flows.*

Being out of sync is like the chain falling off your bicycle - you are still pedaling but no matter how fast you pedal, you are not getting anywhere. Lots of effort, but little result, creates exhaustion and overwhelm.

Many years ago, I was a stressed-out single mom and business owner. I had about a million things to do each day, or at least it felt that way. I remember waking up each morning under an energetic blanket of overwhelm and anxiety. I didn't want to get out of bed and face the day, but I had to - at least until I realized that *I didn't have to.* That idea took me by surprise and contradicted everything that I had ever believed about myself and my life. I questioned this new concept but it secretly gave me relief, peace and resolve.

I began to start each morning by surrendering my day to a higher power. In the recesses of my mind I would whisper, "Today, I don't have to do anything." Ahhh..., I could breathe – the layers of the heavy blanket began to dissolve.

Sweet Surrender

We humans are incredibly resilient and tenacious, but at some point, we get so exhausted and stressed-out that we have no choice but to eventually surrender. Things just aren't working and we don't have a clue on how to fix them, so as a last resort, we let go. Of course, letting go is exactly what we need to do.

Here's the thing, by letting go of everything, before my feet even touched the ground, I allowed my True-Self to move into the captain's seat and, as a result, I suddenly had the energy and desire to take inspired action but without the urgency, stress or strain that previously engulfed me. By telling myself, "I don't have to do anything today," I became at choice with my days – with my life. I realized that despite how things might seem, I always had the choice to do – or not do. My life was the way it was because it was my choice – and at any moment I could make a different one. From this perspective, I was no longer in a rush – I was no longer stressed. At some point, I felt the tectonic plates of my life slip into place – anxiety began to melt and I realized that the overwhelm which once swallowed me up could not exist if I was *conscious and present in this moment.*

When we surrender the stress and release the rush, we immediately drop into the present moment, naturally re-aligning with our True-Selves. No matter how off-center we have been, *alignment can happen in an instant, simply by letting go.*

The first sign that we are aligned and in sync with our True-Selves is that we feel better. We feel calm, peaceful and we are in the moment. No rush. No urgency. Just here now in the present moment. The second thing we notice is that things get done easier and quicker, and sometimes they might even appear to get done on their own.

Synchronicity is simply being in sync with Life, and when you are in sync, everything good-and-fine lines up for you – you manifest what you desire with ease and grace.

So, I did just that - I slowed down, I chose my life and I became really, *really* present. Then the most amazing thing began to happen – not only did I feel better, my life began to get better. I was suddenly in sync with the rhythm of the Universe. Everything got done that needed to get done – kids got fed, money got made and even books got written, but there was no longer stress or grief. There was the sweet dance that became my life. The things that once took all my energy, because I was resistant and not present, now seemed to get done without effort.

Ironically, I discovered that the more I slowed down, the more I accomplished and the better the results.

At some point, I realized that my sweet dance was the sweet dance that the Universe had in store for me all along – so, as I had been trying to force things, make things happen and do everything myself, I was actually causing unnecessary pain and hardship. *The mere act of slowing down and letting go, allowed the Universe to do her magic, which is infinitely more powerful than anything I could ever do in many lifetimes.*

What does it take to get in sync with the natural speed of life?

To help you determine what shifts might make the most difference in your life, I offer the following:

You are Not Alone

Sometimes we move *faster than the speed of life* because we believe that we are all alone, and we must do everything ourselves. Despite how it may seem, you are not alone on this journey. You are an intricate part of the Universe – of life itself. When you believe that you are doing it all alone, anxiety and stress are the results. But it is those very emotions that tell you that you have unplugged from the rhythm of life, and it is time to let go so that you can plug back in.

Running from yourself?

Often, we keep super busy because we are afraid of meeting ourselves in the quietude. We are afraid that if we are alone and still, we might confront our weaknesses and have to deal with the shadows we have been avoiding. So, we run from one thing to the next - switching roles, playing identities and hiding behind the illusion of busyness. Yes, it may be uncomfortable to "meet yourself" at first, but you cannot be in sync with life, if you don't know *who you really are.* Whether it is your body or your mind that runs a mile a minute, in order to get in the flow of life, you have to stop, and be still - so that you can hear the quiet voice of your own True-Self.

Stress is fear disguised as desire...

The voice of stress says, "*I have too much to do and not enough time to do it.*" Stress is a liar! In fact, it is stress that shortens time and gives you more to do. When you think thoughts like, *"I don't have enough time"* you are telling the Universe, don't give me enough time. And when you think thoughts like, *"I have too much to do,"* you are telling the Universe, give me too much to do. Your thoughts program reality, so you must consciously program peaceful and harmonious thoughts.

Work Smarter – Not Harder

Our EGOs have us brainwashed with "work ethics' that tell us that in order to succeed we must work incredibly hard and sacrifice ourselves for the success of our desires. This is a myth - the only thing that you have to sacrifice in order to succeed is the belief that you must work so very hard and sacrifice yourself.

Yes, success requires an exchange of energy – things don't materialize out of thin air (at least not yet), but, as the saying goes, work smarter not harder. Working smarter does not just mean innovation and efficiency, it also means *state of mind.* If you are working from a state of overwhelm and stress, it is the EGO at work, and you are likely giving out more energy than you are getting back. If you are multi-tasking and not focused, you are also not getting an equal return for what you put in. However, when you are relaxed, focused and in a state of flow, your True-Self is aligned and the energy that you give out through your work is exponentially returned to you tenfold. Working smarter means, first and foremost, embodying your True-Self, and, as a result, engaging the power of the Universe on your behalf.

In the Flow...

Being in the flow with the Universe doesn't happen by forcing things or trying to control things – it only happens by letting go and trusting that flow, wherever it takes us.

Does this mean that we really let go of control? Well, in some ways, yes, but it also means that we take our power back as creators which is well beyond the petty control of details. When it comes down to it, the only control that we really have is the control of our minds. You can make a huge difference in your life by beginning each morning by pre-paving your day. By envisioning your perfect day, you are telling the Universe what to create for you, and the Universe will respond by giving you intuitive guidance and inspiring you into specific actions that will support your desires.

Ask the Universe

Like a good parent, the Universe will allow you to do whatever you want to do on your own, and not interfere, but as soon as you ask for help, the power and energy of the Universe conspires on your behalf. When we try to do anything ourselves, we experience more effort and less results and when we invoke the magic of the Universe, we experience less effort and more results. The key is asking! There is an infinitely great Source that loves you unconditionally and eternally, and this Source is always conspiring for your highest good, even when it appears otherwise.

Use Love

One day, I was making my boys peanut butter and jelly sandwiches, when I realized that my focus was elsewhere. I immediately recalled my energy and I put my entire attention on the task at hand, and as I did, I could feel my love enliven the sandwiches that my children would soon be eating. In that moment I got it – I needed to put my love in everything! And, when you do, it comes back to you in abundance.

Drop Multi-tasking

Despite how it might seem, we are not equipped to multi-task. You can really only do one thing at a time. Multi-tasking causes stress, and stress makes us less productive. As you focus on one thing at a time, be present doing it. Don't be daydreaming or thinking about the next thing that you have to do. Be here now, and be present to the experience that you are having, as if it is the first and only time you will be doing what you are doing. Remember, being present aligns you with your True-Self.

Mishaps – warning you to slow down

When we move *faster than the speed of life*, big and small mishaps are designed to slow us down, and get us back on track. This includes slow drivers who cut in front of you on the highway, when you are in a rush to get somewhere and all sorts of unforeseen delays. Nothing is random – everything in your reality is specially selected. The Universe is conspiring to wake you up! But first, you have to slow down, and quiet your mind, so that you can hear that wake up call.

Turn-off Auto Pilot

Get real with yourself, and ask yourself, *"Is this really something I want to do?"* You might surprise yourself by answering yes, but, if the answer is really no, then turn off automatic pilot and find a better way to live your life, or a better state of mind to do what you are doing. Life does not change until you ask it to change. You must be willing to let go of the way things are and willing to embrace new possibilities.

Give up Identity

It is often our identities that keep us from being truly present and in the flow. Maybe we are so busy playing the good mom or dad that we forget to pay attention to our children, or we are so caught up in playing a career role that we forget who we are beyond the performance. So instead of being superman or super woman, just be present. There is no stress in being present.

Detox your Mind

It is often self-judgment that causes us to stress-out and go *faster than the speed of life*. When we drop criticism and self-judgment and we allow ourselves to be (without "have to's," or "shoulds"), we become free to grow and flourish with life. Also, remember, *Perfectionism is just another word for self-judgment.*

Your #1 Priority

If you are overly busy or stressed-out, chances are you are putting yourself last, but this is the worst thing that you can do. In order to get in the flow of life, you must make yourself a priority. So, instead of "seeing if you have time" for working out, meditating or getting a massage, you must make self-care your number one priority. Your body has immense wisdom, but in order to access that wisdom, you must take care of yourself, and you must listen to your body, when it has guidance to offer - which is literally every day. Your body is the first to tell you when you are moving *faster than the speed of life*.

Happiness is Your Guide

You are meant to be happy, and, if you are not happy, you are not in the flow of life. Unhappiness is your inner guidance system telling you that you are going in the wrong direction. If you get to the end of the road and you are stressed-out and unhappy, turn around and find another way. Resistance to change is like digging a deeper and deeper ditch in a place you don't want to be.

Nature Knows

Nature is always in resonance with life. You never see a flower unnerved because it is not blooming fast enough, or a cloud upset because it didn't make a deadline. When you spend time in nature, the rhythm of your body begins to sync up with the rhythm of nature, allowing you to slide into resonance with your True-Self.

Breathe

Breathing deeply brings you back into your body and aligns you with the present moment. Just ten deep breaths tell the body and mind that it is safe to relax. While you are breathing deeply, you might as well imagine that you are breathing in beautiful golden light, and you are enveloped by the love of the Universe.

Life does not have some grand finale, nor is it a game to be won. *The beauty of your life is right here in this moment*, and, if you are not going to pay attention to it, you will have missed an enormous gift that only you can experience – *and appreciate*. If you are not going to live your life, no one else can.

Life loves you and desires to make all your dreams a reality – this means that, firstly, *you must dream* and secondly, you must align with those dreams by getting *in sync with the divine speed of life*. Only then can the "synchronicity of miracles" shower you in abundance.

Let's Recap:

- Time is relative to whether you are living life through the EGO or True-Self.
- When you are living through the EGO, stress, pressure and rushing condense time, and, as a result, you experience a scarcity of time.
- When you are living as your True-Self, time expands to accommodate your needs.

- There is a natural rhythm to the Universe and when we are in sync with this rhythm, life unfolds seamlessly.
- By rushing, we may actually *move faster than the speed of life*, resulting in avoidable challenges.

Synchronicity is being in sync with life, where you can manifest what you desire with ease and grace.

Chapter 43

Tired of Being a Negative Energy Sponge?

Certainly, it would be a great deal easier to live as our True-Selves, if we lived alone on a mountain and didn't have to relate to others, but that's not realistic, nor the point of life for most of us. Since taking on other people's negative energy is a prime cause of True-Self displacement, let's now address this issue.

Do you ever find yourself taking on the negative energy of others? If so, you are not alone. Most of us come in contact with numerous people every day - who bring us down and trigger our EGOs.

We all feel it. We know when we are with someone who is high-spirited and happy or someone who is low and unhappy, but why is it so easy for others to affect us in negative ways? Some of us cannot even go into supermarkets without taking on the woes of everyone in the store.

I worked as a crisis counselor at a well-known crisis center in New York for about seven years. I quickly figured out that if I was going to be successful at helping people, I couldn't take on any negative energy. Because I uncovered the secret to keeping my energy clean and clear, I was able to assist thousands of people in dire need without once being adversely affected, and, in fact, I consistently felt energized and fulfilled. If I can do it, anyone can.

In order to shield ourselves from negative energy, we must first understand how our energy is infiltrated by others.

Energy Infiltration

Whenever you encounter someone, whether in the morning rush to the bathroom or over the conference table, an exchange of energy is at play. There is *your energy* and there is the *other person's energy.* At some point in space the energies meet. If you could be a fly on the wall, you would witness an interesting dance of vibration - with the strongest energy leading the dance. This means that if you are not centered in your energy field, your energy could be infiltrated by that of your friend, spouse, child, friend, parent or perhaps a stranger. So even if you are having a good day (embodying your True-Self) and you meet someone who is spewing their bad-day-energy onto you, your True-Self is kicked to the curve, EGO takes over and your good day turns bad. You have been hit by Energy Infiltration.

This all happens without consciousness, but what if you actually brought a higher state of consciousness to all your interactions and relationships? What if you could be responsible with your energy and not be negatively affected by anyone's lower vibe? What could this do for the quality of your life? And, for the quality of your relationships?

This means that it is all about you, and you don't have to change anyone but yourself.

Your Energy is Your Most Valuable Resource

If you are going to protect your personal energy, you must first realize that your energy is your *most valuable resource.* In other words, how you feel on any given day is your greatest source of power and attraction. If you feel good, you likely embody your True-Self and, therefore, you are more connected to your power and to your ability to consciously create. If you feel down, the EGO is likely in charge and, therefore, you are less connected to your power, and you are likely unconsciously creating - more of what you do not want. When we allow the negative or incongruent energies of others to affect our energy, our True-Selves become displaced, and, as a result, we give away our power and we lower ourselves to a level where we do not have the ability to consciously create.

This is why it is essential to make "how you feel" the most important part of every day, and not compromise your energy for anything or anyone. So, how do you do it?

12 Ways to Reclaim Your Energy and Prevent Energy Infiltration

1. **Don't Use Negative Emotions as Tools for Connection**

   It's natural to want to connect with others, but we often do this unconsciously by matching emotions. In other words, if your friend is sad, you become sad in order to connect with her, or, if your partner is annoyed at something, you mirror that annoyance in order to get on the same wavelength. The thing is, every time we use negative emotions as tools for connection, we compromise our own energy, and even if we want to help our friend, spouse, child or co-worker, we cannot offer effective support or guidance at the low emotional level of the problem.

   How can you help anyone if you are suffering with them?

   If your friend is depressed, you don't need to match his "down state" in order to connect with him. It is possible to offer compassion and understanding without compromising your energy. If you can maintain a higher level of emotional vibration, you can be of greater service, simply by creating a safe space for your friend to express his feelings without bringing you down.

2. **Let Go of Responsibility**

   The quickest way to be affected by another's negative energy is to feel responsible for them or their experience. Every time you feel responsible for another, you take on the responsibility as if it belongs to you, and your body, mind and spirit responds as if you really are responsible and you must fix the problem. This means that you take on worry, stress and pressure that belongs to someone else.

   Feeling responsible for another is like accepting their baggage as your own; hence, walking around with their weight on your shoulders. How many people can you do this for without getting overwhelmed or even sick? Sometimes our illnesses are the result of carrying problems that aren't even ours. How much of what you carry doesn't even belong to you? Really think about this.

No matter how much you care about someone, you are not responsible for them or their issues. You are responsible for you and your experience of them, but not for them.

Don't think that you can help someone by taking on their stuff as your own. The best help you can ever provide is by being your True-Self, and inviting others "up" to meet you where you are. They may or may not come up, but that is also not your responsibility.

Once you release responsibility, you can actually show up in a more responsive way and possibly be of service, instead of part of the problem.

3. **Stop Playing Judge**

   The act of judging immediately connects us to the source of our judgment. This means that if the other person's emotional vibe is low, your vibe will quickly match, thereby compromising your energy in exchange for judgment.

   As soon as you judge someone's experience, even if it is silently to yourself, you invite the energy of their experience into your own energy field. Because the mind does not know the difference between real and imagined, judging something about another opens you up to taking on the energy of whatever you are judging, as if it is happening to you. This includes gossip.

   When we allow everyone their own experiences, we don't take on their energy or the energy of their issues. If it is not about you, keep out. Your mental interference in someone else's life is not worth the risk to your energy.

4. **Drop the Sympathy**

   The moment you sympathize with someone, you energetically take on the symptoms of the person you are feeling sorry for. Yes, sympathy is when you feel sorry for someone. This means that you can catch a cold over the phone or feel pain in your body when you experience sympathy for another.

   Feeling sorry for someone is actually judging their experience - so when you feel sorry for someone, you lower your vibe to match theirs – taking on all that negative energy.

   When you feel sorry for another, you are actually imagining that they are stuck in their predicament and they are powerless to heal, change or consciously create a new reality. How does it help anyone when you are imagining the worst for them?

   You cannot feel sorry for someone and imagine them empowered at the same time. When you imagine others empowered, you also empower yourself.

   The evolution of sympathy is compassion. Compassion allows you to maintain a space of love and understanding for others without compromising your energy in anyway. Can you love someone and allow their experience without feeling sorry for them? Can you trust that their experience is somehow perfect for growth, evolution and awakening?

5. **Don't Give Anyone Power Over You**

   We tend to allow our energy to be influenced by those who appear to have power over us: parents, teachers, bosses, authority figures, etcetera. If someone in authority is having a bad day, and spews it on us, we don't hesitate to accept it, or maybe we even allow these people to dictate how we feel about ourselves

When you remember that everyone is a reflection of your own consciousness, it is easy to see that no one ever has power over you. They only have the power that you give to them through your thoughts, beliefs and actions.

6. **Let Go of Thinking that You Know Better**

   When we think that we know better and we try to change others, we instantly allow their energy to infiltrate ours. If you don't want anyone to affect your energy, then it is important to allow everyone their own experiences and their own choices. Don't even have opinions about their opinions. In trying to convince someone of your "know-how," you are likely to compromise your own energy. Remember how you feel is your most important asset - sacrifice it for nothing and no one.

7. **Stop Reacting to Others**

   Are there people in your life who attempt to get their energy through drama? In other words, they try to invoke negative emotional responses from you, in order to "get energy." Maybe you are even doing this unconsciously to others?

   The moment you react, you give your power away and you also accept the negative energy of the person causing you to react.

   In order to be angry, resentful, jealous, etcetera, you must lower your vibration, and as soon as you are an emotional match to the other person, their energy infiltrates yours.

   If you want to own your energy and stay positive, it is just not worth reacting. The cost is too great. This doesn't mean that you cannot speak your truth and set boundaries in a way that supports you and the relationship. This can be done from a space of clarity and compassion.

8. **Don't Take Sides**

   Others may want to use your energy to support their cause, but, if it is not about you, don't make it about you. Allowing yourself to get in the middle of another's squabble or cause, when you know it doesn't concern you, is basically a waste of your valuable energy. You can support others without getting in the middle, and without allowing your energy to be poisoned by another's issues.

9. **Do Not Accept Blame**

   Even if someone blames you or is angry at you, you don't need to take on their energy. My five year old grandson spilled his ice cream in the car and blamed me because I hit a bump in the road. We talked about him blaming me so that he could feel better about the loss of the ice cream, but he really felt worse. People blame us all the time for things that are out of our control. Just because someone blames you, doesn't mean you have to take it on. If you are responsible, be responsible and rectify the situation, but don't allow yourself to be someone else's scape-goat. You do not even need to react to the blame - just let it pass.

10. **Say "No" to People Pleasing**

    If you are a people pleaser, you are likely very good at giving your energy away and, therefore, being affected by other's energy. Because people pleasers put others before themselves, they are not responsible with their energy, and, therefore, they become energy sponges for everyone with whom they are trying to please. It is not your job to please the world. In fact, you would do much better at pleasing others if you first pleased yourself, putting your own needs and wants in first place. It is okay to say, "No" and set boundaries that create a safe haven for you to be responsible for your own energy.

11. **Stop Believing Others Beliefs**

    When two people meet, the one with the stronger beliefs about life often dominates the energetic dance, but only if you are not grounded in your own beliefs. You may consider various beliefs presented by others, but don't be bullied by someone who thinks that they know best. Sometimes others will even think that they know what is best for us and they try to infringe their beliefs upon us in the name of caring, but only you know what is best for you. Follow your own inner guidance.

12. **Mind Your Own Business**

    This might be a hard one, but it is none of your business what other people think about you. You cannot please all the people all the time, but it is also not your job to please anyone. It only matters what you think, and feel, about you. As long as you try to control other people's thoughts and feelings about you, you subject yourself to their energy. It's like you are telepathically saying, "Please tell me how I should feel about myself today." When you no longer have interest in what the world thinks about you, something truly amazing happens. Your confidence soars and you become super attractive - energetically and even physically. As a result, others will actually think more highly of you, but you won't care, and that is the point!

Be Responsible with Your Energy

Most people are not responsible with their energy, but this doesn't give you permission to be irresponsible with yours. This means being consciously responsible for the energy that you receive and the energy that you project. Once you are completely responsible with your own energy, it doesn't matter if someone is regurgitating their energy onto you - you won't take it. Ironically, it will also happen a great deal less.

If you do take on another's energy, it is important to remember that once you take it on, it becomes your energy - not theirs. If this is the case, notice in which of the 12 ways you have allowed your energy to be infiltrated. Take responsibility for it. No one can force you to take their energy. As long as you blame another, you have no power to release it, thereby giving even more of your energy away.

Over time, you can train your energy upward to a threshold where others cannot bring you down. It might take some conscious effort to get there but once you do, life flows with ease and grace and you become a beacon of love and light for others.

Let's Recap

- Your energy is your most valuable resource and your greatest source of power and attraction.
- When you feel good, you likely embody your True-Self and are more connected to your power and to your ability to consciously create.
- When you feel down, the EGO is likely in charge and you are less connected to your power, and you are likely unconsciously creating what you do not want.
- When you allow the negative energies of others to affect your energy, your True-Self becomes displaced.
- With focused intention it is possible to avoid external negativity and not take on stuff that doesn't belong to you, and, with practice, you can train your energy upward to a threshold where others cannot bring you down.

Chapter 44

THE SECRET TO HAPPINESS

Chasing happiness, or acquiring things or experiences in order to find happiness, is a sure indicator that the EGO is commanding the quest. It is possible that the EGO does, in fact, *buy you happiness*, but there is an inflated cost involved, and, as soon as required conditions are lost or fail to be met, happiness goes with it. Direct observation demonstrates that happiness is only experienced when certain conditions are met, and only for as long as they are met, therefore, it is accurate to summarize EGO-driven happiness as temporary, elusive and fleeting.

There is also a good chance that your *happiness baseline* grows higher over time, and it takes more and more conditions, with higher standards, to make you happy and keep you happy.

> *Signpost on the path*
> *True-Self is the key to everlasting happiness!*

Depending on the EGO for happiness is like riding a roller coaster ride without safety restraints – the combined force of gravity and thrust of inertia takes you on a wild out-of-control ride. When happiness is extrinsic, you are subject to the highs and lows of life, leaving your emotional wellbeing unstable.

EGO says, *"Pain before pleasure, because you must prove that you deserve happiness."*

By now, most of the world agrees that money can't buy happiness, nor will the acquisition of even the finest things in life, but, it is still commonly believed that happiness comes from doing what we love to do, yet this is also not the whole picture. If it were, we would always be happy when we do the things we love to do, but this is simply not the case. If you are doing what you love to do, but you have guilt that you should be working or doing something else, or you are overridden with stress and you just can't relax, no amount of joyful activities will elevate your emotional state.

When the truth about happiness is exposed, it becomes apparent that happiness is conditional, and, in fact, happiness depends on desirable "*happenings.*" Therefore, if things don't *happen* according to plan or expectation, the end result is inevitably unhappiness. This means that in order to be relatively happy, you must be able to control life's *happenings* at all times, and since we all know that this is quite impossible, it turns out the road to happiness is covered with disappointment and discouragement at every turn. Could it be that the quest for happiness is simply not a good strategy for *being happy?*

Do you recall that any emotion is simply *Energy in Motion?*

Emotions are your mind's interpretation of moving energy, and depending on the speed and intensity of the energy moving in your body, the mind interprets anger or joy, or anything in between.

EGO-driven happiness results whenever the EGO generates an abundance of energy that can be interpreted by the brain as happiness. This requires a high functioning "motor(s)" that successfully proves worth, but the moment the "motor" slows down or stops for any reason, happiness is the first to go.

Mary is a perfect example; her EGO utilizes the Role Motor by identifying with being a good mom to her two kids, and, therefore, she proves her worth in this way. When all goes well during the day, she feels worthy, and, as a result, the "motor" generates enough energy to create a feeling of happiness. However, it is not the role of mother that creates happiness, but, rather, Mary feels happy because fast moving energy is flowing through her body, and her brain interprets this specific flow of energy as happiness.

Sounds pretty good, but it is unsustainable because Mary's happiness is dependent on having good days and feeling successful as a mother. This means that if anything goes wrong and Mary doubts her worth as a good mom, the Role Motor will not produce enough energy for her to feel happy. At the end of a challenging day, Mary will likely feel exhausted, and the slow, inhibited energy in her body is then interpreted as sadness, overwhelm or some equally debilitating emotion. Like most, Mary is only as happy as the conditions of her life allow.

Let's look at a different spin to this same dynamic; Mary's husband Mark is success-oriented and one of the many "motors" that his EGO operates is the Acquisition Motor, where he gets a sense of worth from acquiring new things, and, as a result, he constantly chases after the newest high tech device, the most desired car and the pinnacle of high-echelon status symbols. The Acquisition Motor motor-vates Mark to continuously acquire the next big thing that will improve his worth and generate energy.

Signpost on the path

Trade in conditional happiness for unconditional Joy!

As your True-Self, you are aligned with the Universe, allowing Life Force Energy to flow abundantly through your body, and your mind interprets this sensation as joy.

No doubt, perpetually acquiring things that will improve Mark's worth takes a great deal of energy, especially since the next big purchase is always out of reach, requiring tons of energy to make it his own. Mark frequently takes time out of his extremely busy days in order to prospect and acquire, but he also needs to make heaps of money to afford his lifestyle and operate the "motor." This dynamic splits his energy and divides his attention, causing an energy deficit, thereby inhibiting the flow of energy to such a degree that the slow moving energy in his body is interpreted by his brain as despair, and sometimes even depression.

However, when everything lines up and Mark completes his latest acquisition and he feels a sense of increased worth, energy floods his body and he experiences a momentary rush of exhilaration. For an instant, he feels happy, but it is short-lived because once something is acquired, it no longer proves or improves worth in the same way, as when it was first conquered. Thus, the cycle begins again with Mark seeking the next big thing. Mark spends an enormous amount of time feeling unhappy with only momentary sparks of happiness fueling his fire for more.

Life lived as the EGO is full of drastic ups and downs. Even a tiny bit of happiness has a big cost, making the conditions for happiness just too unreasonable to meet. As long as the EGO runs your life, happiness will be like a carrot on a stick, always out of reach, and, even if you catch it every once and a while, you will discover that the payoff doesn't even come close to justifying the cost.

If you truly want to experience and sustain joy, the EGO is not the way to go.

So, what is the secret to happiness?

The secret to happiness is being *who you really are,* except it's not really happiness - *it's joy!*

Truly Living in Joy!

Simply by being conscious in the present moment, the fast moving energy of Universal Consciousness is available to you, and, therefore, being conscious in the present moment automatically provides access to unlimited Joy.

Joy exists intrinsically within consciousness as an inseparable attribute.

For all intents and purposes, consciousness and joy are not two separate things, they are one in the same. The essence of joy sparkles within consciousness, and, in fact, when the sun hits the air just right, and you can see delicate light sparkles in the air, you are seeing the tangible manifestation of joy.

Despite strong EGO motor-vation that compels us to control all the moments of our lives so that we might be happy, true joy is not contingent on the happenings of this moment or any moment - what happens in the *space of now* has no bearing on joy, whatsoever.

Not only is joy not dependent on what happens in the present space - joy is the space itself; not separate from the space, not dependent on the space and not fueling or sucking energy from the space. Joy fills the space, and, in fact, ***it is the space.***

Joy is eternal, infinite and unchanging.

Joy is an intrinsic state of being that is not dependent on *happenings or non-happenings.* It encompasses feelings of peace, wellbeing, centeredness, connectedness, inner confidence and *trust in something greater.* Joy is eternally rooted within our intimate relationship with life, making even the smallest details full of delight.

Self-expression

Life is so much more joyful living as your True-Self due to the fact that you naturally embrace the willingness to express your authenticity, and, when you do, uninhibited expression invokes the flow of increased Life Force Energy. Indeed, when you do what you love to do as your True-Self, joy overflows, but it also overflows even when you are not doing your favorite things. Since joy is induced by being *who you really are,* in the present moment, it is not dependent on conditions.

However, if you resist following inspiration, and you repress expression, your True-Self becomes misaligned and you inhibit the flow of Life Force Energy - the result is slow moving or stuck energy, which your mind interprets as some form of unhappiness or sadness, with long-term suppression often resulting in depression.

Location, Location, Location

Joy can only be accessed in the present moment, so, if you really want lasting joy, you must "locate" to where joy exists, and that just happens to be right here - right now.

As they say in real estate, it's all about location, location, location, except the location we are speaking about is actually found in the now.

The EGO is not programmed for this "location" because it is not needed to operate when you are conscious and present in the moment, so it remains dormant. However, as soon as you go unconscious, get distracted or dissociate from the present moment, for any reason, the EGO automatically activates and takes command.

Every time you refocus your awareness in the present, you come a bit closer to transcending EGO programming; it doesn't matter how many times you need to refocus your awareness in the now, as long as you consistently do it, for as long as it takes.

If you desire to experience joy, you must go where joy awaits – not at the end of a four year college degree, not when the ink dries on a marriage contract or divorce decree and not on the next birthday, xmas or anniversary. Joy is not located at any house of worship, elite organization or fortune 500 company, nor can it be found on a paycheck, winning lottery ticket or big inheritance.

If you don't greet joy where it can be found, better health, wealth or love will not elevate your mood or tip the scale in your favor. You cannot fool joy – it knows all the tricks and will not play any games. If you truly want joy, you must dive in deep and find it for yourself within the vast cavern of Consciousness.

True-Self Practice for Joy

Instead of relentlessly trying to meet all the made-up conditions of happiness, it's a better investment of time and energy to embody your True-Self, and experience life in these lovely shoes.

Step 1. Identify

- Identify all the ways in which you now experience happiness.
- What are your conditions for happiness?
- How is this working for you?
- How often are you happy?

Step 2. Disengage

- Once you identify the dynamics of happiness in your life, and the self-imposed conditions upon your happiness, the next step is to release all conditions - this also requires that you disengage from EGO motor-vated behaviors.

Step 3. Presence

- Let go of everything in this moment.
- Release the attachment to all your thoughts – just allow them to float by without believing any of them.
- Breathe deeply and imagine that you are breathing in the energy of joy.
- Focus on bodily sensations: smell, taste, sound, sight and other physical sensations.

Step 4. Expression

- Your True-Self naturally inspires expression; this can mean almost anything, but the most common types of expression include: gifts, talents, music, art, style, voice, writing, fun, adventure and contribution.

Beyond joy there is Bliss.

At a faster frequency than joy, your mind cannot interpret energy as emotion, therefore it is experienced in its pure form, known as Bliss. Bliss is the absence of all emotion.

Let's Recap:

- Happiness is only experienced when certain conditions are met, and only for as long as they are met.
- EGO-driven happiness is temporary, elusive and fleeting.
- EGO-driven happiness results whenever the EGO generates enough energy to be interpreted as happiness.
- Joy is sustainable because there are no conditions.
- Joy is the emotional manifestation of Universal Consciousness, and is accessed by being fully conscious in the present moment.
- When you try to do anything in order to be happy, the "doing" takes you out of presence, and into the future, misaligning you with joy.
- Bliss is the absence of all emotion.

Chapter 45

True-Self Living

This book would not be complete without a final discussion on True-Self Relationships, Parenting and Purpose.

True-Self Relationships

- *When you come from your head, it is likely the EGO.*
- *When you come from your heart, it is likely your True-Self.*
- *Whereas the EGO is closed, your True-Self is open and expanding.*

Most of us have only known EGO-based relationships where the EGO drives us to have relationships in order to get our emotional needs met, while also depending on others to validate our existence and make us feel complete, and while playing the Worthiness Game, we need others to play with us in order to compete for worth – using comparison and competition as a means to judge our own value and to know if we are worthy in comparison.

EGO-based relationships are not self-generating, and, therefore, to generate energy, we need other people in order to operate most of our "motors," and as we struggle for our share of energy, we simultaneously struggle for power, and because we are out of balance, we need others for balance and reassurance. Our dysfunctional ways of relating in EGO-based relationships perpetuate individual disempowerment and every relationship issue imaginable.

Fortunately, we are at a pivotal turning point, and the fact that you have made it this far in the book is a sign that you are on the leading edge of transformation. Along with millions of others, you play an important part, and, therefore, on behalf of humanity, I graciously thank you!

New Paradigm of Relationship

Once we are living as our True-Selves, we won't need others in the same way, and without the need for EGO-based relationships, some of us may realize that we don't need very many people in our lives, and we may not want to pursue many relationships.

However, the relationships that we do pursue and cultivate will be immensely more meaningful. As we explore new and exciting ways of relating, we will discover the power and fulfillment of co-creation and collaboration.

From a space of individual wholeness, relationships can allow us to know ourselves and each other more intimately.

Without EGO-driven power struggles, we can join energy with others and energy can exponentially increase, allowing us to discover that what we can create together is so much greater than what any of us can create alone. With limitless potential to develop individual and collective gifts, we express mutual encouragement and inspire each other to new heights, while offering positive reflections and feedback.

This inspiring paradigm will transform all our relationships, with the most profound impact on intimate partnerships.

The True-Self Couple

The True-Self Couple calls forth a new paradigm of intimate partnership.

If you have ever wondered why the divorce rate is so high, it is because most relationships involve two EGOs battling against each other for power and energy. Even when a couple starts out in love, if they don't live as their True-Selves, sooner or later, their EGOs are bound to sabotage the relationship. Even minuscule threats to the EGO can result in an all-out war, with plenty of bloodshed and no winners at the end. As long as the EGO is in control, relationships are doomed to fail - everyone ultimately loses when EGOs go head to head.

However, when two people live together as their True-Selves something amazing and magical happens.

When both partners know and own their unconditional worth and they don't depend on each other to feel worthy, the relationship has the potential to flourish – bringing out the very best individually and collectively.

Living as their True-Selves, each person is self-empowered and responsible for their own experiences, and, therefore, no one gets blamed or feels shamed. In such relationships, it is safe to express one's authentic self without fear of punishment or negative feedback.

True-Self partners are self-reliant, connected to their inner power and secure within their own being. They don't rely on each other for happiness or stability, but together they create even more of it.

While never taking each other for granted, they frequently express love and admiration - deepening the bond in an ever expanding love consciousness.

It is common for True-Self partners to share similar beliefs about life, purpose and the world, but when they do find themselves at odds, they respect each other's thoughts and opinions, and, therefore, they are quick to find resolution. Instead of sacrifice or compromise, they create a space of inspired collaboration – finding solutions that support and empower them equally.

They support each other's dreams, desires and self-expression, while, at the same time, they hold each other accountable – if for any reason, one of them is out of integrity, or the EGO has taken hold, the other speaks up, offering truthful yet empowering feedback - without taking their partner's actions personally, they can gently point out the misalignment.

True-Self embodiment sets the stage for higher-level thinking and expanded consciousness with the result being clear and empowering communication; resulting in the ability to express uninhibited truth - without lying or defense, and without withholding love.

Due to the fact that they are each highly responsible for their own energy, they do not take on the other's energy, or take responsibility for their partner's feelings. In consciously responding to the relationship, and each other, they are each responsive without being responsible for the other.

Built on a foundation of mutual respect and trust, there is plenty of space to explore intimacy and deep, profound connection. As their True-Selves, sex is conscious and exciting - allowing both partners to experience the ecstasy that comes when you combine intimacy with consciousness.

Rooted in their own individual spiritual foundations, they cultivate an open hearted relationship, effortlessly practicing forgiveness, understanding and compassion.

No longer controlled by unconscious programming, an indescribable type of relationship is possible.

When all your thoughts, beliefs and choices originate from unconditional self-love, your life grows and blossoms in magnificent ways, and you are able to attract, create and sustain relationships built on unconditional love and mutual empowerment.

Being your True-Self is the Master Key to *finding love in all the right places.*

When a True-Self Couple has children, those children are born into an extremely healthy and loving dynamic. As children model their parent's behavior, they learn to love themselves unconditionally and they take ownership of their intrinsic worth. They are taught how to manage the EGO and also how to master and express their thoughts and emotions so that they can embody their True-Selves full time. Children experience a highly nurturing environment, where they are encouraged to express their authentic selves, and, as a result, they learn how to think for themselves and become self-reliant.

But, how, exactly do you raise True-Self Children, if you are a parent who is just now awakening as your True-Self?

Raising True Self Children

Raising True-Self Children requires an entire book on its own, which will be published in the near future, but, for now, I want to offer a thought provoking overview.

My little disclaimer is that some wonderful True-Self adult behaviors, like questioning the rules and thinking for oneself, are often discouraged in children because parents don't know how to respond to conscious children. Raising a conscious child, in this way, isn't always easy but the ultimate rewards are well-worth the journey. Of course, the best way to raise a True-Self Child is to be a True-Self Parent, or at least on the path to being so.

Even if your children are teens, it's never too late to become a True-Self Parent. Yes, it may require some very different parenting skills and undoing some old patterns, but you can do it.

The following is a synopsis of the most important elements of Raising True-Self Children:

Unconditional Worthiness

Most parents see their children as unconditionally worthy, but, due to their own unconscious programming, they send a completely different message. Your job as a True-Self Parent is to consistently send messages that tell your children that they are unconditionally worthy.

Here are some things that send the wrong message:

- Making children prove that they are worthy.
- Comparing children to each other.
- Asking children to compete with each other.
- Labeling children in anyway.
- Withholding approval or acceptance.
- Any form of judgment (children are more sensitive than most people realize, so respect their sensitivity).

Don't make anything more important than your child's wellbeing and sense of worth. This means many things, but, especially, don't make your child's worth depend on performance or grades in school. You can support your children to do their best and unleash their potential without attaching their worth to any of it.

No matter what you say to your children, or try to teach them, they will learn most by example. Children unconsciously model their parent's behavior, even if the parent intends to teach them something quite different. In other words, you can't teach a child about his or her unconditional worth, if you are still playing the Worthiness Game yourself. If you desire to raise a True-Self Child, you must at least be in the process of owning your worth; you don't need to be perfect. However, it is important to be conscious of the behaviors that your children witness in you, so, if you are still healing some worthiness issues, do your best to keep it separate from your children. If you have emotional triggers and feelings of unworthiness,. heal privately. If any of your children witness your wounds, depending on the age, talk about it appropriately, and reassure your child that everyone is unconditionally worthy, but sometimes people forget, and they have to remember.

Emotional Needs

Children absolutely need all their emotional needs met because when a need is not met, the child associates his/her worth with that need being met, and it becomes a primary emotional need for life, or until he/she wakes up. So, yes, do your best to meet every emotional need - give your children approval, acceptance, understanding, appreciation, validation, respect, etc... Listen to your children, and make them feel valuable and important, while also emphasizing their unique gifts and beautiful attributes.

Your children will likely tell you, if one or more emotional needs are not met, so pay attention. If your child says, you don't listen to him, listen to him. If your child says, you don't appreciate her, appreciate her. If your child says, you don't accept him, accept him. If your child says, you don't understand her, take the time to really understand. Keep in mind that your version of acceptance, approval, understanding, etc... could be very different than what your child is asking for, so don't just assume - communicate with your child and find out what he is really asking for, and when he tells you, don't argue about it; don't try to convince him that he's wrong, shouldn't have this need or insist that you already meet this need. Whatever your child tells you, believe him/her and respond accordingly. If you don't believe your children, they will learn to doubt themselves.

Take Responsibility

Teach your children to take responsibility for their behavior, actions and the results, but this doesn't mean punishment or judgment. If you always punish your children, or even judge them, when they tell you the truth about their "undesirable" actions or behavior, they will inevitably lie to you to protect themselves from punishment and particularly from your judgment. A parent's judgment is a million times worse than any punishment, because parental judgment makes a child feel unworthy, consequently causing her to fear rejection or abandonment.

If the behavior does require a consequence, you can absolutely enforce it without the use of judgment. In fact, reassure your child that he/she is unconditionally loved - separate the behavior from the child.

Intrinsic Power

It is very important to allow children to feel like they have some power. If you are always the one to make the final decision, or play the, "I'm the parent card, so you must do as I say," you will teach your children to be powerless, and they will react by trying to get control, resulting in all sorts of behavior issues. The power you give to a child must be appropriate for their emotional age, which may be quite different than their chronological age.

Make Decisions

Allowing children to make age appropriate decisions supports individual thinking and shows them that they have some power. When your child is very young, you could allow her to choose between the green shirt and the yellow shirt, and, as she gets older, the choices naturally expand in complexity. I always gave my kids just a little bit more power than I felt comfortable with, and that always turned out well, but you know your kids best.

You might also find other ways of giving your children power, for example, when my youngest son was just five, I would ask him to hold the keys; silently telling him that I trusted him with something really important allowed him to feel empowered. Even though he never lost them, I always had an extra set, just in case. The more you trust your children, the more trustworthy they become.

As your children grow, teach them how to make their own choices, by offering thought provoking questions. Learn to ask questions in a way that will teach children how to think about their options and see the bigger picture in any situation. For instance, "What do you think might happen if you choose to __________?" Ask follow up questions that guide your children to thoughtful and empowering answers.

Believe

Children learn to believe in themselves based on how much their parents believe in them. Hence, focus on all the positives and support your child in overcoming any challenges. *Believe in your children and they will believe in themselves.*

Feeling Emotions

Teach your children about their emotions and create a safe space for them to feel their emotions. Never judge what your child is feeling - even if you think he/she is over-reacting.

Self-love

Self-love is the golden key to life - if you want your kids to be happy and successful, they must love themselves unconditionally. This is a big topic so you might want to review the self-love section in this book, and consider how you can better teach your children to love themselves.

Communication

True-Self Children need plenty of space for communicating. They need to feel like they can talk to you about anything and you won't judge them or undermine their thoughts or feelings.

Encourage Creativity

Children of all ages express themselves and explore potential and possibility through creative play, so, make sure your children have the time and space to play every day. Even better, play with them!

Mind Mastery

The mind is the greatest quantum computer in all of creation, but it needs a conscious operator. By teaching your children to master their thoughts, you give them the grandest gift imaginable. Teach them how to focus on what they do want, and not on what they don't want. Do your best to help your kids avoid all forms of negative thinking, and especially self-judgment. The one unchangeable rule in my home has always been, "We are not allowed to judge ourselves."

If there is another parent involved in your child's life, who doesn't agree with a True-Self Parenting approach, don't argue or get into conflict, just do your best as a conscious and awake parent.

Even with all this, your children will still have issues, so don't take it personally. Growing through issues on their own definitely supports maturing children, so trust the process, and know when to help and when to get out of the way.

Chapter 46

Living Your Purpose

When you live as your True-Self, your path effortlessly finds you.

Despite the intrinsic drive and overwhelming desire to fulfill our purpose, why is it that so many people spend a lifetime searching for purpose, but never finding it?

Maybe it is because we don't understand what we are really looking for, and, therefore, we miss it completely.

The good news is that when you know the true meaning of purpose, your purpose unfolds naturally, but you don't have to wonder or search a moment longer, because I am going to tell you what your purpose is right now.

Your one and only purpose is to be you. That's it, your purpose is to experience and express your True-Self - simply to be *your real authentic self.*

The Infinite Universe specifically manifested You, and through You, the mystery and magic of the Universe is revealed!

Do you really think that you were an accident that just randomly came into being or maybe you came off an assembly line stacked with similar models and packaged for duplication? No, absolutely not!

You were carefully created, right down to the most minuscule details, and after providing you with the perfect blueprint for everything you would need, you were intentionally sent to this plane of existence in order to experience life as only you could, and, as such, through you the Universe experiences a special version of life that only you can provide.

Just by being you!

Your perceptions, opinions and preferences are unique and in their uniqueness they are sacred. Through your eyes, ears, thoughts and all your finely tuned senses, your journey is one of a kind and can never be duplicated or repeated. Just by being you, the entire Universe expands and Consciousness grows.

Your Prime Purpose is to be your True-Self.

If you are not going to be you, then who will? Maybe you can take out a classified ad, "Seeking man/woman to be me. Must like ice cream, dogs and the beach." You could interview a million people for the job and not one could even come close to being you. There is only one you and of all the billions of people on the planet, including all those who have ever lived or will ever live - there is only one you.

The EGO Can't Discern Purpose

Maybe the reason why we don't discover our purpose is because the EGO is usually the one searching for it , but the EGO can never find your purpose because the EGO filters everything through worth – often disregarding anything that could be risky to your worthiness quotient, and, it just so happens, according to the EGO, the most risky thing you can do is be your real authentic self – an untrained EGO would never run the risk of judgment and rejection, so it ignores the fact that your true purpose is to be yourself.

If the EGO searches for purpose, it will miss it by a mile, but, if you embody your True-Self, you automatically fulfill your purpose.

What does it mean to live as your True-Self?

As your True-Self, you are fully alive - uninhibited in creative expression, you are confident, curious and adventurous. You approach life fearlessly optimistic with an openness to all experiences. Without masks or excuses, you don't do one thing in order to get another, and you don't justify why you need to play parts that don't suit you. As a result of your divine authenticity, you are naturally in sync with the flow and rhythm of life.

But, is that all there is?

You might be thinking, *"There has to be more to life than just being me. What about having some purpose in life?"*

Usually when people speak about finding their purpose, they are really wanting to remember their mission. Your purpose is being you, but your mission is the specific thing you chose to do during this lifetime – usually this means providing contribution in some way. Prior to your birth, you received instructions for this lifetime that included the precise mission to fulfill, and along with this mission, you were given the proper gifts and natural abilities in order to fulfill it.

Your childhood was perfectly orchestrated so that you would be prepared; the choice of your parents, place of birth and certain life experiences were all intended to propel you toward your mission. In addition, your challenges perfectly set you up with the desire and inspiration, and, if it were not for these life challenges, you might forget or miss your mission completely.

Despite the elaborate planning and execution that goes into preparation, if you deny your core purpose of being you, in all likelihood, you will miss your mission - because your authentic self naturally aligns you with your mission.

You cannot know your mission until you are living life authentically.

So, here is the problem... if the EGO is running your life, you are probably hiding behind masks and pretending to be someone you are not, thereby derailing you from ever discovering the true reason for being here. When worth is dependent on others finding us worthy, we conceal any expression that might be judged negatively, and we tailor our behavior according to what others find acceptable, sacrificing our real selves in exchange for approval and acceptance, and, as a result, we fail to fulfill our one purpose, thereby misaligning with our mission.

Sometimes we make excuses for living unfulfilling lives, *"If I knew what I was supposed to do in this lifetime, I would do it."* We fail to realize that we must simply be our True-Selves before we can discern what we came here to do.

Expressing your gifts, desires and abilities, as the True You, ultimately leads to discovering your mission.

The Vision

As you are guided by the calling and expression of your authentic self, a vision will begin to emerge. This vision contains the instructions for your mission. You may not receive the full vision initially. Oftentimes, we are only shown the next step and as we take that step, the following one is revealed, and so on, until the vision has manifested as our divine path.

Another important component is trusting your inner guidance - if you don't trust your intuition, you might not recognize the vision when it comes, or you might "doubt it down" - giving it little importance or justifying why you are ignoring it.

If you are suppressing your real self, or pretending to be someone you are not, chances are your inner guidance is also inhibited, and, if this is the case, you might miss the vision when it comes.

> *Signpost on the path*
>
> *Your purpose is connected to your mission through a vision.*
>
> *Your purpose leads to your vision and your vision contains the instructions for your mission.*

Oftentimes, your mission will ask you to step fully into your life, probably out of your comfort zone, and you will need to know your intrinsic power in order to walk your path, but sometimes a mission is as simple as living in a specific part of the world - just to offer your unique energy signature, or quite possibly, simply to bear witness to a certain type of life experience.

Everyone comes here with a mission. Even the "bad guys" have a mission. It could be that they are here to wake-up humanity, by making people pay attention to issues so that we seek solutions. "Bad guys" point out what is wrong - not by telling us but by showing us. Behind the bad guy rap may be a loving and kind soul who agreed to perform a difficult mission for the betterment of humanity. Playing the role of a "bad guy" can be just as noble and important, as playing the role of the good guy who saves the day. Keep in mind that in order to play the "bad guy" one must agree to forget his True-Self during that enactment.

What if you uncover your mission but you don't like it? Even though you agreed to your mission prior to being born, you still have free-will to say yes or no, but, usually, our mission brings joy and fulfillment so we want to follow it. In addition, by following your calling, you are naturally in sync with the Universe, from which all abundance flows, and you are also able to unite with like-minded people who share your mission or contribute in some way.

Look around, can you see that all those who are fulfilling their missions have one thing in common? Each one is living authentically - fearlessly expressing who they really are. If you haven't realized it by now, this divine expression requires freedom from subconscious programming, including the Fitting-in Program.

Turning Off the Fitting-in Program

Thankfully, with the help of the Fitting-in Program, our ancestors fulfilled their mission by sustaining the human race, but that is not the end of the story. In fact, humanity is now rebirthing a New Paradigm of Reality and the story is just beginning...

> ☙*Signpost on the path*❧
>
> *Follow the call of self-expression*
>
> By no means coincidence, the current pull toward self-expression calls us to awaken.

We have reached a glorious time in human evolution where we are about to transform humankind from overwhelming disempowerment to grand scale freedom and awakening. Embarking on a new paradigm that focuses on love, healing and abundance, we must learn how to harmoniously co-create and collaborate so that every being on Earth, thrives in love, wellness and prosperity.

We are privileged to be alive now, having the rare opportunity to participate in the greatest show on earth!

At this pivotal moment in history, if we are to walk our paths and do what we came here to do, we must be willing to express individual authenticity, so that we can turn our dreams into reality, but in order to express our True-Selves, without the EGOs persistent resistance, we must first turn off the Fitting-in Program.

Flipping The Switch

As you now know, belief is the on and off switch for all subconscious programs, therefore, to turn off the Fitting-in Program you must release the belief that keeps it active.

The Fitting-in Program operates on the belief that *self-expression is dangerous and may result in shame or even death.* But, here's the thing, if you repress yourself because you are afraid to be shamed or shunned, you are telling your subconscious mind that you believe that it is risky to express yourself, thereby perpetuating the program. Therefore, to turn off the program you must convince your subconscious mind that it is safe to express yourself, without fear of shame, rejection or abandonment.

Turning off the program requires you to courageously express your authentic self - speak your truth, dance your dance, sing your song, follow your inner guidance and *choose yourself* for the starring role of your life, without *worrying about what others think.*

We are each here to express the beauty of individual creativity through our unique gifts, specific talents and authentic curiosity, ultimately, resulting in innovation and collaboration for all. This collective dance of co-creation has the power to transform life on earth, but we must all play our parts.

The path is revealed to you as you allow yourself space and time for creative expression. If you are always trying to fit-in, you will not have access to your vision and you might miss your path entirely. Only by having the courage to go outside your box, will you discover what you are here to do.

By being your authentic self, listening to inner guidance and trusting intuitive perceptions, you will access the desire to make a difference, the vision on how to do so and the inspiration to see it through.

Your greatest value to the world is expressing *who you really are* because this is who the Divine chose you to be. When you express your True-Self, you allow the desires and dreams of the Divine to be expressed through you, and as you. You do your part and walk your path simply by exercising the freedom of expression, and as you follow your dreams, you are following Divine Guidance.

You are a unique masterpiece awaiting full expression!

- It no longer suits you to worry about what others think or say.
- It no longer supports you to hide behind a wall of shame.
- It is time to come out of the shadows and shine in the light.
- It is time to claim your place in the world.
- It is time to sing your song and dance your dance.
- *It is time to be who you really are!*

What about those you love?

Do not worry about anyone but you. Your only job is to turn off the program in yourself, but, when you do, you will naturally hold the space for those you know and love, so that they may model your courage and follow in their own unique form of expression. When you are authentically you, it invites others to be themselves, as well, and that's when the party begins! Imagine living in a world where everyone joyously expresses *who they really are*; where no one suppresses, represses or depresses their unique creativity in anyway.

One day, future generations will only know how to be themselves and the idea of not being yourself in order to fit-in will be unthinkable. We are now here to bridge that gap; we are ones who must turn off the program in order to free future generations.

There is a new song playing - inviting us to dance to the music of possibility, collaboration and collective evolution.

Please take your time to answer the following question:

- In what areas of your life are you purely authentic? What is it like?
- In what areas of your life are you suppressing your real self? How is it impacting you?
- In what relationships are you open and expressive? What is it like?
- In what relationships are you suppressing your real self? How is it impacting you?

- If you stopped worrying about what others think or say, who would you be? How would that change your life?
- What actions and behaviors would you need to express in order to be your authentic self?

If you are not going to be yourself, then who will? Ponder this for a moment. Can you think of anyone who would be better suited to be you?

Chapter 47

The Gift of Being Your True-Self

The open secret to living as your True-Self is being true to yourself.

When you unlock the memory of your intrinsic worth, you connect to the Source of your worth, and as you do, you connect with the Source of all. *This infinite and all loving Source can be expressed as the True You*, and, in fact, your free-flowing expression allows Source to flow through you, and this is the secret to accessing your greatest intrinsic power.

Knowing your worth is not selfish nor does it make you better than anyone else. When you truly know your Source-Given Worth, you also know that everyone is equally as worthy, because we are all connected to the same one Source. It is not a different Source for each of us - there is only One and that is why it is called Source.

When we are connected to Source, the wisdom and guidance that we receive is in harmony with the wisdom and guidance of everyone who is also plugged in as their True-Selves, and, as such, we are each given intuitive direction regarding our unique piece of the puzzle, and our piece fits perfectly with all the other pieces. This guidance includes every detail: how to live our lives, how to relate to each other, what to do (and not do) and how to treat our home planet for sustainable living. Because the same One Mind works through each of us, world harmony is inevitable. When we believe that we are separate, we must fight, compete and get ahead, but when we remember that we come from the same Oneness, we naturally support each other through unconditional love and mutual empowerment.

As more of us experience our True-Selves on a consistent basis, and we come together, a powerful and positive dynamic unfolds. All our relationships evolve into higher expressions of co-creative collaboration, while our closest relationships have the potential to elevate us into an enlightened realm of utopian possibilities - one we have yet to manifest on this planet.

Abundance and wellbeing are natural byproducts of conscious and awake beings living as their True and Wise Selves, and as we connect with each other through our individual True-Selves, we embrace the joy and peace that naturally accompanies Oneness.

We are not diminished through Oneness, but, instead, our unique expression shines through and we expand exponentially as our own magnificent expression of divinity.

The key to creating Heaven on Earth lies in the embodiment
of our True-Selves – only then can we create our dreams
and live our lives as they were meant to be lived.

Bonus Chapter

When all our "motors" fail, what happens?

Hitting Rock Bottom

Although we may arrive at "rock bottom" from different paths, the dynamics of the destination are always one in the same.

When we hit rock bottom, it can only mean one thing; the EGO has essentially failed.

At this point, it is clear – none of the ways in which the EGO motor-vated us to prove worth have continued to work. If even one "motor" is still operating, we wouldn't be at rock bottom. Likely, we would still be playing the Worthiness Game.

Rock bottom is the result of completely losing the Worthiness Game with no hope of regaining status or standing.

Dark Night of the Soul

The dark night of the soul is another way to describe the experience of hitting rock bottom, but it would be more accurate to call it, "The dark night of the EGO" - for all intents and purposes, your soul is your True-Self, and no matter what name you use, darkness is not an attribute. *Who you really are* is pure love and light, and, if you experience a "dark night" it signifies the *falling away* of the EGO and the reemergence of your True Being, *but only if you fully surrender.*

Meet Gil

According to societal standards, Gil did everything right - he got good grades in school, he landed a well-paying career, he married a beautiful woman and even managed to achieve high status in his field. However, Gil was never happy because he suffered from "Never Enough Syndrome" – no matter how much money he made, how many awards he received or how good his life *seemed* to be, it was never enough. He always needed more money, more importance, more success and more respect, and even when he surpassed his latest goals, it still wasn't enough.

Can you see how the Worthiness Program motor-vated him to get good grades, a well-sought after career, financial abundance and relationships with highly valued women? Gil's primary emotional need was respect, and it did a great job of motor-vating him to spend his whole life trying to get respect and keep respect, so that he would feel worthy. But, as you can see, there is no end to the Worthiness Game.

Year after year, Gil was under constant stress in order to maintain the illusion of success. At some point, the endless overwhelm and anxiety led him to drink, and when that wasn't enough, he indulged in more serious mind-distracting substances. His current wife (#3) tried to help him overcome his addictions but that made him feel like she didn't respect him, and, as a result, he sought respect outside the marriage, and it wasn't long before he started having a series of extra-marital affairs.

When his wife found out, she immediately filed for divorce, and forced him to move out of their luxurious family home, but not before bad-mouthing him to all their friends and anyone who would listen. When Gil lost the respect of his wife and friends, his EGO concluded that the Relationship Motor was no longer a good energetic investment; with this being his third failed marriage, Gil's EGO calculated that the energy needed to motor-vate him to pursue a new relationship outweighed the energy received from boosting his EGO via respect, and, therefore, the Relationship Motor was a bad investment. Making this assessment, the EGO turned off the "motor" and despite the fact that Gil was quite lonely and desired a romantic partner, he no longer had any sort of motor-vation to look for a new relationship.

Life at work was equally disappointing, and it became apparent to Gil that his job would never fill that emotional void. Well sought-after promotions, awards and recognition brought respect and boosted his EGO, but only for a moment and the moment was gone. Year after year, it took more and more respect to boost his EGO, but, since it never lasted, he always felt empty inside.

Gil progressively lost interest in work, doing the bare minimum just to get by and not be noticed. He probably could have remained on auto-pilot indefinitely, if it weren't for the fact that he got a new boss with new *unrealistic* expectations, at least according to Gil. Disappointed by Gil's performance, the boss criticized Gil publicly on a daily basis, causing Gil to feel incredible disrespect.

With Gil's Success Motor wearing out, and the need to defend his worth at work, the EGO activated the Anger Motor, which had been mostly dormant for twenty years. Now generating energy from anger, Gil attracted one anger-triggering situation after another, demonstrating the law of attraction at work. The energy generated from anger kept Gil going, at least until a devastating blow up in the office, and he was fired.

The Success Motor had already been wearing down but it was operating just enough to motor-vate Gil to go to work each day, but now that he got fired and he left work feeling judged and disrespected by the whole office, his EGO once again calculated that this "motor" was a bad investment, and, consequently, turned it off. Now unemployed, Gil had absolutely no motor-vation to find another job.

Of course, it doesn't end there.

Would it shock you to know that, at about the same time as losing his wife, home and job, Gil made some bad financial decisions and lost a great deal of money? The Money Motor, which once operated on full steam (successfully proving Gil's worth left and right), was now also failing, and he had no further motor-vation for any financial investments, nor the money to invest.

With the loss of Gil's primary "motors" (success, relationship, money), the EGO needed another way to generate energy for Gil, thereby turning his casual interest in sex and drugs into two full blown "motors" for energy generation.

Although the "sex and drugs" lifestyle never brought Gil happiness or respect, for about two years, these "motors" produced enough energy to keep Gil going, but they were not without cost. Alienated from his former friends, his new "friends" were very challenging to cope with and extremely unconscious in relating. Consequently, Gil's anger was typically triggered several times a day, which, of course, generated quite a bit of energy, but it also resulted in perpetual emotional turmoil and physical violence - ultimately, costing this "motor" more energy to run than the pay-off. Of course, Gil had no idea that his EGO had been using anger to generate energy; he just knew that he no longer had any energy to fight so he avoided confrontation, but his lack of aggressiveness was interpreted as weakness and this set him up for victimhood.

Also having to deal with drug-related lying, stealing and cheating, and needing to do the same in order to survive, Gil lived in a perpetual state of anxiety and stress. For a time, lying, cheating and stealing were also "motors" for energy, but they also created chaotic problems to combat, with unconscious solutions resulting in even more chaos.

Feeling worthless and blaming himself manifested as shame.

Feeling powerless and blaming the world manifested as victimhood.

It's probably not surprising to hear that Gil ended up penniless, purposeless and alone, and along with being homeless, he suffered from a wide array of untreated health issues, but this was not the worst of his troubles.

Slowly, but surely, all Gil's "motors" wore-out. Not one "motor" generated more energy than it cost to operate, so the EGO systematically turned each one off. Without a single "motor" to generate energy and full-on energy deprivation as a result, Gil's EGO went into code red survival mode, leading to a full-on conservation of energy; deep depression ensured that Gil would not use energy for non-essentials. With barely enough energy for vital life functions, and zero energy allotted for anything other, Gil could hardly speak or move his weary body. Feeling less than worthless and completely powerless, Gil felt as if a dark, dense cloud swallowed him up.

Buried beneath guilt, shame and regrets, the EGO had failed, and Gil hit rock bottom, ultimately facing *his darkest night ....*

Not a morsel of energy left for hope, rock bottom is void of all possibility.

If you have never hit rock bottom, you might wonder, "Why doesn't the guy just pick himself up and get some help?"

If we hit rock bottom, but, at least one "motor" is running, the EGO can dig us a way out, so it's not really rock bottom, but when all "motors" have failed and the EGO is operating in "death mode" the EGO is not going to save us.

With barely enough energy for basic needs, there is no motor-vation to try something new, save ourselves in anyway or climb up from the bottom, and with no energy to live, suicide often becomes a viable option.

When the Worthiness Program results in worthlessness and the Powerlessness Program ends in powerlessness, the EGO is defeated and the EGO program is corrupt.

Without the EGO operating in its usual manner, we are lost in a dismal pool of despair because we have little or no experience living without the EGO. When the EGO is not in charge, there doesn't seem to be anyone to run the show. This is an interesting dynamic, indeed. The EGO has failed and subsequently lost control, but there is nothing else to take its place.

I know what you are thinking, where's the All-Knowing True-Self?

Well, chances are, on the way down to rock bottom, the EGO was super-active, trying every last ditch effort to save the day – controlling us more than ever in order to keep the programs operating and the "motors" running, all the while over-riding inner guidance, and, besides, all the fear, anxiety and stress doesn't create a good habitat for a high-vibing True-Self. In most cases, a byproduct of hitting rock bottom is total True-Self displacement.

So, here we are at rock bottom with no EGO to motor-vate us "up and out" of this dismal mess, but also no True-Self to step in and guide us to better days. Isolated, desperate and lost, this is truly being alone in the dark - at the bottom.

Some people do opt out of life at this point, but many more discover that rock bottom has a hidden back door.

No longer playing the Worthiness Game and nothing more to lose, the outward quest for importance is done and over, and now the journey inward can begin.

With nowhere else to go, many "rock-bottomers" turn to religion or spirituality for answers. Religion may prove rewarding or it may be another trap for the EGO, if the EGO identifies the religion, or religious role, as a new source of possible worth, and starts up a brand new "motor."

Indeed, spirituality can also become a "motor" for the EGO, especially, if we identify ourselves with a particular spiritual modality and we attach our worth to meeting the conditions of the practice. Just about anything can be a "motor" if we are unconscious, but, if we embark on a spiritual path that is not encumbered by rules, regulations and doctrine, and we stay conscious along the way, the journey could lead us to discover *who we really are,* ultimately aligning us with our True-Selves.

If we truly surrender our lives to *something greater,* rock bottom can be filled with incredible opportunities; when the EGO is no longer in the way, solutions to our biggest challenges can easily and effortlessly manifest like Radical Miracles.

Another back door leads to AA ...

Alcoholics Anonymous can be a literal life-saver, and, in fact, many of the twelve steps override EGO-driven behavior while also supporting True-Self embodiment, but AA is built on a perpetual system of dependency – training members to believe that they need the organization and other members in order to be empowered. This dynamic perpetuates the Worthiness and Powerlessness Programs.

Sobriety is energetically rewarded with praise and acceptance – adding up to worth.

Non-sobriety is energetically punished with judgment and disapproval - adding up to not worthy.

AA is an incredible resource and has helped millions worldwide, but unless you are conscious in the process, the EGO will use it as a replacement "motor." When something becomes an identity, like AA often does, the EGO is sure to create a new "motor" based on using that newfound identity to prove worthiness. Should this be the case, the EGO will motor-vate you to follow rules, adhere to guidelines and measure worth accordingly.

However, with conscious awareness, AA can be a powerful healing modality that supports True-Self embodiment, for example:

- Don't just depend on others for support.
- Develop a relationship with your True-Self.

- Don't form an identity around being a "former addict" or a lifelong AA member.
- Align with your True-Self by partaking in a daily spiritual practice that connects you to Source.
- Create a life outside the organization, including relationships, interests, mind expansion, creativity and anything that helps you to get to know yourself.
- Practice unconditional worth until you turn off the Worthiness Program.
- Practice being empowered until you turn off the Powerlessness Program.

Surrender is Life's Fail-Safe

The absolute worst experiences could happen, but there is always a "fail-safe" to life.

The precise point we feel the most worthless and powerless is the furthest we stray from our True-Selves, but we might actually be closer than ever before, because there is a *fail-safe* mechanism designed to literally wake us up.

The pressure, pain and suffering of feeling shame and victimhood is designed to keep intensifying until there is nothing to do but let go. To some, this might mean exiting the world and hoping for instant relief in the afterworld, but that exit strategy misses the whole purpose.

The higher purpose of suffering is to force you to release the source of your pain, so that you will free yourself, and you will be propelled out of the painful illusion and back into your True-Self.

When nothing about life works and everything falls apart, desperation and hopelessness force you to give up, but instead of being done, you have really only just begun

With nothing left and no resistance, you are closer than ever to *who you really are,* but you must do this one thing.

The key that unlocks a new reality is surrender.

If you surrender but you are still closed, you haven't really surrendered - you are still holding onto whatever it is that allows you to be closed, and, if you are closed, you are no closer to discovering your real self.

Each of us has a different threshold for emotional pain, so suffering, and the point where we let go, is never the same, however, surrender is always the same.

Total surrender requires you to release absolutely everything, so there is nothing left to close you down. Only then, does your openness reveal the inner unknown, where the hidden becomes found. Nothing has to necessarily change in your life, but your relationship with everything and everyone must change, so that nothing comes between you and the Source of *who you really are.*

As you undo your grip on reality, and you let go of the illusion, the True You will shine through!

Your True-Self is only a surrender away.

Certainly, you don't have to reach rock bottom to find your True-Self – it's actually much easier if you don't, but you do have to make the conscious choice to live as your True-Self.

Living as your True-Self is not just a new practice, it is an entirely new paradigm, but to experience this new paradigm you must participate in an ongoing conscious practice. It is an everyday choice – one choice after another, one day after the next, until you ultimately reach the magical moment when practice becomes mastery.

What About Gil?

If you are wondering about our friend Gil, he found his way out of rock bottom - *in the dark night of the EGO he discovered his True-Self.*

Indeed, it took time, but by doing the inner work to discover *who he really is,* he learned how to embody his True-Self on a regular basis, and step by step, he reclaimed his life by making conscious choices that reflected his inner guidance and supported his authentic being. Finally following his true dreams, and listening to his heart, he built a fulfilling life on a sustainable foundation, and from there, he discovered anything and everything is possible.

Final Signpost on the path
You are love, you are light
and All is Well!

In love, grace & gratitude,

Nanice

The Story Behind this Book

In the search for comprehensive instructions on how to consciously create life, I spent decades researching books, teachers and ancient knowledge around the world, but even the best of the best only offered bits and pieces of the full puzzle. Never losing sight of my desire, I relentlessly searched for clues that would allow me to finally put the abstract pieces of the puzzle together so that the full body of knowledge would be as clear as crystal. My life formed around solving this mystery - for myself and also so that I could share this tangible wisdom with the world.

Upon discovering the last pieces of the puzzle, I began to write the book I was born to write, "Seducing the Field." The Field represents the quantum field and the book compiles the wisdom of the Universe into an instruction manual for life, with a central focus on how to communicate with the quantum field (aka Universe) so that it hears you and complies with the manifestation of your dreams and desires.

So, with endless exhilaration, hundreds of pages poured out of me, but as I neared completion, I experienced an incredible download of knowledge and information that was integral for manifestation but beyond the scope of the book I was writing, and no matter how much I wanted to complete Seducing the Field, I couldn't stop thinking about this new knowledge, and how it was intended to be written as another book. Believing this new book was only going to be fifty or so pages, I took what I thought would be a brief break from completing Seducing the Field, in order to write the new book, but fifty pages turned into more and more and more, and days turned into weeks and then months. That supposedly short but highly inspired book turned out to be the book you have just read. I suspect the Universe knew what it was doing all the time, so instead of Seducing the Field, I was joyfully *Seduced by the Field.*

Seducing the Field has a publication release date of fall 2016 - available on ***www.Nanice.com*** and Amazon.

True-Self Living Programs

Individual True-Self Coaching

Learn to apply the principles of True-Self Living to your relationships, career and all other facets of life. Overcome your personal sticking spots, and live as the True You. Couple and Group Coaching also available. Worldwide Coaching by Skype. Find out more at www.Nanice.com

True-Self Coach Training

Get professionally trained to be a True-Self Coach and bring your coaching practice to the next level. To apply, or find out when the next training begins, go to www.Nanice.com/CoachTraining

True-Self Seminars, Workshops and Keynotes

To have Nanice speak at your organization, please email info@Nanice.com for rates and availability.

Books By Nanice

- The Infinite Power of You!
- Out of The Jungle
- Even Gandhi Got Hungry and Buddha Got Mad!
- LipPrints
- What *if...*
- Is There A White Elephant In Your Way?
- The Matrix of Depression
- The Gratitude Journal
- I Am
- Zest Point

Nanice is available for Workshops, Presentations and Keynotes, as well as Tele-conferencing and One-on-One Coaching sessions.

Visit www.Nanice.com for free classes, podcasts, articles, videos, meditations, downloads and more books!

INFO@NANICE.COM

WWW.NANICE.COM

CPSIA information can be obtained
at www.ICGtesting.com
Printed in the USA
LVOW09s0143020517
532864LV00015B/502/P